The Swiss
WITHOUT HALOS

A SWISS
BANNER
BEARER
WOODCUT
BY
URS GRAF,
SWISS
ARTIST
AND
SOLDIER
(C. 1485–
C. 1527)

The Swiss

WITHOUT HALOS

(1948)

J. Christopher Herold

NEW YORK
COLUMBIA UNIVERSITY PRESS

[1958]

Contents

Illustrations

ILLUSTRATIONS AND MAPS

Maps

The Swiss
WITHOUT HALOS

I: The Polyhedral Paradox

Surely no country in the world can boast of more diversity per square mile than Switzerland; diversity not merely in landscape, as advertised in every Swiss travel prospectus, but also in language, customs, social and economic structure, and even in government. At the same time, few other countries offer a comparable spectacle of harmony, stability, and integration. Small wonder if the concept of Switzerland as a microcosm, an orderly little world of its own, reflecting the reconciled components of the greater, but disorderly, world around it, has caught the fancy of not a few dispensers of good advice. Good little Switzerland is held up as a shining example to the indocile hoodlums of this world. The peaceful, virtuous, industrious Swiss, we are led to believe, have avoided the pitfalls into which other nations have been stumbling throughout the centuries and have achieved a state where Latin and Teuton, Papist and Calvinist, worker and banker, cow and milkmaid are all living together in peace and harmony, enjoying the benefits of democracy and watchmaking. Perpetual neutrality; streets so clean that perverse perfectionists have thought of eating off them; prosperity; yodeling; the Four Freedoms; chaste and simple morals; hospitality to the persecuted; numberless other charms and virtues—all these are put into the composite picture of the country that all other countries should imitate.

To some extent this picture of modern Switzerland, though incomplete, is true. There is small profit in dwelling on the less edifying aspects of the Swiss scene; compared to conditions in most other countries, they are trifling. But the road to such exemplariness was not easy. It was not always followed by free choice. From 1291 to 1848 the history of Switzerland was one of foreign and domestic warfare. Interminable internal squabbles caused repeated foreign interventions—not to weaken the Confederation, but to keep it from breaking up altogether. The result of all this was the union of an area which in America would not even constitute one fairly large state. Besides good will, wisdom, industry, and virtue, there was a concourse of compelling circumstances. The world, now far more divided than Switzerland ever was, can scarcely afford five more centuries of conflict to evolve to the Swiss solution. Moreover, unlike Switzerland, it has only itself to fear: there are, as yet, no neighbors from Mars or the moon whose threats or mediation force its components to unite. The existence of a nation as diversified and as united as the Swiss may well be considered proof that the thing is not impossible, that there is reason for hope. The road that led them to unity can scarcely be pointed out as a way to be followed slavishly.

This book does not pretend to dissect the Swiss guinea-pig in an attempt to find a remedy for the world's disorders. Switzerland is worth knowing for its own sake, even if its study offers no therapeutic benefits. Travel and books on travel have familiarized large sections of the American public with the physical beauties of the Swiss scene, or rather scenery; a few studies, mostly uncritical, have acquainted a much smaller public with the outline of Switzerland's formation and the apparent miracle of its cohesion; and many are the stale jokes dealing with the Swiss navy, the Swiss language, and the methods of perforating Swiss cheese. That Switzerland is inhabited by live beings other than hotel personnel, that it has a rich and proud past, that its culture has deeply influenced the entire western world, and that its economy might properly be called a work of art—if art is defined as the creation of something out of nothing—all this has escaped general attention.

In the present world we can spare neither the time nor the interest for a detailed study of the labyrinthine complexities of Swiss history, institutions, and culture. For all those who are neither Swiss nor specialists the importance of such matters is remote, and the taste rather dry. But a few glimpses of the Swiss scene in its most typical aspects and retrospects should prove neither taxing nor unrewarding. This manner of presentation may be haphazard but it will serve the purpose better than to skim everything and penetrate nothing.

II

Switzerland—a country slightly larger than the combined areas of Vermont, Connecticut, and Rhode Island—has on some occasions been described as the heart of Europe, a term with somewhat debatable connotations. It might as well be called an antechamber, with its doors leading to the main rooms of the European apartment. The four adjacent rooms—France to the west, Germany to the north, Austria to the east, and Italy to the south—have their own connecting doors, it is true, but since they are invariably locked and bolted whenever the tenants cease to be on speaking terms, the most convenient routes from Germany and northern France to Italy and from Austria to France lead through Switzerland's windowless antechamber. It is windowless in the sense that Switzerland is landlocked; in order to get air, it must keep its doors to the surrounding rooms open at all times, even when the neighbors barricade their own interconnecting doors.

Like all similes, the antechamber concept of Switzerland has obvious limitations. It is valid only to describe the Swiss position with regard to the rest of Europe. In other respects Switzerland may appear to some as the roof of the Continent. While it lacks the figurative air of ocean trade, it has prodigious supplies of literal mountain air—so rarefied and precious that it is profitably sold in numerous resorts—and an equal supply of ultraviolet rays, for which the sun bathers of the European apartment house are no less handsomely charged.

Nonmetaphorically speaking, the natural frontiers of Switzerland are, roughly, the Rhine in the northeast and north, the Jura in the west, and the Alpine crests in the south. The natural limits are only approximately observed by the political borders, especially in the south, where the canton of Ticino, covering the southern (or Italian) slope of the Alps, forms an appendage to Switzerland. It is not accidental that the Ticino, though held by the Swiss for centuries, is far more typical of Italy than of Switzerland in landscape and character and that its cultural contributions were made mainly to Italy.

These boundaries, narrow though they may be, encompass a land of which almost one fifth is totally barren, and which supports more than four million people. The Jura region is sparsely populated. Its valleys and plateaus were apparently fashioned with a view to insuring maximum coolness and ventilation, for there is nothing to stop the north wind from blowing through its entire length, and the winter temperatures are Siberian. For a living its inhabitants have depended, for two centuries and a half, mainly on the watchmaking industry. Le Locle and La Chaux de Fonds are known to the whole world as watchmaking centers; much of the industry, however—especially in the past—was carried on in individual homes, and work used to be specialized in the usual sweatshop manner. Largely of Huguenot stock, the people of the Jura have found little in their stern surroundings and their meticulous occupation to upset their austere faith and frugal manners.

As the Jura slopes down the wine growing banks of Lake Neuchâtel and the thickly settled Aar basin, both climate and customs tend to thaw somewhat under a friendlier sun. The rolling country that stretches from the Rhine to Lake Geneva and from the Jura to the Alps is the main source of Switzerland's supply of home-grown food and contains its most important industries. Berne, the federal capital, and Zurich, the commercial and cultural metropolis, are its principal cities.

The southern and the eastern portions of Switzerland—the tourists' Switzerland of chalets, cowherds, mountain guides, and William Tell—form a segment of the Alpine semicircle that extends from the Mediterranean to the Black Sea. This area boasts the largest number of snow-capped peaks, ice fields, and glaciers, and cradles two of Europe's mightiest rivers, the Rhine and the Rhone. Both spring from the very heart of the Swiss Alps, within a few miles' distance. The Rhine, at first divided, issues from the mountains of the St. Gotthard group. Near Chur it joins a second headstream, the Hinter Rhein, which rumbles through the deep and narrow gorge of the Via Mala. It then fills the huge basin of Lake Constance, the "Swabian Sea," drops some sixty feet at

Schaffhausen, and finally accommodates itself to navigation at Basel, whence it takes a steady northward course toward the home of Siegfried. The Rhone bursts forth, miraculously, a full-fledged river, from an opening in the precipitous, jagged, and multicolored Rhone glacier. Sweeping a straight path between the peaks of the Bernese and the Valaisan Alps, it enters Lake Geneva. After leaving the lake, it narrows to a mere trickle when entering France at Bellegarde, as though it wanted to hide from a customs inspection. Once safely past the border, it widens again and, after traversing Lyons, rolls south majestically to the land of Mireille.

The two rivers, symbols of two opposing civilizations, characteristically seem to flee in opposite directions at the very instant they come into existence. But Switzerland, with its Alpine passes, has done its part in bridging these civilizations. From Germany, the country is easily accessible across the Rhine. The Austrian frontier is far more difficult of access, however, and against France the Jura presents a solid wall, open only at its two extremities, Basel and Geneva. These cities and Constance were until the last century the three main gates through which travelers from northern and northwestern Europe had to pass in order to reach Italy. If they entered from Constance, they were likely to take the ancient route across the Splügen Pass or the Julier Pass, both leading down to Lake Como, in Lombardy. It was at its northern entrance that an Irishman named Gall built himself a hermit's cell about 613 A.D. Thanks to its strategic position, it soon became the powerful abbey of St. Gall, whose monks exercised a profound cultural influence over Europe.

The travelers who entered through Basel were more likely to choose the perilous, but more direct, St. Gotthard route, which became practicable in the thirteenth century when a bridge was built across the Reuss River.

From Geneva or Lausanne the usual road to Rome led across the Great St. Bernard, best known of all the passes because of its monastery, its brandy-bearing dogs, and the publicity Napoleon received for leading his armies over it (actually a minor feat). The Simplon, more difficult of access, has been widely used only since the construction of a modern road early in the nineteenth century.

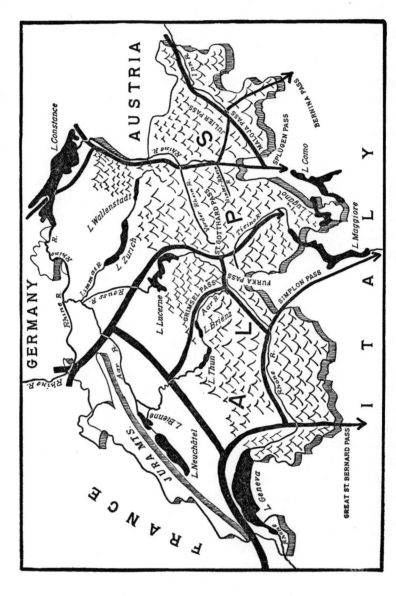

HISTORIC THOROUGHFARES OF SWITZERLAND

Connecting the main valleys of Switzerland itself are a number of other passes used since antiquity: the Lötschberg, cutting across the Bernese Alps into the Rhone Valley; the Grimsel, leading from Interlaken to the Rhone Glacier; and the Furka, which rises alongside the Rhone Glacier and links the Grimsel with the St. Gotthard. There are, of course, dozens of lesser passes. The daring and ingenuity of Swiss road and railroad engineers who have adapted these small paths and trails to the requirements of modern transportation enlivened the otherwise drab history of nineteenth-century Switzerland with some epic moments.

Though Switzerland straddles several of Europe's main highways, its own internal communications are necessarily poor. With the trifling exception of navigation on the larger lakes, a few canals, and a section of the Aar River, traffic is landbound. This limitation is not too inconvenient in the relatively flat country of northern Switzerland, but in the Alpine parts lengthy detours are sometimes necessary to connect localities just a few miles apart. The roads are not always passable, being snow-blocked or endangered by avalanches for many months each year, or, in some cases, having a one-way traffic schedule. Because of these difficulties it is generally thought that the inhabitants of the Swiss Alpine valleys have lived in isolation from the rest of the world for hundreds of years. This is absolutely false. Only a few outlying valleys suffered—or, perhaps, benefited—from such isolation. By and large, the people of even the remotest corners were obliged to entertain relations with trading centers, and were by no means alien to the currents of outside life. In the eighteenth century—a time when most French or Italian peasants were illiterate—travelers in the Swiss Alps commented with amazement on the high degree of education, even in the humanities, that they encountered in the most unlikely places. Perhaps the Alps were too great an obstacle for most prophets to go to the mountaineers—but the hardier mountaineers could easily go to the prophets.

Natural obstacles did not prevent the Swiss from keeping in contact with each other, but in all justice it must be added that they did not encourage them to do so either. Distances which would seem short to plainspeople still seem long to the Swiss, and regional differences which without natural dividing lines would now be effaced, have survived in costumes, speech, and ways of thought. Almost every valley of the high Alps has retained its very distinct character. But localism, though it takes on very extreme forms in Switzerland, must not be confused with the backwardness that stems from real isolation. The physical and material handicaps imposed by nature have been overcome by the Swiss to a remarkable extent; it was only the psychological effects of living in narrow valleys that they could never fully overcome.

III

The political structure of Switzerland is largely the result of its physical map. In the historical core of Switzerland, the fragmentation into valleys has resulted in the development of quasi independent communities of minute dimensions; in the west and the north the nature of the agricultural country was more proper for the formation of large states dominated by large cities. These states and communities, which joined in a confederation, are called cantons. Modern Switzerland consists of twenty-two such cantons, but, since three of them are subdivided into half-cantons, which are politically as autonomous as the full cantons, the total number of political units amounts to twenty-five.* Typical of the large agricultural state is the canton of Berne, while the minute subdivision in the Alpine districts is best illustrated by Unterwalden.

One of the all-too-numerous peculiarities in Swiss history is that

* The following is a list of the Swiss cantons (half-cantons in italics):

Canton	Square Miles	Population	Canton	Square Miles	Population
Zurich	668	674,505	Schaffhausen	115	53,772
Berne	2,658	728,916	*Appenzell-*		
Lucerne	576	206,608	*Ausser-Rhoden*	94	44,756
Uri	415	27,302	*Appenzell-*		
Schwyz	351	66,555	*Inner-Rhoden*	67	13,383
Upper Unterwal-			Saint Gall	777	286,201
den (Obwalden)	190	20,340	Grisons	2,746	128,247
Lower Unterwal-			Aargau	542	270,463
den (Nidwalden)	106	17,348	Thurgau	388	138,122
Glarus	264	34,771	Ticino	1,086	161,882
Zug	93	36,643	Vaud	1,239	343,398
Fribourg	645	152,053	Valais	2,021	148,319
Solothurn	306	154,944	Neuchâtel	309	117,900
Basel-City	14	169,961	Geneva	109	174,855
Basel-Land	165	94,459	Total	15,944	4,265,703

the large agricultural cantons are traditionally called city cantons, while mountainous districts, like Schwyz, where scarcely any agriculture exists, are called rural cantons. It will be noted, however, that only the "city cantons"—Berne, Zurich, Solothurn, etc.—derive their names from their capitals. The most typical "rural cantons," such as Uri, Schwyz, and Unterwalden, on the other hand, have no real towns; their capitals are mere villages or meeting places. The only true city cantons in modern Switzerland are Basel and Geneva.

By its present constitution, adopted in 1874, Switzerland is a union of twenty-five states whose sovereignty is slightly wider than that of the states of the United States of America. All the sovereign functions transferred from the cantons to the confederation are specifically enumerated in the federal constitution and its amendments. They include, of course, all matters of general foreign policy and tariff legislation. The legislative branch of the federal government consists of two chambers: the Council of the Estates, in which every canton is represented by two members, and every half-canton by one, and the National Council, elected by universal male suffrage through a system of proportional representation.*

The two legislative chambers unite to elect, for a four-year term, the members of the executive branch, or Federal Council. Here the Swiss constitution differs radically from the American, where the chief executive is elected, in practice, if not in theory, by direct popular vote. The "president" of the Swiss Confederation, in the true meaning of the word, is a board of seven men, the members of the Federal Council. The nominal president and vice-president of Switzerland are selected from among them each year by the Federal Assembly.

The importance of the Swiss legislature is weakened because the larger part of its acts is subject to review by means of the popular referendum and because its failure to legislate can be made good through the popular initiative. Both these forms of govern-

* The members of the Council of the Estates are elected or appointed according to the election laws of the canton they represent, and their salaries are paid, not by the Federal treasury, but by their respective cantons according to their means. Extracts from the Swiss constitution are to be found in the Appendix to this book.

THE CANTONS OF SWITZERLAND

ment by direct democracy are guaranteed by the federal constitution, and are the salient features of Swiss political life.

The judiciary branch of the Swiss federal government, the Federal Tribunal (which has its seat, not in Berne, but in Lausanne) is not comparable to the Supreme Court of the United States, for it is concerned exclusively with legal matters. The specific nature of the Swiss federal constitution leaves no room for interpretation—the characteristic function of the Supreme Court.

The variety of the cantonal constitutions is limited only by the guarantee, contained in the federal constitution, that the republican form of government be observed in all cantons. This may appear as a mere formality to those who think of Switzerland as having been a traditionally republican state for the past seven centuries. Actually, Neuchâtel, one of the cantons, was a principality until 1848, when its inhabitants expelled their governor. The prince of Neuchâtel, who was no other than the king of Prussia, renounced his claims to the principality only in 1857, and numerous members of the local aristocracy continued to serve him as Prussian subjects; Pourtalès, the German ambassador to St. Petersburg in 1914, was one of them.

Despite variations in details, most Swiss cantons are now governed by essentially similar constitutions, providing for a unicameral legislature and a directly or indirectly elected executive cabinet. Referendum and initiative with regard to cantonal legislation exist, in varying shades and degrees, in all cantons, except in Glarus, the two Appenzells, and the two Unterwaldens. The latter canton and half-cantons have retained an ancient form of direct popular government; their legislatures, known as Landsgemeinden (commons), consist of all male adult citizens, who meet once a year in an open-air assembly to elect their officials and magistrates, vote the budget, pass on naturalizations, and accept or reject legislation. The oldest of the still existing Landsgemeinden (Nidwalden) dates back to 1309.

Swiss citizenship is always dual—federal and cantonal—and independent of residence. If a citizen of Zurich settled in Geneva in 1880 and spent the rest of his life there, and if his son has never set foot outside Genevese territory, his son's son will nevertheless still be a citizen of Zurich unless he (or his father or grandfather) has been granted citizenship in Geneva. However, it is sufficient for a male citizen of Switzerland to be a resident of a canton in order to exercise his right of franchise or to be eligible to a public office. Moreover, no Swiss citizen can be denied residence any-where within the Confederation unless he makes himself "unde-sirable" as a criminal or as a public charge, in which case he may be expelled from any canton except his own.

A non-Swiss may be expelled, for similar reasons or for being politically undesirable, either from a canton or from the entire Confederation. Such expulsions are rather frequent. To become a Swiss citizen, a foreigner must comply not only with the federal naturalization law but also with the naturalization laws of the canton in which he resides. The names of prospective citizens are publicly posted, and any Swiss citizen may challenge their fitness. On the whole, naturalization has become increasingly difficult, and a large part of the three to four hundred thousand aliens resi-dent in Switzerland are merely tolerated.

A country in which every elector is at the same time a legislator and where in some districts abstention from the polls is punishable by a fine may well be expected to have the best educated electorate in the world. As far as internal politics go, there are, with the excep-tion of the Icelanders, probably no better informed citizens than the Swiss. As for foreign policy, they would be slightly less ignor-ant than most other nations if they were not so entirely preoccu-pied with local politics. At the same time, they are among the world's most conservative peoples. This does not necessarily mean that conservatism is the fruit of political wisdom; correct knowl-edge does not guarantee correct action. In most respects however, Swiss hostility to all but very gradual changes is probably justified in a country whose very existence hinges on the preservation of the *status quo*. Yet, in one respect it is difficult to see what advantages Switzerland may gain from being behind every other democratic country in the world: Switzerland has no female suffrage. This is the more (or perhaps the less?) remarkable as Swiss women enjoy a very advanced social and professional status. But somehow the idea of female suffrage appears unthinkable to a large number of Swiss—and if we consider that in order to extend the vote to women the proposed change would have to be voted on by all Swiss citizens except the women, it is difficult to see just how and when an end can be put to this impasse.

I V

There are several popular misconceptions concerning the language situation in Switzerland. Some believe that the Swiss speak a language called Swiss. Others (surprisingly many) are convinced that every Swiss speaks French, German, Italian, and possibly even English, all equally well. Actually, most Swiss speak dialects and few know more than one language well.

Officially, the Swiss constitution declares that German, French, and Italian are all official and national languages of Switzerland. An amendment of 1938 declares Romansh, a Latin dialect spoken in parts of the Grisons, especially the Engadine, the fourth national —but not official—language of Switzerland. The distinction between *national* and *official* is made in order to avoid the necessity of translating all federal state papers into Romansh. Indeed, all federal documents are translated into the three official languages, all three versions being equally authoritative. Complicated as this may sound, it is simple compared to what follows.

In Switzerland German is not a spoken, but a written language. Official papers, newspapers, and most literary works are written in German. The spoken language, called Schwyzerdütsch, is largely unintelligible to anyone but a Swiss German. Varying from canton to canton, it is called *Bernerdütsch* in Berne, *Baslerdütsch* in Basel, and so forth. Schwyzerdütsch is not a mere vernacular, however. Indeed, Switzerland was virtually an independent nation before Luther, through his translation of the Bible, created the language which became standard German. In the meantime Swiss writers who wrote in the vernacular, that is, who did not write in Latin, used their own Alemannic dialect as a matter of course. In the Renaissance period even those Swiss cantons that were, like Fribourg, predominantly French-speaking, adopted Swiss German or Latin when dealing with their confederates. No importance was attached to the difference of languages, which was taken for granted. In the late seventeenth century French became the literary language of many Swiss Germans, but in this they followed only the general German trend, exemplified by Leibnitz and Frederick the Great. Vernacular literature, which never completely disappeared, was revived in the nineteenth century. One Swiss poet of that period, August Corrodi of Zurich, even went so far as to translate the poems of Robert Burns into Schwyzerdütsch. At present there again is a rising tendency among Swiss German writers to write in their Alemannic dialect.

Schwyzerdütsch is distinguished in still another respect from dialects in the ordinary meaning of that term. It is spoken by all Swiss Germans, regardless of class. The educated upper classes, it is true, are well able to speak standard German, but they rarely do so.

All in all, there are three varieties of German spoken in Alemannic Switzerland: Schwyzerdütsch, by everybody; standard German, occasionally used in formal speeches and by the large German colony; and standard German pronounced like Schwyzerdütsch, a mixture useful in dealing with German-speaking foreigners. Where the French element has exerted a strong influence, as in Berne, it is represented by a strong admixture in the local dialect. A watch, for instance, is known in *Bernerdütsch* as a *kellörettli*, obviously derived from *Quelle heure est-il?* (The diminutive ending, -*li*, is characteristic of many Swiss German words, particularly proper names.) This somewhat ludicrous mixture of French and Germanic is not confined to Switzerland, but extends into Alsace-Lorraine, parts of the Rhineland, and Holland.

While German is only perfunctorily taught in the schools of French Switzerland, French is the second language of a very large number of German Swiss, notably those connected with business, commerce, and the hotel industry. Though spoken fluently, it is massacred pitilessly. The rough and guttural singsong of Schwyzerdütsch is all-pervading and is applied with murderous effectiveness to any language a German Swiss may choose to speak. Natives of French Switzerland will often point out that they have no quarrel with "good" German, but that the unrefined sounds produced by the German Swiss turn their stomachs. The German Swiss, on the other hand, regard the German spoken in

Germany with such hatred that they often prefer to flounder in French than to admit that they can understand or speak the German of Germany. This has been particularly true since the days of Hitler.

The German Swiss are accused by the French Swiss of massacring French; the French Swiss are accused of the same crime by the French French. This accusation is to a large degree unjustified and rests on a confusion between the French spoken by the literate natives of French Switzerland and the French used by officialdom. The former, though somewhat provincial and occasionally quaint, is, on the whole, proper French. As for the official French, accurately nicknamed *français fédéral*, it is largely the creation of bureaucrats, with a heavy Swiss German influence. As a living language, it may be disregarded.

Besides the French as spoken in Geneva, Lausanne, Neuchâtel, and other towns (which certainly is superior to what passes for French in Belgium), a patois akin to Savoyard has survived in some rural areas. Though rapidly dying out, it lingers in many place names and family names. Endings in *z* or *x* (usually not pronounced) are typical, as in Bex, Château d'Oex (pronounced *deh*), De Traz, Ramuz, etc. Controversy is still raging between Parisians, who pronounce Chamonix with the final *x*, and the Genevese and Savoyards, who do not. Old patois have their deepest roots in the outlying valleys of the Valais, where they are related to the French dialects spoken in parts of Italian Piedmont. The Genevese patois has, moreover, survived in the national anthem of the city, which begins with the words

> Cé qu'è laîno, le Maîtré dé bataillé,
> Que se moqué et se ri dé canaillé,
> A ben fai vi pe on Desando nay
> Qu'il étivé Patron dé Genevois.*

* The following are translations into English and standard French:

"He who is above, the Lord of battles, Who scorns and laughs at the rabble, Has plainly shown, on a Saturday night, That He was the patron of the Genevese."

"Celui qui est là-haut, le Maître des batailles, Qui se moque et se rit des canailles, A bien fait voir, par une nuit de samedi, Qu'il était le patron des Genevois."

The word *Genevois* in the patois version is, of course, to be pronounced *Genevoué*, in accordance with the pronunciation of old French.

This is much as though the people of New York City had their own anthem and sang it in seventeenth-century Dutch.

The Italian-speaking Swiss, who almost all live in the canton of Ticino, are somewhat at a disadvantage. German is spoken by 71 percent of the Swiss population; French, the language of 22 percent of the Swiss, is a second language in all German Switzerland; Italian, spoken by only 5 percent, is nowhere taught as a compulsory language outside the Ticino. As a result, the Ticinese are obliged, in all cultural fields, to look to Milan rather than to Switzerland, while those engaged in commerce or politics must learn one or two additional languages. As for the rural population, they speak much the same dialect as do the people of northern Lombardy, around Lake Como, Maggiore, and Lugano.

There remains only Romansh, which sounds and looks like a mixture of one third Latin, one third Italian, and one third Schwyzerdütsch. Whether or not this is an exact analysis, this writer is not qualified to assert. Though spoken by only a handful of people, it is the oldest language of Switzerland, for it is the only one that has persisted without interruption from Roman times to the present day. As a result, Romansh has an old and extensive literature. Nevertheless, and in spite of official pronouncements, it is a dialect rather than a language, being merely a branch of the Rhaeto-Romanic tongue, which is spoken in the Italian Tyrol and in Friuli as well as in Switzerland. In some regions it is known as Ladin rather than Romansh. Fanatic Ladin-speakers are likely to assert that their dialect is closer to Latin than any other tongue, a belief no doubt based on the name of the language. Romansh people seldom go so far, but then they are the only Rhaetic people who can boast that their dialect has become a national language.

It is a mistaken assumption to believe that linguistic differences ever stood in the way of Swiss unification. Unification was completed in 1848, when modern nationalism had not yet reached the point at which people of different tongues automatically assumed that they were made of different stuff. It was only after the outbreak of the First World War that friction between Alemannic and Romanic Switzerland became acute, and even then it did not constitute an internal problem, but one of foreign policy. The French and Italian population of Switzerland are minorities only in numbers, but not minorities in the accepted sense. They enjoy absolute equality with the German-speaking majority, their languages are equally valid in all parts of the Confederation, and in this respect it is true that there is a Swiss language which is manifested, like a trinity, in German, in French, and in Italian. This is difficult to visualize for anyone who thinks of minorities as of foreign elements in the body politic, as is somewhat the case even in the United States and much more in Central Europe. The antagonism between the Swiss language groups is not one of language, but of culture, a conflict between latinity and teutonism, and it rests less on linguistic differences than on differences of temperament, manners, sense of humor, and other such subtle causes of division. A young man from Geneva will forgive a Swiss German girl her dialect, but not her clothing or make-up habits.

It is incontrovertibly true that the rise of nationalism has, in Switzerland as well as elsewhere, deepened the linguistic division, but it also has operated in an opposite direction, and to a much larger extent. The growing Swiss consciousness of belonging to one nationality, regardless of a language, proves that language is not the only or even a particularly important bond of a nation. It proves another thing as well, namely, that the fusion of peoples speaking different languages has not been achieved in a spirit of internationalism, but of nationalism.

II: The Perpetual Status Quo

SWITZERLAND, Montesquieu said, is the image of freedom. There was only one thing they lacked, Gibbon told the Bernese a few years later: freedom.

"Free—the Swiss?" Goethe exclaimed at the end of Montesquieu's and Gibbon's century. "What one cannot make people believe!" Not much later, Schiller began to plan his *William Tell*.

Unhistorical though Schiller's play may be, it contains a line which helps to explain why Switzerland has been at all times a symbol of freedom as well as reaction. It is the third line of the oath which the representatives of Uri, Schwyz, and Unterwalden pronounced, according to legend, on the clearing called the Rütli: "Wir wollen frei sein wie die Väter waren" [We wish to be as free as our fathers were].

As free as our fathers—not more, not less. Schiller meant, in this phrase, free *like* our fathers, but the ambiguity of his expression contains more truth than he realized. The whole political history of Switzerland, with but a few interruptions, was an attempt to maintain the *status quo ante* through thick and thin and for all eternity. The only thing that changed with the times was the idea the Swiss entertained as to what precisely the *status quo ante* had actually been. Even that did not change much. Everything else in Swiss history—if Switzerland as a whole is considered—was purely accidental. There never was any design common to all the cantons, except that of maintaining what had been there before.

Before what, one might ask?

The exact definition of the word *ante* in *status quo ante* differed from case to case, so that a comprehensive definition must degenerate into a brief history of the Swiss people. Well, let it degenerate!

Whatever happened in Switzerland before the disintegration of the Roman Empire belongs to the history and prehistory of Switzerland, but not of the Swiss. The early history of the Swiss has little to do with the lake dwellers who inhabited Switzerland in the New Stone Age, or with the Helvetii and the Rhaetii, the partly Celtic, partly Liguric tribes that Caesar encountered in the Gallic Wars. A temple of Jupiter still stands in ruins atop the Great St. Bernard Pass; great cities, such as Aventicum, where hundreds of thousands once lived prosperously under Roman rule, have been unearthed; innumerable place names have survived from Roman times to this day; and automobiles are rolling over roads and bridges built on the foundations that the Roman legions laid. But the Swiss past lies not there: it lies with the laws and customs of some barbaric tribes of Germany.

Three of these tribes were to conquer Switzerland. The Burgundians settled along the western fringe of Helvetia—not as enemies, but as allies of Rome. The Alemanni came as conquerors, taking over all but the core of the Rhaetic provinces. In the sixth century both tribes were subdued by the Franks under Clovis. Until the disintegration of Charlemagne's empire, in 887, the larger part of the country was, in theory at least, under Frankish administration. From 887 until 1032 (the dates are somewhat arbitrary), western Switzerland from Basel to Geneva was part of the kingdom of Upper Burgundy, while the rest passed to Germany.

During that period the larger part of Switzerland underwent pretty much the same process as all Western Europe. The imperial or royal officials gradually established themselves as feudal dynasties. In addition to their territorial fiefs, they acquired rights of jurisdiction in territories held by ecclesiastical lords, and even in free communes. When the Upper Burgundian kingdom dissolved, in the eleventh century, and all Switzerland passed under the Holy Roman Empire, the feudal system seemed fairly well established. The bishops of Basel, Lausanne, Geneva, Sion, and Chur, and the abbots of St. Gall and Einsiedeln were raised to princely rank, holding their dominions in fief directly from the emperor, and great families like the houses of Zähringen, Lenz-burg, and Kyburg became virtual sovereigns over vast tracts of land inside and outside Switzerland. However, as in the rest of Europe, the feudal institutions here carried the germs of their own decay. Cities grew from military outposts, and by the thirteenth century the most powerful among them were made Free Cities of the Empire—in other words, they were placed under the immediate jurisdiction of the emperor and freed of their feudal relations with the local nobles.

In most of Western Europe the birth of nations in the modern sense was the result of the growth of towns and the increasing importance of the bourgeois elements. The evolution proceeded in a forward direction, with few backward glances. Not so in Switzerland. The origin of the Swiss nation is to be found, not in the towns, where feudalism had been overcome, but in the Alpine valleys, where it had never taken root. Here the *status quo ante* meant the conditions which had existed, or were imagined to have existed, before feudalism began to make its inroads.

In the valleys of Uri and Schwyz the local administration had consisted, since times immemorial, of a *Markgenossenschaft*, the body of all inhabitants regardless of their feudal status. Under the vague feudal superstructure created by the Frankish rulers, Uri had been deeded in 853 to the convent of Fraumünster at Zurich by Louis the German. If the suzerainty belonged to the nuns, however, the temporal jurisdiction belonged to the house of Zähringen and, after its extinction in 1218, to the counts of Hapsburg. In Schwyz, where originally the vast majority of the population had been freemen, the situation was still more confused. What is clear is that in the thirteenth century the right of jurisdiction also passed to the Hapsburgs.

The feudal structure was deceptive. By maintaining their popular assemblies, the *Markgenossenschaften* continued to assert their democratic rights inherited from the old Germanic institutions. The fact that most of the population were freemen, and thus had the right to bear arms and to serve abroad, gave them delusions of grandeur and independence. They consequently seized upon the first opportunity to free themselves of all feudal obligations toward any lord except the emperor himself.

The opportunity came when the emperor, Frederick II of Hohenstaufen, entered upon his long struggle with the papacy. The House of Hapsburg, which had become the first power in Switzerland, sided with the pope, and it was vital for the emperor to entice its subjects in central Switzerland to switch their allegiance from the Hapsburgs to himself. Indeed, they dominated the indispensable St. Gotthard Pass, and thus held a key position. As a result, Frederick II was only too glad to grant, in 1231, letters patent to the people of Uri, who had bought back their rights from the Hapsburgs, and to put them under the immediate jurisdiction of the Empire. In the case of Schwyz, it was not even necessary for the people to buy themselves off. Through the Charter of Faenza, in 1240, the Schwyzers received the same privileges as Uri, as a reward for having taken sides with Frederick II against the pope.

As far as the people of Uri and Schwyz were concerned, matters stopped there. Unfortunately for them, Rudolph of Hapsburg, who did not share their views, became emperor in 1273. One of his first acts was to revoke the Charter of Faenza. However, considering the turbulent disposition of the Schwyzers, he promised to place them under his direct and personal jurisdiction.

But Rudolph I was a busy man. His family, from its modest beginnings in the ancestral castle of Habsburg near the Swiss town of Aargau, where its ruins still stand, had come to rule over a considerable section of Germany and Austria, and the imperial dignity added to his many duties. It was unreasonable to expect him to spend his time in some forsaken Alpine village, sitting in judgment over cases involving stolen goats. The Swiss, however, were unreasonable; this was precisely what they expected him to do. When he began to send bailiffs to their communities in order to administer justice in his name, they were outraged. A bailiff, a servant, possibly a man of servile origin, sit in judgment over free men? They would not dream of it.

In fact, the mountaineers had real cause for anxiety. Rudolph had tripled their taxes, he levied tolls at the entrance to the St. Gotthard Pass, and he acquired magisterial rights in neighboring Glarus, Einsiedeln, Lucerne, and Unterwalden. If things were allowed to go their course, he soon would have them as firmly under his control as much of the rest of Switzerland. Consequently, immediately after learning the news that Rudolph was dead, they resolved to reaffirm their old rights before another emperor was elected. On August 1, 1291, the leaders of the three communities of Uri, Schwyz, and Lower Unterwalden signed the Eternal Pact, in which they affirmed their independence from the Hapsburgs and promised each other assistance against any encroachment on their real or fancied rights.

The three communities had succeeded in becoming as free as their fathers had been. In the general confusion that followed Rudolph's death it was easy for them to uphold their claims and to throw out their bailiffs. Since no more Hapsburgs were elected emperor for a considerable period, they also had the blessings of the imperial court, which favored everything that diminished the power of the great feudatories. Their status of immediacy under the Empire was confirmed upon several occasions by subsequent emperors. Against Austria, of which the Hapsburgs had become dukes, the Confederates defended themselves successfully at Morgarten, in 1315, and again at Sempach and Näfels, in 1386 and 1388. By that time their Confederation had increased to eight members.* Having renewed their oaths of confederation in 1393, the Swiss cantons had become firmly established as a national entity.

To the rural cantons of central Switzerland the adherence to the league of towns like Zurich and Berne was a mixed blessing. It strengthened their military position, but at the same time it threatened the continued existence of the beloved *status quo*. In no case would they allow the balance between city cantons and rural cantons to incline in favor of the cities. Thus, from the admission of Berne, in 1353, until 1481 the rural cantons successfully opposed the admission of any new members.

They also fought a civil war to prevent Zurich from increasing its territory in the direction of the rural cantons. The quarrel, known as the Zurich War, broke out in 1336 over the distribution of the lands belonging to the extinct family of Toggenburg. It resulted in the temporary secession of Zurich, which was ulti-

---

* The five additional members were: Lucerne (1332); Zurich (1351); Glarus and Zug (1352); and Berne (1353).

mately defeated, and the intervention, in favor of Zurich, of Charles VII of France. The bone of contention, by the way, the county of Toggenburg, was finally purchased by the abbot of St. Gall.

Civil war seemed imminent again in 1481, when cities and rural cantons were divided over the admission of Fribourg and Solothurn, two more towns, into the league. Tempers were so hot that only a saint could have calmed them down. Providentially, a saint appeared. He was a hermit, Nicholas of Flue, who has been canonized only recently. Hermit though he was, he seems to have followed political news rather closely, for it was in the nick of time that he made his dramatic entrance into the diet, which was held in the village of Stans. There he made a short speech, in which he advised the Confederates to settle their differences by compromise rather than war. The towns should be admitted, he suggested, and in return they should abandon their separate alliances. It was a sensible speech such as any sensible man would have made, yet sensible speeches have seldom impressed statesmen. Nothing is more justified than the canonization of Saint Nicholas, for anyone who can make politicians listen to sense must be a saint. What is more, Saint Nicholas returned to his hermitage immediately after he had fulfilled his mission—a fine precedent and one that arbitrators should keep in mind.

Fribourg and Solothurn were admitted on condition that they remain neutral in any conflict that might divide the original eight cantons. On the same terms two more cities—Basel and Schaffhausen—were admitted in 1501, and one more rural canton—Appenzell—in 1513. From then until 1798 the number of Confederates remained thirteen, although applications for membership were not lacking. The reason for this exclusiveness was not any perverse preference for the unlucky number, but again the sanctity of the *status quo*.

The *status quo* was maintained in more than one respect. In the course of the fourteenth, fifteen, and sixteenth centuries the individual cantons had acquired, through purchase, conquest, or alliance, a considerable number of territories. Switzerland as a whole —then still commonly known as the Confederation of the Leagues of Upper Germany—was no longer made up simply of the members of a league, but had become an extremely complex organism, for the simple reason that the *status quo* was maintained in all newly acquired territories.

First of all there were the thirteen cantons, of which only the first eight were fully equal partners. These cantons were by no means political units in the modern sense of the word. In the case of the city cantons, only the full citizens of the towns of Berne, Zurich, Basel, and so forth were actually members of the Confederation. The lands which they ruled and their inhabitants were held in subjection. The reason for this state of affairs was simple: the original compact had been entered into only by the sovereign burgesses of the towns, and they saw no reason for extending to the rural population privileges which they had not held before. The feudal domination which they themselves rejected they regarded as perfectly proper for their subjects, who by passing under their rule had simply changed masters. Serfdom, it is true, was abolished by the fourteenth century, but not because of libertarian principles. The citizens of the Swiss towns insisted on being as free as their fathers had been, but they also insisted that their rural subjects should remain as unfree as *their* fathers had been. However, serfdom, which was on its way out throughout Western Europe, was particularly unpracticable in states where the lord was not a single, concrete person, but a corporate body of citizens. The subject population of Switzerland, though theoretically consisting of free men, was more limited in its rights before the French Revolution than the vast majority of the French under the *ancien régime*.

The same situation prevailed in the rural cantons. Only the original communities which had joined in 1291 were really free. Districts which had been acquired subsequently retained the status they had held at that particular time. In Schwyz, for instance, the larger part of the land and the people were held in subjection by the smaller part.

The Confederation, however, was not merely composed of the thirteen cantons, or *Orte*, as they were called in German. Among its other components were the so-called subject territories. Uri and Schwyz had conquered, in the fourteenth and fifteenth centuries, the triangular area between the St. Gotthard

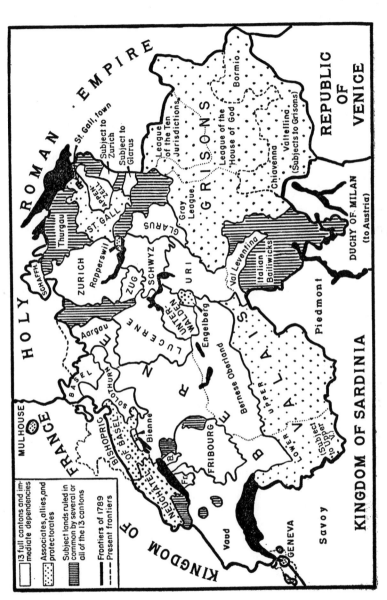

SWITZERLAND IN 1789

and Lake Lugano, the present canton of Ticino. Here, again, they perpetuated the feudal conditions which had prevailed before the conquests. From the forbidding castles, which still seem to threaten the sunny landscape from almost every hilltop, the bailiffs of Uri and Schwyz ruled the valleys of the Ticino far more harshly than the Austrian bailiffs had ever ruled in Uri and Schwyz.

Aargau, Thurgau, and Vaud were seized by the Confederates between 1415 and 1536. The lion's share went to Berne, but some of the subject territories were ruled jointly by one, several, or all members of the Confederation. These were called "Common Bailiwicks" and "Free Bailiwicks," none of which was governed in exactly the same way as any other, since here again the *status quo* was faithfully preserved.

So far, things are relatively simple. Unfortunately, there were still other components: associates, allies, and protectorates. The Grisons, itself a confederation of three separate leagues, was an associated power. In turn, the Grisons held a subject territory, the Valtellina, which extend as far south as Lake Como. Among the other associates were the prince-abbot of St. Gall; the Upper Valais (which in turn held the Lower Valais in subjection); the town of Mulhouse in Alsace; and Geneva. Between associates and allies there was little distinction, except that the bonds of alliance were not as permanent as those of association. Strasbourg and a number of Swabian towns were Swiss allies at some time or another. As for protectorates, they included the territory of the abbey of Engelberg and a number of other small districts.

The whole of this rambling organism, which was Switzerland before the French Revolution, was held together by no central government of any kind. The federal diet, which met irregularly and had no fixed meeting place, had no power in itself, but was merely a conference of ambassadors, whose votes were tied to the instructions they received from their governments. All its acts were in the form of treaties or covenants concluded between quasi-sovereign states. When the Reformation split Switzerland into two camps, these agreements largely fell into desuetude, and the diet even ceased to meet.

By the end of the fifteenth century, however, Switzerland had a remarkable degree of national cohesion, which was based mainly

BATTLE BETWEEN THE SWISS AND THE BURGUNDIANS
AT NANCY, 1477
Pen drawing from a chronicle, c. 1500

on its common military organization. Within forty years the Swiss decisively defeated three of Europe's most powerful monarchs: Charles the Bold of Burgundy in 1476, Emperor Maximilian I in 1499, and Louis XII of France in 1513. The first and the last of these victories, though they enhanced the military reputation of the Swiss, had no effect on their national status. The victory over Maximilian in the battle of Dornach was something else again. It was the Confederates' way of answering Maximilian's attempt to impose an imperial tax on them. As a result of his crushing defeat, Maximilian was obliged to sign the Treaty of Basel, which specifically exempted Switzerland from all obligations to the Holy Roman Empire. The cantons now held much the same status as that of the Irish Free State within the British Commonwealth: they were part of the empire, but only in so far as it suited them.

The beneficent results of national independence and unity were entirely destroyed by the Reformation. Preached first by Zwingli in Zurich about 1523, it spread rapidly to Basel, Berne, and Schaffhausen and made inroads in Solothurn, Fribourg, Appenzell, and Glarus. Only in the Four Forest Cantons—as Uri, Schwyz, Unterwalden, and Lucerne came to be called—did it meet with utter failure. The fact was that the Reformation favored the economic and political interests of the city cantons and harmed the rural cantons. However, whether they welcomed the Reformation or opposed it, all the cantons took their position in the name of the *status quo ante:* to some, it meant the state of the church before its corruption; to others, the church before the introduction of new doctrines. Those who saw in the Reformation a possibility for establishing a more equitable social order—the Anabaptists—were ruthlessly suppressed by Zwingli.

In the inevitable war which resulted from Zwingli's missionary zeal, the Catholics were victorious. Zwingli himself fell in the battle of Kappel in 1531, and peace was made in the same year. By its terms, the *status quo* was established as the permanent religious division of Switzerland. Needless to say, the subject districts were forced to adopt the creed of their masters.

As a result of the Peace of Kappel, the Protestant cantons, with a combined population far larger than that of the rest of the Confederates, faced the prospect of being systematically outvoted in the diet by the less populous, but more numerous, Catholic cantons. Applications for full membership by Protestant states, such as Geneva, were doomed, since the Catholics feared the loss of their majority. Finally, in 1586 the seven Catholic cantons,* under the leadership of Lucerne and with the blessings of Saint Charles Borromeus, archbishop of Milan, joined in a defensive and offensive league. The Borromean League, as it was called, thenceforward met in a separate diet.

Despite this fateful division, which obliterated almost all traces of national unity, Switzerland remained neutral during the Thirty Years War. This apparent paradox was actually the logical consequence of Switzerland's division, since every individual canton could, by furnishing mercenaries, support either the Protestant or the Catholic side in that conflict. Only the leagues of the Grisons, where almost every community and every castle was autonomous, became a theater of war, with France and Spain fighting over the possession of the Valtellina. As the Catholics took up arms for Spain, and the Protestants for France, the Grisons became the scene of some of the most fratricidal mayhem ever perpetrated in history.

The Thirty Years War was barely over, when again a religious war broke out in Switzerland, in 1656. Again the Catholics were victorious, and the *status quo* was maintained. Finally, in 1712, the Protestants could take their revenge. War had broken out once more over a quarrel concerning the religious status of some communes in the Toggenburg which belonged to the prince-abbot of St. Gall. The Protestant cantons intervened, and this time soundly defeated the Catholics. The victory was somewhat belated. Except for some minor concessions, conditions remained as they had been since the Peace of Kappel. They have been aptly summed up by Hamilton and Madison in Number 19 of the *Federalist:*

The connection among the Swiss cantons scarcely amounts to a confederacy; though it is sometimes cited as an instance of the stability of such institutions.

---

* The Four Forest Cantons, Zug, Solothurn, and Fribourg. Appenzell, moreover, split into the Catholic half-canton Ausser-Rhoden and the Protestant half-canton Inner-Rhoden in 1589.

They have no common treasury; no common troops even in war; no common coin; no common judicatory; nor any other common mark of sovereignty.

They are kept together by the peculiarity of their topography; by their individual weakness and insignificancy; by the fear of powerful neighbors, to one of which they were formerly subject; by the few sources of contention among a people of such simple and homogeneous manners; by their joint interest in their dependent possessions; by the mutual aid they stand in need of, for suppressing insurrections and rebellions, an aid expressly stipulated, and often required and afforded. . . .

. . . The controversies on the subject of religion, which in three instances have kindled violent and bloody contests, may be said, in fact, to have severed the league. The Protestant and Catholic cantons have since had their separate diets, where all the most important concerns are adjusted, and which have left the general diet little other business than to take care of the common bailages.

II

At the cost of three "violent and bloody contests," the Swiss had managed to maintain the *status quo* of distribution of the different conceptions as to what was the original *status quo* of their religious beliefs. During that period they had also made great strides backward in their social and political make-up.

In all the cantons, where they were ruled by corporate guilds, as was Zurich, by aristocracies, as were Berne and Lucerne, or by a privileged citizen class, as were the rural cantons, the prosperous oligarchies had lost interest in territorial aggrandizement. Their main concern was to consolidate and increase their riches, to limit the number of citizens with whom they had to share them, and to put down rebellion wherever it raised its ugly head.

In the towns the population was still very small, but nonetheless it had been relatively increased by the influx of peasants who sought employment in the rapidly expanding textile and watch industries. To such newcomers full citizenship was denied. Intermarriage between citizens and subjects, which in former times had enabled members of the subject classes to secure citizenship for their descendents, was discouraged or forbidden. While the ranks of the underprivileged were thus gathering more and more recruits, the ranks of the actual governing class became ever more restricted.

The burgher class, which constituted the bulk of the free citizenry, were more concerned with increasing their own wealth and with keeping out upstarts than with exercising their political prerogatives. The tedious routine of government they were glad to delegate to a thin crust of aristocratic families. These aristocratic families, in turn, saw to it that government should become their exclusive privilege, lest the burghers should chance to change their minds. To some degree every town in seventeenth- and eighteenth-century Switzerland was ruled by a self-perpetuating oligarchy which had originally been appointed by a plutocracy.

The underprivileged classes, in descending order, were the *natives*, born in the ruling town, but prevented by their ancestry from becoming full citizens; the *new settlers*, whose descendents would join the ranks of the natives; and the *subjects*, who formed the rural population. In the so-called democratic, or rural, cantons the situation was much the same.

The system described above was reaching its full flower at the time when Montesquieu declared that Switzerland was the image of freedom. Among the Swiss themselves there were many who thought differently. Rebellions, as the *Federalist* pointed out, were frequent—especially for "a people of such simple and homogeneous manners," who had "but few sources of contention." The editors of the German *Universal Lexicon*, published in 1738, remarked on the subject of Lucerne that "the rural folk are inclined toward rebellions, which they have often stirred up, notably in 1571, 1653, and 1712, but in which they have regularly lost out." The same could have been said of almost every Swiss canton. Even among the bourgeoisie there was a growing movement toward more liberal social order.

Indeed, a situation had once more arisen in which the Swiss no longer agreed on what exactly constituted the *status quo ante*. The ruling classes held that the state of things such as it then existed was the same as it had always been, and consequently the best and sacred. The propagandists of Enlightenment, on the other hand, contended that the *status quo* had been upset, that originally the Swiss had been free, and that they should once more unite in order to reconquer the freedom of their fathers. In the seventeen nineties some politicians in Vaud pushed this theory to an extreme. They called on the French Revolutionary government to help them restore feudal privileges which their Bernese rulers had suppressed.

The most vocal among the advocates of a return to ancient liberties, including Jean Jacques Rousseau, were obliged by the cantonal governments to seek refuge outside Switzerland. In Paris, particularly, there was a flourishing colony of expatriate Swiss at the time of the outbreak of the French Revolution. Unfortunately, their ideas were far in advance of those held by the majority of their countrymen, who had stayed at home. Their constant agitation to stir up in Switzerland enthusiasm for the Revolution found but a weak echo there, except in the subject districts. Indeed, their political program involved weakening the power of the cantonal governments and setting up a central government—an innovation which seemed excessively bold to most Swiss. What is more, it would have scrapped all the petty feudal privileges enjoyed, in one way or another, by nearly every class of the population. To many, these petty and often peculiar rights, cherished for generations, meant more than equality under the law.

The Swiss liberals in Paris were more successful in their dealings with the French Revolutionary government, which they tried to convince of the necessity of freeing Switzerland from its aristocratic rulers. By the end of 1797 the French had grown tired of waiting for the Swiss to strike the first blow for liberty, and by the beginning of 1798 a French army, commanded by General Montesquiou, invited itself to assist the Swiss in making up their minds. This intervention, which brought foreign troops into Switzerland for the first time in its history, was largely due to the growing influence of General Bonaparte, who was to seize the power in the following year. Two main objectives were in his mind: to seize the treasure of Berne—which, though large enough, had been exaggerated to fabulous proportions and had become legendary in the circles of the money-starved French government—and to dominate the Swiss mountain passes. Both were accomplished. The gold of Berne was seized and sunk immediately into Napoleon's Egyptian campaign, the aristocratic governments were overthrown, the Helvetic Republic was proclaimed, and all resistance, notably in the Four Forest Cantons, was repressed with a brutality which is still remembered.

The constitution of the Helvetic Republic, the first that Switzerland ever had, set up a uniform state and reduced the cantons to administrative districts. The former subject districts were emancipated, social equality before the law was established, torture and other medieval survivals were abolished. One might think that the larger part of the population would have accepted the change with gratitude, but the contrary was the case. Except in the liberated subject lands, the constitution, changed six times between 1798 and 1803, satisfied only a small minority. It was made unworkable by ceaseless internal squabbles, jealousies, and constant conflicting requests by the Swiss statesmen asking the First Consul to intervene in their quarrels.* Even modern Swiss historians, though mindful of the cruelties of the "French yoke," are likely to overlook the positive side of the constitution and to gloss over the inglorious aspects of Swiss statesmanship during the Napoleonic period. The sad but obvious truth was that the Swiss proved unable to govern themselves and unready to be a democratic nation. It was Napoleon's realization that the Swiss were far more eager to preserve ancient rights than to promote any new-fangled freedoms that ultimately led him, in 1803, to go back to the old order of things.

The weakness of the Helvetic Republic was clearly demonstrated when the French troops were withdrawn: political chaos resulted immediately, and the Helvetic government was saved only by the return of the occupation troops. Bonaparte, on the other hand, was not eager to continue the occupation. A neutral Switzerland was more useful to him than an occupied one—especially since, in his own rather frank words, Swiss neutrality could exist only so long as he pleased. But a neutral Switzerland was not viable as long as it depended on the presence of French bayonets. Bonaparte solved this seemingly insoluble dilemma through his celebrated Act of Mediation, which was probably the astutest diplomatic feat of his career.

* Chaos was increased by the fact that in 1799 three armies—the French, the Austrian, and the Russian—were fighting out the war of the Second Coalition on Swiss territory.

Broadly speaking, the Act of Mediation re-established division into quasi-sovereign cantons. However, by constituting the former subject districts of Aargau, Thurgau, Vaud, and Ticino and the former associated lands of Grisons and St. Gall into six new cantons, he deprived Berne of its former predominant position. Being leaderless, the federal diet (over which Napoleon set a president, or *Landamman*) was entirely subservient to Paris. As for their internal government, Napoleon allowed the Swiss to express their love for individual freedom by re-establishing such cherished customs as judicial torture.

Though it was neutral—and for that matter a state—only by the grace of Napoleon, who took the official title of Mediator of the Swiss Confederation, Switzerland knew relative peace and order under the new regime. A reasonable facsimile of a *status quo* seemed to have been achieved. By 1813, however, after Napoleon's defeat in the battle of Leipzig, the conservative elements felt their hearts glowing at the prospect that the real *status quo*, the *status quo* which had existed before 1789, might be re-established. They were not mistaken, for within a short time, with Metternich's advice prevailing over Tsar Alexander's, an Austrian army crossed the borders of the Confederation. Except in the former subject cantons, which feared for their continued existence, the invaders were greeted as liberators.

On the heels of "Liberation" came the return of the aristocrats to power and a general scramble among the cantons to secure for themselves as many advantages as the allies would permit them. At Zurich the representatives of the Big Four—Austria, England, Russia, and Prussia—were supervising the efforts of the cantons to arrive at a new Pact of Confederation. It is likely that without their guidance, or rather bullying, the Swiss would never have arrived at even as loose a form of federation as they ultimately reached. The fact that the four Great Powers, at loggerheads in so many respects, were able to act in agreement and thus were able to overcome the discord that reigned among the representatives of one of Europe's most insignificant nations, should serve as food for thought, especially for those who proclaim that the Swiss have shown Europe the way to harmony. It is true that two of the four representatives—Capo d'Istria of Russia and Stratford-Canning of England—were somewhat above the ordinary run of diplomats.

After much wrangling, the Federal Pact was finally accepted by the Swiss late in 1814 and ratified on August 7, 1815. Leaving the details of the territorial borders for discussion at the Congress of Vienna, the Pact provided for a confederation of sovereign cantons and a federal diet which, as in the past, was little more than a conference of ambassadors. The few federal executive functions for which the Pact provided were exercised in turn by the governments of the cantons of Berne, Zurich, and Lucerne for two-year periods. The nineteen cantons of the Mediation period continued in existence—in other words, the former subject lands retained their independence—and three new cantons were admitted: Valais, Neuchâtel, and Geneva.

At the Congress of Vienna, where every single canton was represented, the present borders of Switzerland were established with a few very minor exceptions. The Valtellina, detached from the Grisons in 1797, was given to the Lombardo-Venetian kingdom; but for the lackadaisical attitude of the Swiss, it might easily have been restored to Switzerland. Geneva acquired some small tracts of land from Sardinia, and Berne received the former bishopric of Basel * (the Bernese Jura) as partial compensation for the loss of its subject lands. In the Final Act of the Congress, the four Great Powers, later joined by France, promised to guarantee the neutrality of Switzerland.

Even before the Final Act was signed the allies were exerting pressure on Switzerland, whose neutrality they were about to guarantee, to declare war on Napoleon, who had returned from Elba. In the opinion of the allies, there was little point for the Swiss to stick to neutrality at a time when Napoleon's armies threatened to reduce the guarantee to a shred of paper. The Swiss did not regard the matter in this light and preferred to stall for time. Finally, on June 12, 1815, six days before Waterloo, they ratified their alliance with the Coalition. Austrian troops began to cross Switzerland on their way to France, and on July 3 a Swiss army invaded French territory. On July 22 the campaign was

* The lands of the prince-bishops of Basel; it should not be confused with either the city of Basel or the half-canton of Basel-Land, where the bishops held no more power since the Reformation.

ended as far as the Swiss were concerned by the simple fact that the Swiss troops had decided to go home. This episode, which the Swiss have fairly well succeeded in eradicating from their national memory, was the last occasion on which Swiss soldiers other than mercenaries set foot on foreign soil, and the last time that armed foreign soldiers set foot on Swiss soil. With the Treaty of Paris, signed on November 20, 1815, the perpetual neutrality of Switzerland was solemnly recognized.

In Switzerland, as elsewhere, the period between 1815 and 1830 was one of unbridled reaction. In 1817 Switzerland joined the Holy Alliance, and the main object of Swiss foreign policy became to appease the fears of the monarchs, who considered Switzerland a hotbed of exiled political agitators. The press was curbed, and laws dating to the reign of Emperor Charles V were put back on the statutes. Internal customs barriers between the cantons became so cumbersome that Switzerland even ceased to be a highway for international trade, a situation which was not improved by the fact that each canton coined its own currency.

This period, traditionally known as the Restoration, gave way about 1830 to the "Regeneration," which continued the struggle begun in the Age of Enlightenment for the reconquest of the lost freedom of the fathers. Though following the main trend of Western Europe, the movement took on peculiarly Swiss characteristics. While in the rest of Europe it culminated in a few, but highly explosive, revolutions, in Switzerland its course rather resembled the popping of a string of small firecrackers.

The nationalist and liberal elements of Switzerland, now joined in the Radical party, agitated for centralization of the federal power, economic unification, popular rule, and in the Catholic cantons for an anticlerical program. In 1830 the first crackers began to pop, quite harmlessly, in Aargau, in Vaud, in Fribourg, and in Schaffhausen, where the country people organized armed expeditions against their capitals. Without shedding any blood, they succeeded in overthrowing their respective regimes. In Berne the aristocratic government relinquished its powers of its own accord in 1831. Zurich, Lucerne, Solothurn, St. Gall, and Thurgau followed into the Radical fold in quick succession. In other cantons things went less smoothly.

In Basel a state of war existed between the town and the country-side from January, 1831, until March, 1832. In September the independence of Basel-Land as a half-canton was finally recognized, but as late as the summer of 1833 an attack by city troops on the rural capital, Liestal, was repelled. The townspeople lost sixty-three lives. In Neuchâtel, where the monarchic constitution proved an additional cause for strife, there were chronic riots, *coups d'état*, and revolutions. As late as 1831 the local authorities of Neuchâtel tried to discourage rioters by sentencing them to life imprisonment, putting them in chains, placing them in the pillory, and flogging them. More tempests in the teapot were raging in Schwyz at the same time, where the district of outer Schwyz declared its independence from inner Schwyz in 1832 and the inner Schwyzers retaliated by occupying Küssnacht in 1833.

In 1831 the seven cantons that had adopted liberal constitutions formed the so-called Concordat of the Seven as a defensive measure. In the following year the reactionary cantons replied by forming the League of Sarnen. Declaring that they would refuse to sit in the same diet with representatives from Basel-Land and Outer Schwyz, they met in a separate diet. In August, 1833, the Federal Diet sent troops to Basel-City and Schwyz, and the League of Sarnen broke up.

While the internal and the external Schwyzers were undergoing their internecine convulsions, the people of Lucerne reconsidered their position. In July, 1833, they decided that old things were better than new ones after all and restored a conservative government to power. Through their defection from the liberal fold, the rift between reactionary and liberal cantons became identical with the division between Catholic and Protestant cantons. Lucerne from now on was the capital of both Catholicism and conservatism in Switzerland.

The reasons for this combination were manifold and had very little to do with religion. The Catholic rural cantons had always been the most conservative elements of Switzerland. They had always opposed the cities. The smallness of their populations and of their territories put them in great danger of losing what influence they had on federal affairs if a centralized government were created. There was reason enough for them to band together, even if the religious question had never come up. When that question did arise, however, it injected an element of passion into their separatist tendencies which was bound to lead to violence.

In 1841 the Radical government of the canton of Aargau committed the blunder of secularizing a number of convents. Lucerne answered by recalling the Jesuits, a gesture which the Radicals for some reason considered a most insolent outrage. Two armed risings were organized by the Radicals of Lucerne, who received the assistance of volunteer bands from other cantons. In their second attempt, which occurred in April, 1845, 100 volunteers were killed and 1900 captured. In the same year the leader of the Catholic peasant party in Lucerne was murdered. No less outraged than the Radicals, the seven Catholic cantons,* whose combined population was but a fifth of Switzerland's total, concluded a separate alliance, the *Sonderbund.*

On July 20, 1847, the federal diet, where the Radicals had held the majority since Geneva had adopted a liberal constitution, ordered the Sonderbund dissolved, on the ground that it violated the Federal Pact of 1815. Defied by the Sonderbund, whose leaders pointed out that the Concordat of the Seven had also been a separate alliance, the diet, on November 4 ordered the federal army to begin hostilities.

The campaign lasted three weeks and cost the Federals exactly 78 lives. The losses of the Sonderbund were still less. General Dufour of Geneva, who led the Federals, seized Fribourg without trouble and from there proceeded to the Forest Cantons, where he defeated the Sonderbund forces at Gislikon, the very unmurderous Swiss Appomatox. Characteristically enough, Dufour, who led the Radicals, was a dyed-in-the-wool conservative, while Ulrich von Salis-Soglio, the commander of the Catholic troops, was a Protestant.

It was a good thing for the Swiss, in more ways than one, that the campaign turned out to be so brief. Indeed, Metternich, who took the view that the four Powers which had guaranteed Swiss neutrality were also responsible for the enforcement of the Federal Pact, had succeeded in convincing the government of Louis-Philippe that the reactionary Catholic cantons should be sup-

* Uri, Schwyz, Unterwalden, Lucerne, Fribourg, Valais, and Zug.

ported against the rising tide of radicalism. Together, Austria and France approached the English government to obtain its approval of intervention. Lord Palmerston, in his usual way, said that he agreed in principle, but that the question required further study. Through his tactics of what came to be called "masterly inaction" Palmerston succeeded in stalling long enough to face France and Austria with the *fait accompli* of a federal victory, and the matter was dropped.

The victors were not particularly vindictive. They contented themselves with expelling the Jesuits from the Confederation for all time, with levying fines on the recalcitrant cantons, and with bringing to a quick conclusion the revision of the Federal Pact, which had been begun just before the outbreak of the war. The result was the Federal Constitution of 1848. In the inevitable cliché of all Swiss textbooks, it changed Switzerland from a confederation of states into a confederate state.

For the first time in its history—excepting the ephemeral Helvetic Republic—Switzerland had a federal government. For the first time democratic constitutions were in force in all its cantons. To the victorious Radicals this merely meant the final realization of the liberties won by the Swiss in 1291. A few more revisions were needed, and they were incorporated in the constitution of 1874, described earlier in this chapter. When at last the popular referendum and initiative were introduced, the Swiss had indeed gained the popular democracy that had characterized the old *Markgenossenschaften* of Uri and Schwyz and the still older popular assemblies of the ancient Germans. There was a return to the *status quo ante*, which went as far back as any one could wish.

Having accomplished this return, the Radicals could settle down. They now were as free as they cared to imagine that their fathers had been. It was time for catching up with the rest of Europe by industrializing their country, exploiting its resources, and increasing their capital. With the advent of the Social-Democrats, the Radicals were completely pushed back into the folds of respectability. They had become the liberal conservatives, and their former opponents the reactionary conservatives. Joining their forces, the two parties have, up to the present date, succeeded most admirably in maintaining the *status quo*.

III: War for Export

THERE ARE SEVERAL ways in which a nation can make good an unfavorable balance of trade. It may mine gold, it may make foreign investments, it may attract tourists, or it may sell its services to foreign nations. The Swiss always had an excess of imports, but they never had gold mines, and their tourist trade dates only from the nineteenth century. As a result, they always had to rely to some extent on the sale of services and on foreign investments. Beginning in the late Middle Ages, they sold military service to foreign powers in the form of mercenaries. In order to exercise their military profession undisturbed and to enjoy its fruits in peace, they soon adopted a policy of neutrality—that is, the territory of Switzerland became neutral, while its citizens took part, on an impartial business basis, in every European war for several centuries.

Thus it happened that the Swiss, who consider themselves the first free and peaceful nation of the Continent, gave their name to an occupation usually involving both servitude and belligerency. Just as now the word Swiss evokes in many minds the picture of a watchmaker or a cheese expert, there was a time when it meant, to most Europeans, a professional soldier, and a ferocious one at that. The belligerent tradition of the Swiss might be traced back to the Helvetii, whom Julius Caesar called the bravest of all the Gauls (though earlier he reserves that distinction for the Belgians), but this would be stretching the importance of heredity a trifle too far. The present Swiss, though strains of the ancient tribes may have persisted, can only remotely be identified with the hardy fighters of Orgetorix that Caesar encountered. A better explanation of the warlike character of the Swiss can be found in their geographic situation, which assuredly has conditioned their methods of warfare. Infantry tactics are natural in mountainous terrain, and the Swiss have always been footsoldiers par excellence. Geography, moreover, accounts for another Swiss characteristic, shared with most highland nations: tribal or local warfare, which they have waged almost continuously from Caesar's time until not long ago. In their continual quarrels the Scots, the Afghans, and the Swiss have a great deal in common.

Yet, despite these traits in common, the Scots, the Afghans, and the Swiss did not develop along precisely the same lines. The Swiss, as distinguished from other highland nations, found themselves in a paradoxical situation. They were protected from the surrounding powers by obstacles of terrain, and at the same time, they perched upon the most important crossroads of Western Europe. No conqueror, no statesman, from Hannibal to Hitler, could make plans for major European conquests without taking Switzerland into account. The Swiss cantons, moreover, were situated in the midst of the possessions of the principal Powers of the Middle Ages and the Renaissance: the emperor of Germany, the pope, France, and Spain. Thus, thanks to the inaccessibility of their habitat, the Swiss could gratify their tribal sense of independence; and, thanks to their strategic situation, they could at the same time play an important political and military role in the contests between their neighboring powers.

Highlanders not only cherish a tribal sense of independence; they also are said to cherish the penny. The insufficiency of their economic resources drives them to thrift or, if that is not enough, raiding their richer neighbors in the valleys or, if that still is not enough, looking for a livelihood in other lands. The Swiss did all three of these things. Their thrift became proverbial. They extended their conquests from their original mountainous core to the fertile shore of Lake Geneva and tried to dominate Lombardy. And many hired themselves out as mercenaries, though retaining enough sense of independence to refuse to fight if they were not paid. Hence the famous dictum: *Pas de sous, pas de Suisses* (No pay, no Swiss). Yet it is unjust to assume that the Swiss fought exclusively as hirelings, though the very word Swiss began to acquire that meaning in the fifteenth century. The wars which established their military reputation were largely fought in their own right.

The Eternal Alliance of 1291 of Uri, Schwyz, and Unterwalden was a defensive alliance. When their initial aim—immediacy under the emperor—was secured in 1309 through its recognition by Henry VII, the economic and political threat of the Hapsburgs was by no means ended; to end it, the Confederates passed on to the offensive. Two hundred years later Maximilian I of Hapsburg, the last champion of feudalism and chivalry, hat in hand and short of cash, was begging the unchivalrous Swiss for military assistance.

It was 1315 that the House of Hapsburg received its first warning of Swiss toughness. Emperor Henry VII had died in 1313, and two rivals contested his succession: Louis the Bavarian and Frederick the Fair of Austria, a Hapsburg. The Swiss naturally sided against the Hapsburgs, from whom they had everything to fear and nothing to gain. Their intervention began in 1314. Without any provocation the Schwyzers, picking up their pikes and crossbows, proceeded to the neighboring abbey of Einsiedeln, whose abbot supported the wrong party, sacked it, and returned herding a prize consisting of goats, cows, and several captured monks.

Frederick commanded his brother, Leopold of Austria, to punish the Swiss. In the following year the Swiss routed the Austrian army by the unorthodox device of catching them in a defile at Morgarten and pelting them with rocks, tree trunks, and any other available missiles. Three weeks later the three cantons celebrated their victory by renewing their alliance, and in 1316 Louis the Bavarian rewarded them by specifically recognizing the charter granted the Swiss by his predecessor.

So far the confederacy had remained a purely local and semi-rebellious alliance. When, in 1339, the city of Berne made a treaty with the Forest Cantons, the entire feudal aristocracy became aroused and sent an army against Berne. Joined by their allies, the Bernese soundly defeated the attackers at Laupen. This time the success was assured solely by the superiority of the infantry methods of the peasant army over the unprincipled warfare of the feudal lords, and it firmly established the Confederates' hold over the lands south of the Rhine. When the Hapsburgs unwisely dared to reclaim in 1386 what they considered their territory, the Swiss invaded what was left of the Hapsburg domains. Duke Leopold of Austria, the nephew of the loser of Morgarten, answered the provocation and collected an army to crush the Swiss. The Swiss, however, responded by crushing the army of Leopold and killing the duke in the celebrated battle of Sempach. This battle was remarkable in that it demonstrated the superiority of lightly armed foot soldiers over the armored knights who were defeated as much by the heat of that scorching July day as by the prowess of the Swiss.

The outcome of that day, according to one tradition, was decided by Arnold von Winkelried, a man from Unterwalden. The Austrian knights had dismounted to meet the Swiss, and stood immovable, their spears leveled, offering no point of attack to the mountaineers, who were armed with their traditional pikes. Winkelried ended the deadlock by seizing an armful of the Austrian spears and plunging them into his breast. The Swiss poured through the breach he had created for them and made short work of their opponents, who by now were as defenseless as a turtle when it is turned on its back. The truthfulness of this episode was long contested. The controversy which raged on the subject in the nineteenth century came to be known among Swiss historians as the Second Battle of Sempach; at present, even reputable historians seem to accept the tradition, although they question the importance of Winkelried's sacrifice in the outcome of the battle.

The victory of Sempach was followed, after two years, by that of Näfels, won over the Austrians by the men of Glarus and Schwyz. Taken together, the two battles were decisive. Without them Switzerland might have remained an insignificant mountain republic such as Andorra; but having established their military strength, the cantons, whose number had now grown to eight, continued on a career of conquests. While the Forest Cantons, particularly Uri, with their traditional connections with the communes of Lombardy, continued to look southward for expansion, Berne was oriented rather to the west. The Swiss conquests between 1403 and 1536 have been outlined in the second chapter. For an ephemeral period, Swiss power was supreme from Strasbourg to Milan. Had they lost the battles of Sempach and Näfels, the Swiss might easily have gone the way of so many other leagues within the holy Roman Empire. Having won, even their loss of power in the sixteenth century could no longer effect their independence.

Both battles have been commemorated by religious and patriotic ceremonies since times immemorial. The victory of Näfels, particularly, has been celebrated yearly ever since 1389 by a Catholic procession to the battlefield; in more recent days speeches by the president or vice-president of the Confederation have been added, as well as singing of patriotic songs, military honors, and official banquets. At Sempach, where similar festivities take place, prayers are said for the Swiss and the Austrian dead. The dead Austrians involved are probably the only humans who more than five hundred and fifty years after death are still being prayed for by their enemies.

Though city cantons such as Berne conquered larger areas than the other Confederates, they usually represented the peace party in the federal diets. It was the Forest Cantons which represented the belligerent spirit of the "knotty-armed Swiss," as the more patriotic among their descendants like to refer to their ancestors. It is probable that the Schwyzers, the natives of the now rather insignificant canton of Schwyz, lent their name to the entire Confederation because they were at one time its most widely known members—and a nation's fame, then as now, depended mainly on the fear which its soldiers inspired abroad. Constant warfare made the Forest Cantons grow into military states on an almost Spartan model, which soon came to be adopted throughout the Confederation. It was revived in the nineteenth century and forms the basis of the present military organization of Switzerland.

The only European nation in the fourteenth century that had compulsory military service for all its citizens was Switzerland. All men between sixteen and sixty years of age were liable to military service and were obliged by law to provide their own equipment. Towns refused citizenship to individuals too poor to purchase arms. Contribution of military equipment as well as the imposition of maneuvers and military exercises became forms of taxation. Young boys received premilitary training. Somewhat later, marksmanship was developed by the introduction of annual competitions. By the end of the fifteenth century Switzerland was able to put fifty to sixty thousand trained soldiers into the field— as much or more than the most powerful monarchs of Europe. Small wonder that the neighbors of Switzerland, militarily disorganized and less appreciative of the joys of military life, tended more and more to rely on the services of Swiss mercenaries.

Swiss military reputation reached its peak in the wars of Charles the Bold, duke of Burgundy, and in the Italian Wars. Charles's ambition, which he nearly fulfilled, was to reconstitute a sovereign kingdom of Burgundy, reaching from the Low Countries to Provence. His ambition was crushed, not by the Holy Roman emperor, whom he cheated, not by his principal adversary, Louis XI of France, whom he defeated, but by the peasants of Switzerland, whom he underestimated. Charles had alienated the Swiss by his harsh regime in the free towns of Alsace, which were allied to Switzerland, and had thus driven them into an alliance with Louis. After seizing Nancy, the capital of Lorraine, Charles marched against the Swiss. He took the small garrison of Grandson by surprise and ordered them massacred. Only two men survived—they had been spared for the task of hanging their comrades. Taking umbrage at this, the Confederates attacked Charles's army in 1476 and defeated it severely in the battle of Grandson. Charles, a courageous fighter, but a poor tactician, laid his defeat to the element of surprise and raised a new army This did not keep him from allowing the Swiss to surprise him twice more: at Morat, in the same year, and at Nancy, in 1477. This was his last surprise, for it cost him his life—*Gut, Mut, und Blut* (wealth, spirit, and life), as the Swiss saying had it. For the Swiss the three victories earned the name of Europe's best fighters and a fabulous amount of loot.

Nancy had put the Swiss into the proper mood. The people of the Forest Cantons, unaccustomed to the luxury of life they encountered abroad and spurred by the prospects of more looting and rapine, began to organize expeditions on the slightest pretext, not unlike the "Free Companies" which had ravaged France during the Hundred Years War. At least one of these expeditions, affectionately called the "Mad Life," was undertaken as a sequel to a carnival celebration. In February, 1477, a few weeks after the victory of Nancy, about a thousand men from Schwyz and Uri topped their extensive merrymakings with the decision to punish Savoy for having sided with Charles in the recent war. They descended into the territories of Neuchâtel and Vaud, then still under the lordship of Savoy, doubled their number on the way, and looted the countryside as far as Geneva. Their own magistrates dispatched messages after them pleading with them to return if they wished to avert major complications, and they finally consented to leave off, but only after Geneva had paid them eight thousand guilders, promised further payments, and doled out to each soldier two guilders and one drink.

I I

Before the Burgundian wars, mercenary service, already common in Germany, was considered by the Swiss a useful outlet for the overpopulated Alpine cantons. At the time of their victories over Charles the Bold, the Swiss had attained a national unity which, soon disturbed by the Reformation, was not to return until the nineteenth century. The defeat of Maximilan I, in 1499, which earned Switzerland a status of practical independence, was the crowning event of the period. Yet the military reputation of the Swiss, gained in two essentially national wars, was already on the point of being frittered away through the efforts of foreign recruiting agents. As the situation got out of hand, the cantonal governments attempted by ordinances to restrict the agents' activities—all to no purpose, for the supply of volunteers even exceeded the recruiters' demands. Especially in the poorly fed Forest Cantons, there was an almost epidemic rush for service in foreign countries. Restrictive legislation merely tended to make the poorer segments of the population revolt against the magistrates. Indeed, the magistrates themselves were guilty of another form of mercenary activity, which, though less publicized in historical writings, was no less fateful. There was at the beginning of the sixteenth century not a single Swiss statesman who was not openly in foreign pay—in the form of pensions granted by foreign potentates who sought to exploit or to appease Swiss military power.

The pension system had originated in conjunction with the

system of "military capitulations," which soon displaced the old
and carefree system of voluntary enlistments and gradually became the basis of Swiss foreign service. The treaties of military capitulation (euphemistically called, until the eighteenth century,
treaties of alliance) were concluded by foreign powers either with
the Swiss diet or with individual cantons or groups of cantons. By
their terms the Swiss authorities, against payment of a pension,
contracted to furnish a specified number of troops, subject to
certain conditions and privileges. Thus, for instance, Swiss mercenaries were, theoretically, not to be employed in offensive wars.
The pensions were usually distributed yearly to the citizens or
held in trust for them. The distinction between ordinary mercenaries, who enroll in foreign armies for their own account, and
the Swiss regiments, which remained homogeneous Swiss contingents furnished by international treaties, can readily be seen.
It was, by the way, on a similar basis that Hessian soldiers were
leased to the king of England in the American Revolution.

France was the first power to conclude such a military alliance
with the Swiss. The events that led up to it were not without interest. It will be remembered that from 1430 to 1446 Zurich, at
war with the rest of the cantons over the lands of the extinct
house of Toggenburg, had seceded from the Confederation.
Zurich's ally, Emperor Frederick III, besought the king of France,
Charles VII, to take action against the Swiss. Charles seized on the
occasion to rid himself of the "Armagnacs," as the companies of
idle soldiers called themselves, and in 1444 he dispatched an
army of 22,000 under the command of the Dauphin, the future
Louis XI. This army was met at St. Jakob on the Birse, near Basel,
by a Swiss contingent of some 1,400. With the cry, "Our souls to
God, our bodies to the Armagnacs!" the Swiss threw themselves
on the French and did not cease fighting until they had killed eight
thousand Armagnacs and until every Swiss had either been slain
or wounded. The wine grown in the region is still called
Schweizerblut—Swiss blood.

The Dauphin was impressed and began to turn things over in
his mind. Surely these people would be more useful as allies than
as enemies. He broached the matter to his father, who in 1452 concluded the first French alliance with the Swiss. Finally, in 1477,

when Charles the Bold threatened both Louis XI and Switzerland, a more effective pact was signed. Between 1477 and 1830 one million Swiss, it is estimated, had served the kings of France.

Freelance mercenaries continued, of course, to join foreign armies, despite all official measures. Called *Reisläufer* (travelers), they more or less held the status that seasonal migrant workers hold in our day. But the tendency was toward mercantilism and control of exports and imports; there was more and more reliance, especially in the mountainous cantons, on regulating foreign service and monopolizing it as an official source of revenue. Soldiers became an export article, and this was inevitable, for the only export industry then existing in these cantons, the dairy industry, was insufficient to balance the indispensable import of other foodstuffs. The courage and loyalty that became bywords of the Swiss certainly were largely due to their sense of professional dignity and their religious respect for their oath—but it was an economic necessity as well, for they had to compete with the German mercenaries and maintain the high reputation of their export article lest they should be crowded off the market.

In the wars waged in Italy by Charles VIII, Louis XII, and Francis I of France, Swiss mercenaries were inevitably brought face to face in the ranks of opposing armies, but for a long time the sense of national unity tended to prevail on such occasions. Many a battle took an unexpected turn when the Swiss surprised their employers by hailing the Swiss contingent in the hostile camp as their long-lost brothers and refused to fight them. While common in the Italian wars, this phenomenon happened as late as 1590, on the eve of the decisive battle of Ivry between Henry IV of France and the Catholic League, when the Swiss in Henry's camp obtained authorization to grant their fellow countrymen in the Catholic camp an honorable retreat in order to avoid a battle of Swiss against Swiss. The fact that the Swiss cantons had been fighting among themselves without such qualms was irrelevant: the Swiss might fight against each other whenever they pleased, but not whenever they were paid for doing so.

Even when serving foreign powers, the Swiss never lost their national consciousness. In their eyes a victory won by them for the king of France, or the pope, or the emperor was never as much a French, Roman, or Imperialist victory as it was a Swiss victory. They fought under their own officers and followed the flags of their own cantons, the bull of Uri perhaps, or the bear of Berne. Urs Graf, the foremost Swiss wood engraver and draftsman of the Renaissance period, is probably the best contemporary pictorial source on the life of the Swiss mercenaries. His magnificent warriors express their national pride and the vigor of their individuality. They were not, in their own eyes, mere hirelings, but proud soldiers, jealous of their honor, merciless and expecting no mercy, and famous for their loyalty. If they punctiliously upheld their rights and privileges under the terms of their contracts, they fulfilled their duties with equal nicety. They were prized not only for their military prowess but also for their reliability. They might become querulous and difficult to handle if their pay were late, but at least they never changed sides in mid-battle, going over to a higher bidder—a trick for which some German mercenaries were notorious.

When, in 1499, Louis XII of France prepared to invade Italy, which his predecessor, Charles VIII, had so dashingly won and lost within a few months, he concluded a ten-year alliance with the Swiss. His first objective was the duchy of Milan, ruled by the wily Lodovico Sforza. At that time the Swiss had already seized, in addition to the Val Leventina, taken in 1403, several other portions and dependencies of the duchy. In 1478, at the engagement of Giornico, a party of six hundred Swiss had routed fifteen thousand Milanese, by the ingenious device of flooding the terrain with the waters of the Ticino and its tributary torrents, which they had dammed up, letting the Milanese advance onto the slippery terrain and then—with the battle cry *Liga! Liga!*—charging them in a single massed attack. After 1500 Milanese had been drowned or slain, the rest gave up. With his Swiss allies, Louis XII seized Milan, in 1499, without much effort.

However, helpful as they were, the Swiss did not make Louis very happy. When he made his personal entry into Genoa, whose revolt he had just crushed, in 1507, he rewarded the Swiss by letting them enter the town before his own troops; but the Swiss craved remuneration as well as honor, and the former was forthcoming in thin trickles only. Louis became so tired of constant requests for payment that at the end of the ten-year alliance he was contemplating the replacement of his Swiss levies with the less rambunctious sons of Valais, the Grisons, and Germany. Since, however, both Pope Julius II and Emperor Maximilian I were desperately trying at the same time to wrangle a military alliance with the Confederates against France, Louis was obliged to make efforts to renew his own alliance. The somewhat ludicrous spectacle of the king of France, the Holy Roman emperor, and the Vicar of God, all wooing the despised peasants of tiny Switzerland was brought to a conclusion in 1510 through the efforts of Cardinal Matthew Schinner, bishop of Sion, who negotiated with the federal diet on behalf of Julius II. The pope obtained ten thousand Swiss and a defensive alliance with the Confederation. Maximilian also joined Julius' Holy League, designed to eject the French barbarians from Italian soil. The Swiss, in the course of a fruitless attempt to seize Milan from the French, discovered that their allies relied entirely on them to do the rough work. When they realized that moreover Julius II was a still more reluctant paymaster than Louis XII, they decided to intervene on their own account. In May, 1512, the Confederates, making what was to be the last of their military efforts on a nationwide scale, assembled an army of twenty thousand at Chur in the Grisons. Commanded by Cardinal Schinner, they marched on Trento, using several mountain passes, and from there swarmed down to Milan.

Nobody wished to face an army of twenty thousand Swiss, and Milan was conquered without effort, although a French garrison continued to hold out in the citadel. The Swiss installed Massimiliano Sforza, heir of Lodovico, as duke, but made no move to abandon their own grip on the duchy. Their occupation was costly, oppressive, and disorderly.

Meanwhile the French army rallied in the Piedmont and came back for a countercharge. On June 6, 1513, the Swiss met them at Novara. The French lost eight thousand dead, all their artillery and all their stores. The Swiss were masters in Lombardy.

In 1515 Francis I succeeded Louis XII and immediately proceeded to settle an old score. While a powerful French army crossed into Piedmont, Swiss leadership was divided into the peace party, with Berne, Fribourg, and Solothurn as its foremost

COUNCIL OF WAR

Pen drawing by Urs Graf

champions, and the war party, headed by Schinner and backed
by the Forest Cantons. The war party won out, and the French
offers of peace were rejected. On September 10 a Swiss army was
in Milan, and a French army was taking up positions at Marignano
(or Melegnano, as it is now called). The two-day battle of
Marignano began on September 13.

With the contingents of the Forest Cantons leading, the Swiss
attacked in the afternoon. Relying on their usual tactics, they
formed in squares or in triangles or, when attacked from several
sides, in their unassailable hedgehog formations. Although ignor-
ant of the ancient methods of warfare, they unconsciously imi-
tated the Macedonian phalanx, presenting to the enemy a solid
front of pikes that defied all cavalry charges. They were vulner-
able to artillery, but they rarely gave the enemy the opportunity
or the time to set up his cannon, which were very unwieldy. When
night fell on September 13, the battle was still undecided.

It was resumed at dawn. After a few hours, the Swiss were sure
of victory, though staggering losses had been incurred by both
sides. They were confidently charging the French, when they
were suddenly attacked in the flank by a contingent of Venetian
cavalry, which had arrived at the last minute to assist their French
allies. Forced to a halt in order to regroup their formations, the
Swiss gave the French artillery time enough to train their pieces
accurately. Guns were still a fairly recent invention; their usefulness was still subject to debate. With the cannonade of Marignano,
the debate was decided once and for all. About midday the bleed-
ing and battered Swiss began their retreat to Milan. Despite all
their losses, it was an orderly retreat. The wounded were not
abandoned, and the standards were still in possession of the weary
troops. French losses were far too heavy to allow the victors the
luxury of pursuit.

Marignano meant the defeat of the advocates of war among the
Swiss leaders. It was plain now that the Swiss had borne the brunt
of the fighting, while their allies, the emperor and the pope, had
reaped the benefits. Not even monetary aid was forthcoming.
Two days after their retreat to Milan, the Swiss decided to with-
draw from the struggle and returned to their homes. Although
they did not realize it at the time, this move, primitive as it may

seem, was their first step toward the road of neutrality. It was not merely the result of a military defeat. They had suffered defeats before, though none as spectacular, and they were by no means routed or disorganized. But with the new methods of warfare they could no longer maintain their supremacy, and the uselessness of doing all the hard work for their unreliable allies had become all too apparent. Their military reputation was still high, but from now on they would exploit it strictly on a business basis. The era of national wars was ended for Switzerland; the era of mercenary service had only begun.

The Forest Cantons had not entirely abandoned their hopes. In 1516 they once more invaded the duchy of Milan, in alliance with Maximilian I. But the eight remaining cantons had made their peace with Francis I, and some of their men were fighting on the French side. Refusing to fight their fellow Confederates, the troops of the Forest Cantons broke up and returned home. In November, 1516, France and the Confederation signed an "Everlasting Peace." From 1516 to the present day—if we except the comic opera campaign of July-August, 1815, against Napoleon I—Switzerland has not declared war against a single foreign power. Yet the Swiss have by no means lived in peace.

The immediate result of the Everlasting Peace with France was that within thirty years Francis I used 120,000 Swiss levies in his disastrous wars. Thus, in the battle of Pavia (1525), the victorious Spaniards slew 4,000 Swiss and captured Francis—but only after his personal guard, the Hundred Swiss, had been killed to the last man. Machiavelli's prophecy that the Swiss footsoldiers could easily be beaten by the more agile Spanish infantry had turned out to be correct. However, this and subsequent reverses of Swiss arms in foreign pay no longer had the significance of Marignano. Loss of military reputation might harm the Swiss economically, just as they would be hurt now if their watch movements turned out to be inferior, but they did not threaten Switzerland's national existence.

With the revolutionary transformations that Europe's armies underwent in the seventeenth and eighteenth centuries, the only individual qualities of a soldier that still counted were discipline and animal obedience. In this respect the Swiss might have found it difficult to compete with German recruits if by the end of the seventeenth century the formation of national armies had not left the Swiss a kind of monopoly on foreign service. It was inevitable, however, that the once proud and individualistic Swiss soldier-adventurers should be changed within two hundred years into the type of automaton to whom Frederick the Great once put the rhetorical question, "Dogs, do you want to live forever?"

<h2 style="text-align:center">III</h2>

Throughout Swiss history the Forest Cantons remained the most belligerent element in the Confederation, a distinction which became pronounced as Switzerland split into Catholic and Protestant cantons. The military policy of Switzerland was one of the major issues at stake in the Swiss Reformation, which was at least as much a political as a religious phenomenon. Zwingli, it is true, had at first supported Cardinal Schinner in his Italian venture, and even received a pension from the pope, but he turned violently against the practice of mercenary service as soon as he began to preach in Zurich in 1518.

His words fell on fertile ground, for Zurich, which had always pursued an independent policy, had abolished the capitulation system as early as in 1503. Zwingli's opposition to mercenary service was not prompted by any pacifist inclinations. In fact, he was the very image of a soldier. He probably had been at Novara and at Marignano as a field chaplain, and he was to die fighting in the battle of Kappel in 1531. But Zwingli was an ardent nationalist, who thought in terms of a Switzerland unified by his faith, a strong military power, which in alliance with Philip of Hesse and other German Protestant states was to spread his gospel and undo both the Catholics and the Lutherans. Treaties of capitulation could not be reconciled with such a program.

However, though a passionate politician, Zwingli was not a good one. Where he wished to unify, he merely succeeded in dividing. It was very well for Zurich, a rising commercial and industrial city, or Berne, with its rich agricultural hinterland, to renounce the benefits of foreign pensions and the opportunity of employment which the Forest Cantons, with their surplus population, could not do without. Caring more for local independence than for national grandeur, the Forest Cantons resisted Zwingli's program with all their might. Until 1712 they defeated the Protestant cantons in every battle they waged. Numerically inferior, they were militarily better organized.

Although by the beginning of the seventeenth century the Protestant cantons had resumed the practice of furnishing mercenary troops (they could not afford to renounce the alliance with France), the national character of the Swiss militia no longer existed. Foreign service, moreover, had lost its popular appeal—even in the Forest Cantons, where the main burden of the service fell increasingly on the rural and underprivileged population. Swiss youths no longer flocked to the drums of foreign recruiters, but had to be rounded up. They were no longer sought because they were invincible, but because they made good cannon fodder. Existing treaties of capitulation, by which foreign nations once obtained the right—then granted as a favor—to recruit troops in Switzerland, were now invoked by them to force the levy of recruits and became highly unpopular. Soldiers formerly hired for several months now had to sign up for three years. The habit popular with Swiss contingents of going home whenever they pleased now became punishable by death as desertion.

The *Volkslied* "Zu Strassburg auf der Schanz," one of the most popular of the songs in the German collection *Des Knaben Wunderhorn*, tells the sad tale of a young Swiss recruit in the French garrison of Strasbourg. One evening he hears an alphorn on the opposite bank of the Rhine play a familiar *Ranz* (a traditional melody, apparently appreciated by cows and played by Swiss cowherds on quaint instruments which sometimes attain the length of a dozen feet or more). The recruit becomes so obsessed with the melody—which must have been purely imaginary, since Switzerland is far away from Strasbourg—that he is seized by homesickness and driven against his will to try to desert by swimming across the Rhine. He is caught and knows that his story will not be believed, and in his mind he calls out to the firing squad, presumably made up of Swiss like himself, " 'Tis the alphorn has done this to me, 'tis all its fault." This song is merely a sample from a vast literature of Swiss deserters' songs. Its self-pity, though touching in its simplicity, certainly is a far cry from the attitude of previous times.

The Swiss could no longer avoid fighting each other if they were so ordered. In the War of the Spanish Succession (1701-14), 20,000 Swiss served with the French, 13,000 with the Dutch, 4,000 with Savoy, 3,000 with Milan, and 2,000 with the Imperialists—a total of 42,000 Swiss mercenaries from a country which then had little more than one million inhabitants, fighting on two opposite sides.

Louis XIV organized his Swiss on a permanent basis. The king's own military household included the Hundred Swiss, used as a palace guard, and the regiment of Swiss Guards. Besides these, there were several regular Swiss regiments, whose names, such as Wattenwyl, Stuppa, and others, were those of prominent Swiss families which furnished their commanders. (The regular Swiss regiments were under the command of a "colonel general of the Swiss and the Grisons.") According to an anecdote which illustrates the feelings of the Swiss officers in French service, Louis's minister of war, Louvois, with characteristic lack of tact, once remarked to the king in presence of General Stuppa, "Sire, if Your Majesty had all the money which He and the kings His predecessors have given to the Swiss, He could pave the road from Paris to Basel with five franc gold pieces." To which Stuppa replied: "This may be so, but if it were possible to gather all the blood that our nation has shed in the service of Your Majesty and the kings His predecessors it would fill a canal all the way from Basel to Paris."

A noble rejoinder—much nobler, indeed, than the mentality it stood for!

The contrast between the Swiss soldier of 1740 and the Swiss soldier of 1470 is best visualized by a comparison of their contemporary representation in the graphic arts. On the one hand, the vigor, the color, the individualism of the brawling giants of Urs Graf, lustily hacking away at some unfortunate opponent; on the other, as shown in eighteenth-century engravings, the neat squares of little uniformed men, surrounded by the symmetrical clouds of the powder of their musketry and the tidy blasts of their cannon.

Despite the new regimentation, the service of France remained the most attractive and remunerative, and it was in the service of the kings of France that Swiss mercenaries and their officers most distinguished themselves. The political bonds between the Confederation and France were drawn very close at the end of Henry IV's war against the League and again after the Thirty Years War. The French ambassador to the cantons became the real ruler of Switzerland during the reign of Louis XIV; his residence at Solothurn became a powerful little court in itself. The reversal of French foreign policy under the reign of Louis XV, resulting in the French *rapprochement* with the Catholic powers, had a dividing effect on Swiss foreign policy. The Protestant cantons, unwilling to bolster the solid Catholic front of France, Spain, and Austria, allied themselves with the United Provinces of the Netherlands, while the Forest Cantons continued to furnish military contingents to France. After the accession of Louis XVI to the throne, another general French alliance with Switzerland was signed, in 1777, but the bulk of the Swiss regiments was still made up of recruits from the Forest Cantons.

It was in Lucerne, the leading city of the Catholic cantons, that Thorwaldsen erected the famous monument, a lion carved in granite, to honor the memory of the Swiss Guards, who fell in defense of Louis XVI on August 10, 1792. The episode is well known, though its details are confused. The Swiss Guards were left in defense of the Tuileries when the king, threatened by an armed mob, escaped from the palace with his family and sought asylum in a box in the hall of the Legislative Assembly. When the populace invaded the palace, the king sent word to the commander of the Guards, ordering him not to resist. In his characteristic timidity, Louis had ordered his Swiss to commit suicide: five hundred of them were killed, many of them after they had surrendered. The massacre might have been avoided if the Swiss had from the very start offered no resistance, or if they had disobeyed when ordered to cease resistance. As if was, the massacre was largely the result of confused orders, not merely undying loyalty.

Indeed, the rank and file of the Swiss regiments had not always stood solidly behind the *ancien régime*. One of the first acts of rebellion in the French Revolution was the mutiny of the Swiss regiment of Châteauvieux. It was only through the intervention of the French government that the mutineers were eventually pardoned, for the Swiss officers of the rebellious troops had already taken harsh measures against them. It is true, however, that the Swiss Guards consisted of picked troops and enjoyed about the same popularity in revolutionary Paris as did the Hessians in revolutionary America a decade earlier. Their loyalty to the crown was displayed, not so much in the resistance they offered, for they knew only too well what to expect from the attacking mob, as in their obedience to the king's order to stop resisting. It should be noted that their commanding officer was not among the killed.

Ten days after this episode the Assembly abolished the mercenary system in France. A large number of the disbanded units, particularly their officers, joined the antirevolutionary coalition and fought until 1800 under Austrian command and with British pay against the French Republic—a situation somewhat analogous to that of the serving of Free French units with British pay under American command in the Second World War.

After the creation of the Helvetic Republic, in 1798, Napoleon Bonaparte tried to revive the military bond between France and Switzerland. By a treaty in 1803, Switzerland, though declared a neutral by Napoleon, was to furnish France four regiments (16,000 men) for a period of fifteen years and two additional regiments in case of war. The treaty further forbade the recruitment of mercenaries for any states except those in the French sphere, that is, Italy, the Batavian Republic, Spain, and the Papal States. It can be seen from this that Napoleon's notion of neutrality was elastic. As a concession to the Swiss, it was stipulated that no Swiss levies were to serve outside the European continent. Russia was clearly within the European continent: nine tenths of the Swiss who fought in the campaign of 1812–13 failed to return. Those who did return brought back a song they sang during the passage of the Beresina:

> Our life is one long journey
> Through the winter and the night,

> As we seek to find our passage
> Under skies without a light.

One Swiss officer who accompanied Napoleon on his journey through winter and night and made a name for himself in an unconventional manner was the celebrated General Jomini, author of several classical works on strategy. General Jomini, who had served since the foundation of the Helvetic Republic on the Swiss general staff and under Marshal Ney in the French army, had the distinction of holding a general's commission both in the French army and in the Russian army.

Originally a clerk in a Swiss bank in Paris, he had spent his after-banking hours studying the campaigns of Frederick the Great, was recognized as an authority on the Prussian army by Napoleon, and was promoted to the rank of colonel and created a baron. On bad terms with Ney, he applied for a commission in the Russian army in 1808 and received a generalcy. This enraged Napoleon, who called Jomini to Paris and put before him the odd choice of a generalcy in the French army or a prison cell at Vincennes. Jomini chose the generalcy. However, when war broke out between France and Russia he solved his perplexity by serving in the rear echelon of the French command rather than take part in the actual operations. During the retreat through Germany in 1813 he was rudely taken to task by Marshal Berthier for a mistake which he had actually not made. He decided that it was time to change sides and passed over to the Russians, who received him with open arms. Since it would have been against his honor, however, to betray Napoleon, he strictly refused to give any information on what he knew of the French plans.

It is characteristic of the position held by Swiss soldiers of fortune in the public opinion of the time that Napoleon specifically declared in his memoirs that General Jomini had not betrayed him, that he had justified grievances against Berthier, and that, being Swiss, he was not bound by loyalty to either belligerent. The Russians proved no less understanding. Jomini was a Russian representative at the Congress of Vienna, was promoted, eventually, to the rank of full general, and in 1830 founded the Russian military academy. Toward the end of Jomini's life, Napoleon III called him to Paris to consult him on technical matters. The life of General Jomini is a fine illustration not only of the Swiss interpretation of neutrality then current but also of Swiss stubbornness.

The Final Act of the Treaty of Paris, which guaranteed Switzerland's neutrality, did not end Swiss mercenary service. Treaties of capitulation were concluded between the Swiss cantons and France, Naples, the Papal States, and The Netherlands. The troops thus levied were not intended so much for purposes of war as for helping the Holy Alliance, which Switzerland had joined, to keep down revolutions. As before, the Forest Cantons, being the most reactionary, furnished precisely the type of soldier needed for the maintenance of the hated regimes of the Metternich era.

Everybody has heard of the massacre of the Swiss Guards in 1792, but for some strange reason it is seldom realized that in the July Revolution, which cost Charles X his throne in 1830, the Swiss Guards played a far more important role. The Swiss battalions were, indeed, the only troops in Paris that put up any serious resistance, and a large number of them were massacred, along with their commander, Major Dufay, by the revolutionists. The immediate result was the dismissal of all Swiss troops serving in France and increasing reluctance on the part of the Swiss to renew their treaties of capitulation. Only King Bomba of Naples—aside from the Papal States— continued to use Swiss troops.

At the conclusion of the Franco-Austrian War, in 1859, when most existing treaties of capitulation were about to expire, recruiting by foreign powers was finally forbidden by the Swiss federal government. But Swiss troops continued, in defiance of the law, to participate in the wars of the Risorgimento. Once more the sons of Europe's freest nation stood in the pay of the forces of reaction. In the summer of 1859 a papal Swiss regiment, after taking Perugia, terrorized the town and countryside with all kinds of excesses. As late as September, 1860, Swiss soldiers were trounced at Castelfidardo by an Italian army on its march to join the forces of Garibaldi. Most of these were amnestied after they returned to Switzerland. The constitution of 1874 contained an article declaring succinctly; "There shall be no military capitulations," but volunteering in foreign armies continued until its absolute interdiction was enacted in 1927. Until then there was hardly a foreign war in which Swiss volunteers did not take part. About four thousand Swiss fought in the American Civil War, mostly on the side of the Confederacy; one of them, Major Heinrich Wirz, received the distinction of being shot by the Federals for his mismanagement of the Andersonville military prison in Georgia. In the First World War seven thousand Swiss fell in the service of France alone. If the Swiss chose sides in the conflict of 1914-18 by following their convictions, this was not the case in the minor wars that preceded it: Swiss soldiering as a strict business proposition was satirized by Bernard Shaw in *Arms and the Man*, more widely known in its operetta form as the *Chocolate Soldier*.

After 1927 even service in the French Foreign Legion was made a criminal offense. The only exception to the general prohibition of foreign service is the Vatican Guard, founded in 1505 by Pope Julius II, which by the stipulation of its terms requires no combat duty. Service in the papal guard is still considered a high privilege in the Catholic cantons. To qualify for that select body (it has only some hundred members), candidates must be native Swiss, Roman Catholic, of legitimate birth, unmarried, under twenty-five, at least five foot, eight inches tall, healthy, and free from physical blemish. The guard is commanded by a colonel; the privates of the guard draw sergeant's pay; their everyday uniform is the famous costume designed in the Renaissance, and their dress uniform is as splendid as a cuirassier's. Their favorite off-duty pastime is soccer football.

There are other advantages: service involves little work; the uniforms appeal to the Roman ladies; officers often receive papal titles (the only titles of nobility still used in Switzerland); and, all in all, service in the Vatican guard provides a rather pleasant and, according to some accounts, quite exuberant existence for younger sons of pious but idle disposition.

Economically, foreign military service had ceased to be a necessity for overpopulated Switzerland. Essentially an export industry, it was supplanted by the industrial development that Switzerland underwent in the nineteenth century. Even emigration, once the only alternative to foreign service, dwindled to small proportions after the industrialization of the country. Politically, foreign military service was undesirable because it weakened Switzerland's own military strength. It was, moreover, an obstacle to an effective policy of neutrality. Lastly, the rebirth of a national Swiss spirit was hardly compatible with the sacrifice of Swiss lives to foreign interests.

It is curious to observe the full circle described by Swiss military history. At first a small people of shepherds and peasants, they united in defense; two centuries later, a nation of conquerors, they sought adventure, glory, and a livelihood by serving as soldiers of fortune; soon afterward, and for three hundred years thence, the individual spirit of adventure was curbed by a state monopoly on the lease of courage and life; the nineteenth century witnessed the return to the spirit of private enterprise based on sound business principles; until, at last, we once more behold, united for their common defense, a people of shepherds, farmers, merchants, workers, and hotelkeepers.

What remains to be related is the system this people has adopted to insure its defense.

I V

After the virtual dissolution of the federal ties caused by the Reformation, the Swiss military system was based on independent cantonal militias. Since in many cantons the activities of the militia resembled a Sunday family picnic rather than a martial effort, the military organization was put on a partially federal basis in 1817. After the Sonderbund War, a truly national army came into existence.

The Swiss defense system is unique. Based as it is on the very principles that governed the Swiss armies of the fourteenth century, it is at the same time the most forward looking of all defense systems, since it is the most adaptable to the rapidly changing methods of modern warfare. Every Swiss male, unless physically or mentally unfit, is a soldier from his eighteenth to his sixtieth year. After receiving several months of basic training, he is recalled every year until he reaches his forties (the exact age varies according to rank and branch of service) to participate in refresher courses and in maneuvers that last several weeks. He retains his weapon and his uniform and is ready at all times to be called up in case of emergency. Complete mobilization of the entire Swiss army is a matter of hours. Once a year every Swiss of active military age must qualify for marksmanship on the rifle range. If he fails he may be constrained to repeat the rifle course until he qualifies. He is a member of the reserve until his sixtieth year.

Those exempted or rejected from military service are subject to a special tax. Units are made up of citizens of the same canton whenever possible, and the composition of the troops, the maintenance of their strength, the nomination and promotion of their officers are also cantonal functions. The general organization of the army, however, is a federal prerogative. The use of troops is regulated by the federal or cantonal governments, depending on the circumstances.

The highest peacetime grade in the Swiss army is that of a colonel. In wartime or in emergencies requiring general mobilization, one general is appointed. In the recent World War the Swiss army was commanded by General Henri Guisan. The Swiss constitution specifically forbids the maintenance of a standing federal army, and limits the number of permanent troops allowed to each canton to 300. In other words, Switzerland has a maximum of 7,500 professional soldiers, 300 to every canton or half-canton, who form the small, but highly competent, nucleus of the army.

Most Swiss consider their annual training period a welcome vacation, especially if they belong to Alpine or ski troops. And indeed, despite the very harsh discipline of the Swiss army—in wartime, at least—it is quite natural that several weeks spent away from routine work, in locations considered by the rest of the world as vacation spots rather than maneuver areas, and the possibility of playing boy scout once more must be a very refreshing experience. At the end of the annual maneuvers the entire cantonal contingent holds a big parade, proudly watched by fathers, mothers, sisters, wives, and sweethearts, who have flocked together from all parts of the canton for that occasion. Thereupon everybody consumes a few more drinks and returns to his daily work, invigorated in his body and confident in his mind that Switzerland is well defended. Until the next refresher course, unless he is called up for some special reason, his uniform is embedded in moth balls; his rifle, for which he is responsible, is cleaned and oiled regularly and lovingly.

The Swiss militia system not only is efficient in that it keeps the soldiers in constant training and acquainted with all innovations, but also is as democratic as it may be and still remain compatible with military discipline. Strict obedience is maintained throughout the training periods, but in civilian life there is no special distinction between officers and enlisted men. The fact that all citizens of military age are in constant possession of their arms also presupposes a confidence in the democratic system not easily found elsewhere.

If the Swiss militia sounds somewhat reminiscent of comic-opera armies, the impression is fallacious. Besides the technical excellencies of Swiss weapons and fortifications and the efficiency of the training and mobilization system, the Swiss have continued or revived their age-old military traditions in other ways. One of these, dating back to the fifteenth century, is the federal sharp-shooting contest. The first of these is said to have taken place in 1452; until 1683 contests were held at frequent intervals, and they were revived in 1824. Since then they have been held every two or three years, each time in some different town or village of the country, with thousands of participants.

It is hardly necessary to insist on the Swiss reputation for marksmanship; the one story everyone knows about Switzerland is the legend of Tell's feat, and it is a popularly accepted tradition that Admiral Nelson was killed in the battle of Trafalgar by a Swiss sharpshooter from a masthead. However this may be, marksmanship is indubitably a national sport, and training begins early. Boys of premilitary age may enter the so-called cadet corps and practice every Sunday on the local firing range.

The federal contests are held in the midst of powerful eating, drinking, and speechmaking; like the Olympic games of the Greeks, they create a bond among the participating cantons. Other national sports are mountain climbing and skiing, which not only are vital in mountain warfare but also keep Swiss manhood—and womanhood—in excellent trim. The old bellicose spirit also manifests itself in frequent conventions of officers and noncommissioned officers. Though mostly a pretext for drinking and wenching, they encourage a certain *esprit-de-corps* and offset the deep differences and animosities between the Alemannic and the Romanic cantons. Nevertheless, it is only a fair tribute to the French-speaking cantons to admit that the military virtue and enthusiasm of the citizens are less intense than those of their Alemannic cousins.

More local manifestations of the military urge are found in the occasional expeditions of the inhabitants of one valley in order to settle a feud with the next. Though frequent and untainted by unmanly restraint, they usually remain on the level of family quarrels. This also is an age-old tradition, and no doubt many of the intercantonal discords which history has glorified as wars or battles were of the same nature or were merely protracted and magnified tavern brawls. Indeed, as can be gathered in the preceding pages (and they touch only on the main events), the entire history of Switzerland from its origin to the Sonderbund War is marred not only by foreign wars but also by domestic mayhem.

How could so quarrelsome a nation, of so discordant a disposition, succeed in forming the only European state whose inviolability has been respected for more than 130 years? As a partial answer it may be suggested that the majority of the Swiss, even at the periods when national disunity was at its worst, have always considered their quarrels as family quarrels, realizing soon enough that appeal to foreign aid always weakened their cause more than defeat at the hands of their domestic adversaries. The lesson was clearly learned during the Zurich War, when Zurich's request for foreign intervention led to the murderous battle of St. Jakob-on-the-Birse.

The desire for expansion was curbed at an early stage by the realization of Switzerland's economic needs, and export of mercenaries was substituted for imperialistic warfare. The industrial and financial development of the nineteenth century gave the nation stability and prosperity. The victory of liberalism brought a form of political freedom as near to direct democracy as any constitution can provide. Against external aggression Switzerland was protected by the European balance of power, without which national survival of Switzerland is inconceivable over a long period of time. Finally, Swiss control over the vital communications between North and South, combined with the strict Swiss adherence to neutrality in wartime, made an invasion of Switzerland undesirable even for those who did not keep the balance of Europe close to their hearts.

That Germany respected Swiss neutrality in the last war was surely due in part to the fact that the Swiss, who were fully mobilized and jealously guarded their frontiers, would have defended themselves efficiently and patriotically in the case of attack. This fact alone, however, would hardly have kept Hitler from invading and ultimately overrunning the small republic. Swiss neutrality was far better protected by the circumstance that it was more profitable for Germany to pay a neutral Switzerland for the transit of German matériel to Italy than to launch a costly invasion, see the Swiss blow up all their major tunnels by merely pushing a few buttons (as they are able to do), and to spend several years trying to put the tunnels back into operation.

One good reason is better than ten poor ones, but if more reasons for the maintenance must be added, it may be suggested that Switzerland is a most convenient refuge for the leaders and the capital of a nation which happens to have lost a war. To violate its neutrality might spoil its post-war value. Germany's leaders, it is true, were mistaken if they thought they could find asylum in Switzerland after this last war, but they were not mistaken when they deposited several hundred million dollars in Swiss banks and hid an unknown amount of assets both in Switzerland and abroad under Swiss names.

Possibly there were still other decisive circumstances that saved Switzerland from invasion, but surely the factors just cited were by themselves more important than the Swiss military potential. Switzerland's military tradition, no matter how proud and glorious, could never save it from foreign aggression. But it can save, and has saved, the nation from breaking up internally, for it is one of the main elements that make up Swiss national consciousness. Many Swiss believe that they were spared in the two recent world cataclysms because they were strong. Their faith is the more admirable since it has never been tested. Let us hope it never will be tested.

IV: The Mighty Fortress

IN HIS very malicious, but thoroughly unadmirable, mock-epic, *The Civil War in Geneva*, Voltaire introduced the city in these words:

> Below a mount whose scalp the years have peel'd,
> Along the shores where, rolling his fine waves,
> The Rhone escapes his deep imprisoning caves
> And rushes on, to Saône's appeal to yield,
> Geneva's shining city greets the eye:
> Proud, noble, wealthy, deep, and sly.*

At the time when these lines were written the *"noble cité, riche, fière et sournoise"* was in the throes of a profound transformation, the transformation from the status of the Protestant Rome, Calvin's "City of God," a model to all men, to that of a "Little Paris" on Lake Geneva, endowed with theaters, nightclubs, streetwalkers, and a mild form of officially sanctioned roulette game.

Leaving aside for awhile the solid brawn of Alemannic Switzerland, let us consider the rise and fall of that fortress of the brain, that most un-Swiss of all Swiss cities, that most cosmopolitan of all provincial towns. Geneva became a Swiss canton only in 1815, and still stands apart from the rest of the country. Yet there are certain subtle affinities and mutual influences which if conveniently ignored would by their absence falsify the general picture.

---

* In the original:
> "Au pied d'un mont que les temps ont pelé,
> Sur le rivage où, roulant sa belle onde,
> Le Rhône échappe à sa prison profonde,
> Et court au loin par la Saône appelé,
> On voit briller la cité genevoise,
> Noble cité, riche, fière et sournoise."

The "mont" is the Salève, just outside the Swiss border, a landmark of Geneva.

The general aspect of the city, which for a quarter of a century was not only Calvin's Rome or a "Little Paris" but also the "Capital of the Nations," is familiar to many thousands of Americans. All that, though splendid and beautiful, is not Geneva; the real Geneva is known only to a few thousand among the city's 124,431 inhabitants, and can be guessed at by an outsider with great difficulty only. Even Baedeker, otherwise so intimately acquainted with all the family secrets of towns and cities, is stymied when it comes to Geneva. Its compilers will tell the outward story of the place, they will mention the cathedral of Saint Pierre, where John Knox thundered and Calvin forbade, and a few other historical places—but as soon as they can they leave the forbidding walls of Calvin's Rome and overwhelm you with information on "Little Paris."

Little Paris—and the "Capital of the Nations"—lies mainly on the right bank of the Rhone and of the lake. Part of its long quay is named after Mont Blanc, visible from there in all its majesty on fine days, but hidden from the eyes of the inhabitants of the left bank, and part after President Woodrow Wilson, a Calvinist who by making Geneva the "Capital of the Nations," helped to hasten its end as the "City of God."

On the quay, Baedeker triumphantly points out the supreme architectural monstrosity of the nineteenth century, the mausoleum of an exiled duke of Brunswick who left his millions to the city provided it build him a monument of his design. It is a super-colossal replica of the Scaliger tombs in Verona, surrounded by elaborate iron grills; the equestrian statue of the duke, who had never done anything except run away from his duchy, was originally placed on the highest pinnacle of the monumental pastry—but either it actually threatened to come crashing down through the delicate arches or was merely a constant source of psychological uneasiness to the nervous passers-by—at any rate, the statue was ultimately taken down and placed on a solid pedestal adjoining the tomb. The monument, for which no one but the compilers of Baedeker ever had a sympathetic word, has a subtle message, however. As long as it stands it will tell its fascinated beholders that there is hardly a thing that the city of Geneva would not do to inherit a few millions. "If you see a Genevese jumping out of the window," said the Duc de Choiseul, Madame de Pompadour's foreign minister, "jump right after him: there is fifteen percent to be gained."

A few Americans who are not afraid of walking will also have contemplated another monumental mausoleum: the palace of the League of Nations. Craning their inquisitive necks, they have probably been awed by José Sert's hypermuscular giants, who are breaking chains and generally progressing all over the ceiling of the Council room. Those with cultural and historical leanings probably also have visited the cathedral, a fine structure, parts of which are excellent Gothic, but disfigured by a monumental Greek portal, added in 1749, which proves that bad taste existed even before the nineteenth century.

If anyone has business in the medieval town hall, which instead of stairways has a ramp for horses and litters, and where palefaced clerks labor in offices reminiscent of dungeons and torture chambers, he will in all likelihood be surprised to encounter two or three earnest and unmistakable Americans, inquiring for the location of the Alabama Hall. *La salle de l'Alabama* is the council chamber where in 1872 the United States and England settled the dispute arising from the damages inflicted on Federal shipping by the Confederate cruiser "Alabama" and other vessels constructed at British shipyards. That the hall where so prosaic an event was transacted should have become a place of pilgrimage is one of the many things that make Europeans puzzled about Americans.

Even those visitors who, in preparation for mountain climbing, roam the hilly streets, ramps, and stairways of the Upper City (the old and aristocratic left-bank part of the town) cannot penetrate the spirit of Geneva without an effort of the imagination. They will read the plaque which commemorates the spot where Calvin's house stood, but will they ring the bell of the neighboring door, where, if they look, they may discover a smaller name plate: M. Necker? A Monsieur Necker still lived there a few years ago, and presumably still does. For a number of years he had the misfortune of renting the upper floor of his mansion to the International House, a student organization whose energetic entertainments and dances must have shaken the ancestral chandeliers no less than the Revolution of 1789 shook Monsieur Necker.

Between the cathedral, where Calvin preached, and the college, which Calvin founded, the stroller will notice the dark and forbidding old prison, where Calvin kept those who would neither listen to his sermons nor learn his lessons. It is now replaced by the new prison, appropriately contiguous to the college.

The stroller might as well be an inmate of the prison for all he knows of what is going on inside the handsome eighteenth-century mansions that line the streets of the old city. As in Boston, where the Lowells speak only to the Cabots, and the Cabots only to God, the Genevese patricians have only furtive communication with the vulgar world. Yet this was not always so. Though they felt obliged by the tremendous influx of foreigners and other low elements to isolate themselves within a wall of ice, they actually have maintained a tradition of intellectual and social cosmopolitanism which in the eighteenth century made Geneva one of the capitals of the spirit. It is within these icy walls and within the subterranean labyrinths that have undermined the invasion-conscious city since times immemorial that we must look if we wish to learn anything worth while about Geneva.

II

To the schoolboy in the Latin class Geneva is known as *Genava*, an *oppidum* of the *Allobroges*, where Julius Caesar *posuit* his *castra*. Genevese schoolboys are particularly painfully aware of this fact, since they spend several years on the study of the first book of Caesar's *Commentaries*. Any secondhand copy of that work, which has been deplored by so many generations, if bought in Geneva, is remarkable for the grayness and dilapidation of its first thirty or so pages, and the immaculateness of the remainder, which deals with the negligible part of the Gallic Wars that did not center round Geneva.

Caesar singled out Geneva, where he built a bridge across the Rhone, for precisely the same reason that in later ages was to give the city its great strategic and economic importance. It commands the gap between the Jura and the Alps, and thus controls the access to Italy from the west through the St. Bernard and the

Simplon passes, while seen from the east it forms a gate leading into Burgundy and France.

An episcopal see since early times, Geneva, after the disintegration of the Roman Empire, successively passed to the Burgundians, to the Frankish Empire, to the kingdom of Upper or Transjurane Burgundy, and in 1032 to the Holy Roman Empire. During the Frankish rule the royal officials established themselves as the feudal lords of the region, the counts of Geneva. With them the bishops were in a state of unceasing litigation. Under the Burgundian kings, whose reign is affectionately remembered by the Genevese, the bishops were favored over the counts, till finally, in 1124, the temporal power passed virtually into the hands of the bishops. This state of things was undesirable to the citizens of Geneva, who had carried chips on their shoulders as far back as history can remember, and had discovered that having two lords was the best means of extending their own rights. They appealed to the counts of Savoy, who then resided at Chambéry and into whose family the countship of Geneva had passed, and by 1285 the count of Savoy, Amadeus V, was recognized as the civil protector (*Vicedom*) of the burghers. The episcopal power declined. In 1387 the bishop, Adhémar Fabri, officially recognized the rights of the citizens to direct their own affairs.

Things would have continued fine for the Genevese if the countship of Geneva and the countship of Savoy had not been eventually united in one person, Duke Amadeus VIII of Savoy (for now the counts had assumed the higher title). In 1420 the duke demanded to be recognized as the lord of Geneva, but the Genevese stubbornly and politely declined. The duke hit upon another idea: to control Geneva the house of Savoy must unite the countship and the episcopate. The bishops having lost all their power, this was easily done; members and bastard members of the House of Savoy or creatures trusted by it successively occupied the episcopal see; the Vicedom's representatives played into their hands, and they played into the Vicedom's, while the independence of the citizens was whittled away.

The Genevese became seriously alarmed. For protection, they turned to the Swiss Confederation, then at the pinnacle of its military prestige. A treaty of common citizenship was concluded with Fribourg in 1519, and with Berne in 1526. In 1530 the last resident bishop of Geneva, Pierre de la Baume, declared the Genevese to be rebels against their rightful rulers.

It is necessary to know these events to understand the true nature of the Reformation in Geneva. The Genevese were little concerned with religious matters. In fact, they had a reputation of cherishing the sweet pleasures of the flesh, they held gaming in high esteem, they appreciated the wines from the vineyards that rise along the shores of the lake and of the Rhone, and they had a thriving red light district. The extent to which a citizen might sin was regulated by statutes. It was, for instance, a misdemeanor to keep more than one mistress at a time.

The Genevese were artisans and merchants, and they wanted to be left to enjoy themselves as they pleased. They had few intellectual preoccupations outside the writing of bawdy ballads, and they were not tormented by metaphysical anxieties. Not one of the great Genevese reformers was born in Geneva. But Berne, Geneva's principal ally, had accepted Zwingli's reform, and to obtain its aid in a concrete form against their bishop, the Genevese had to become reformed themselves. Guilaume Farel was dispatched from Neuchâtel to Geneva, where he began to preach the Reform in 1532. Disorders broke out between the supporters of the Swiss alliance, called *Eydguenots* (from *Eidgenossen*), and the supporters of Savoy, dubbed *Mamelukes*. In 1533 Pierre de la Baume left Geneva for good and settled in Annecy in Savoy, thenceforward the seat of the titular bishops of Geneva. In 1535 the people of Geneva, won over in their majority to Farel's energetic preachments, invaded the cathedral, tore down about everything except its walls, and amused themselves by bringing their dogs and mules inside the hallowed walls in order to complete its desecration. Defrocked priests trampled on their robes, and what Catholics remained behind witnessed numerous miracles, notably the Hosts of the Holy Eucharist levitating in the sky. All in all, the Genevese had quite a time of it, as though they had a premonition that John Calvin was to arrive within their walls in the following year and that exuberance should have its last fling.

Three men had gained heroic fame in these troubled years: Bezanson Hugues, Philibert Berthelier, and François Bonivard, the Prisoner of Chillon. All three were leaders of the *Eydguenot* party. Berthelier was even decapitated by the bishop's orders in 1519. But it was only the Prisoner of Chillon who gained, largely through Lord Byron, truly universal fame. His story, less known than his name, is the most fitting commentary on the discrepancy between what the Genevese wanted when they ridded themselves of their bishop and what they actually got.

François Bonivard was a Savoyard nobleman born at Seyssel, near Geneva, in 1493. At the age of seventeen he became, through his family's influence, the prior of the Benedictine abbey of St. Victor, just outside the walls of Geneva. The abbey consisted of nine monks, but their young prior was not a monk, or even a priest. In fact, he had four wives in the course of his life, and a considerably larger number of mistresses. His only function as prior was to gather in the revenues. François, against his own interests, which depended on the duke of Savoy, adopted the party of the Genevese in the struggle between the *Eydguenots* and the *Mamelukes*. There is no rational explanation for this choice, except Bonivard's personal friendship with Philbert Berthelier and his general preference for the "Eternal Spirit of the chainless Mind" over tyranny. In 1519, as Berthelier was about to be dragged to the scaffold, Bonivard preferred flight, but was arrested by the duke's men and detained for three years, recovering his priory only in 1527. If this had been all, however, Byron would never have written his sonnet. In 1530 Bonivard was waylaid while traveling to Seyssel to visit his mother and jailed once more, this time for six years and in the castle of Chillon.

For the first two years he was treated with great consideration, but then he was suddenly flung into the famous dungeon where Byron read his name carved into the rock. "I had so much spare time for taking walks," Bonivard wrote in his later age, "that I left a groove in the rock, as though it had been beaten in with hammers." However, he was not "to fetters confined," as Byron would have it, and was given ink, paper, and books to study.

At last, in 1536, the Bernese came to the rescue of Geneva. Combining generosity with profitability, they overran what is now the canton of Vaud (which then belonged to Savoy), crossed the lake, and annexed the district of Chablais. In the course of this expedition they stormed the castle of Chillon, which became a residence of their bailiffs, and liberated poor Bonivard from the "damp vault's dayless gloom."

Lord Byron, who was not addicted to anticlimaxes, did not tell what happened to Bonivard after he had regained his freedom. Returning to Geneva in triumph, the prior was to discover that a few changes had taken place in his absence. Calvin was master, and his priory had been secularized. To compensate him for the loss, the city generously awarded him a place to live and a pension of 200 *écus*, a sum not entirely suited to his former habits of life. But this was not all.

Bonivard's wives were no less prone to worldliness than Bonivard himself. His fourth spouse had the honor of being sentenced for adultery by the Consistory, through which Calvin regulated the morals of the Genevese with painful vigilance. She was punished in a somewhat drastic manner, of which even her betrayed husband could surely not approve: she was sewn into a bag and thrown into the Rhone. The ex-prior's own peccadilloes were viewed with greater leniency, but many were the times when he, the hero of the revolution, was cited to appear before the Consistory for having neglected the sermon or the Holy Table and for wearing a nosegay behind his ear, a habit "ill becoming to one of his age."

However, somehow the authorities put up with him, and even entrusted him with the writing of the history of the Reformation in Geneva—though, indeed, the work was not published until the nineteenth century. Even in this activity Bonivard was not given full run of the Eternal Spirit of the chainless Mind. Though he declared in his history that God "wished to make Geneva his Bethlehem" and that "from its very beginning Geneva has been the chosen city of God to do strange and miraculous works," the Consistory found his style vulgar and occasionally salacious. Privately, Bonivard wrote different thoughts on the Reformation: "The world is like a donkey's back: a fardel leans too much to one side, and you want to lighten it and put it back in the middle—but it will not stay there, it will lean to the other side."

The Genevese had accepted the Reformation with little thought other than of liberating themselves from outside authorities of any kind. Calvin himself was not at first willing to stay in Geneva and face the superhuman task of teaching morality to its citizens. It was only after Farel had threatened him with divine punishment if he refused that Calvin consented to remain. At the end of two years the Genevese had had enough of their new virtue and threw out both Calvin and Farel.

It was well for the Genevese that the duke of Savoy was kept too busy by the struggles of Francis I of France and Emperor Charles V (in the course of which he lost his territories) to pay proper attention to what was going on in their town. As the Genevese were shifting for themselves without Calvin's guidance, chaos increased to the point where they decided, in 1541, to beseech Calvin to return and to re-establish order and discipline. Calvin, after his first acquaintance with the Genevese, had severe misgivings. "Why not rather death?" he wrote. "It would be better to perish all at once rather than suffer again in that torture chamber." But he came, and he came with a vengeance.

Nothing is better known in the history of the Reformation than what Calvin did to Geneva from 1541 to his death. His organization of the church became the organization of the reformed churches of France, Holland, Scotland, Hungary, and North America, where it was carried by the Founding Fathers. In a manner, the history of the New World was given its decisive turn when Calvin returned to Geneva in 1541.

Owing to its location, Geneva was always in danger of attack from all sides. Its ramparts, its secret passages, of which more and more are discovered as the old city is demolished, bear witness to constant preoccupation with the dangers of a siege and explain in part the fortress-mindedness of its citizens. But now, when Calvin came, the city was not only surrounded by hostile states, it was surrounded by the Devil. The Devil was everywhere—but Calvin, though busy with a tremendous correspondence, with his theological writings, his lectures, and a thousand other things, was never caught short by him. Calvin's vigilance was superhuman. Under his iron discipline, a fortress was built, a mightier fortress than those of stone or steel, a fortress against the Devil.

"A Mighty Fortress Is Our God" is the favorite Lutheran hymn—but in Geneva the preoccupation with the fortress grad-

THE ORATOR

Sketch by Ferdinand Hodler for the central figure
of his painting "The Reformation"

ually became so overwhelming and all-encompassing that the text should have been changed by the Genevese to read, "Our Mighty Fortress Is a God."

It may or may not be significant that Luther was stout and clean-shaven, while Calvin was haggard and bearded. At any rate, no one contemplating the impressive Reformation Monument, a modern work of sculpture which graces a wall opposite the University of Geneva, can avoid certain such reflections at the sight of the three austere beards and haggard faces of Calvin, Farel, and John Knox. The fourth, Calvin's successor Theodore de Beza, looks positively cherubic and jovial by comparison.

As one gazes at them, standing some sixty feet high in *haut-relief*, arranged like organ pipes along the wall, and sternly gazing into an enameled goldfish pond at their feet, one might easily reflect that notwithstanding Calvin's uncontested high qualities there was one of which he was utterly innocent: a sense of humor. You cannot preach or believe that the larger part of mankind, regardless of their good deeds or good intentions, are irrevocably doomed to hell, while you yourself, do what you may, are irresistibly elected to saintliness, and yet retain the faculty of laughter or of sympathy with human failings. Since Calvin's doctrine of predestination, which he himself admitted was "horrible to contemplate," permeated all life in Geneva, levity and laughter, no matter how innocent, were necessarily considered the work of the Devil, and all leanings toward them were extirpated at a tender age. Not that laughter could be entirely eradicated; but it was sufficient that it had become the stigma of the nonelect.

Building, he believed, on the theology of Saint Augustine, Calvin intended to transform Geneva into the City of God. That nine tenths of the inhabitants of the City of God were perhaps predestined to go to the Devil for lack of Sufficient Grace presented but a minor hurdle in his task. The solution was simply that the elect were to govern, while the damned were to live a life as saintly as that of the elect, regardless of the little benefit they would reap from it. It was, moreover, very much in the interest of the damned to appear as though they were elect themselves—a fact which greatly encouraged the practice of what La Rochefoucauld called the compliment paid to virtue by vice.

All resistance to salvation was repressed with the utmost cruelty. To sing secular music on Sundays, to play cards at any time, to wear jewelry, or to eat overly appetizing food were crimes punished by the Consistory. We have already seen how poor Mrs. Bonivard was put out of the way like a superfluous cat, and everybody knows what happened to the Unitarian Michael Servetus, who imprudently took refuge in Geneva and was executed, not by drowning, but by being burned at the stake.

Of all the forces Calvin had to fight, none was as resisting as Calvin himself. As he summoned the pastors of Geneva around his deathbed, in 1564, he laid his soul bare before them: "God has fortified me," he said, "so I could always hold out, no matter how timid nature has made me." And two or three times he repeated: "I assure you that I am by nature timid and afraid."

One cannot help recalling another Picard lawyer, another Incorruptible. Maximilien Robespierre was by nature so "timid and afraid" that he resigned his judgeship in Arras because he would not pass a death sentence.

III

In a certain sense, the Reformation had fallen on more fertile soil in Geneva than in Zurich or Basel. Radiation is most powerful when coming from one small focal center, and for that Geneva was eminently suited by its independent status, by its small and fortress-like character, and by its position at the crossroads of three great cultures. What is more, perhaps, the imprint of Calvin's personality was bound to be more profound than that of Zwingli. Zwingli's main preoccupation was to create a state to which everything else was subordinated and in which he, the prophet, was to lead the people. In this, he was perhaps somewhat ahead of his time. At any rate, his successor, Bullinger, though a capable theologian, was hardly a prophet. Calvin, on the other hand, created a church which encompassed the state. His leadership was necessary in the beginning, but it could easily be continued by others. Zwingli ruled through a secret privy council, hardly the ideal instrument in a City of God. Calvin ruled through the Consistory.

Founded by Calvin after his return to Geneva in 1541, the Con-

sistory was probably his most important achievement in the government of his church. It was made up of six ministers and twelve
elders, who were annually elected from among the members of
Geneva's three governing councils, and it sat every Thursday to
hear charges of misconduct and immorality, including heretical
doctrines. It might be said that Calvin's innovation was nothing
very original—in fact, that it was hard to distinguish from the
Spanish Inquisition. The Spanish Inquisition, however, did not
consist of citizens elected to that office. Calvin's form of inquisition, by its very composition, exemplified the concept of a state
in which every citizen was at the same time a churchman. It would
have been illogical if appeal had been possible from sentences
passed by the Consistory, and indeed no appeal was possible.
Though its penalties became a little less harsh as time went by, it
remained the dominating factor in the life of the Genevese to the
eve of the French Revolution.

Calvin, at the time of his death, had secured the permanent success of his institutions. Any fortress less strong than Geneva
would, indeed, have succumbed to the Counter Reform, which
was preached in the region by one of the greatest saints of the
Catholic church, whose personality was the antithesis of Calvin's:
Saint Francis of Sales, bishop of Geneva, who resided at Annecy.
By the end of the sixteenth century the entire countryside lying
south of the Lake of Geneva was won back to Catholicism by the
persuasive saint; in Geneva itself a number of citizens had secretly
remained loyal to the old faith, and Saint Francis, on at least one
occasion, entered Geneva at the risk of his life to celebrate Holy
Mass. But the Consistory was well established and Francis's efforts within the city walls remained primarily of symbolic value.

A more literal threat to the Reformation was the attempt made
in 1602 by Charles Emmanuel I of Savoy to reconquer Geneva.
The episode, which began somewhat like the storming of Troy
and ended rather like a Punch and Judy show, has been celebrated
by posterity as a great feat of arms under the name "Escalade." On
the night of December 11–12 the Savoyards began their assault
on the city, without any previous warning. Several had already
stealthily scaled the walls, when, according to tradition, they
were discovered by an old woman called *La Mère Royaume*,

who poured a pot of hot broth over their heads (some pretend
that the vessel was not a marmite, but one of different nature and
use). Whatever it was, the alarm was given, the citizens, many
clad in nightshirts, heroically repulsed the invaders, at the cost of
several lives. Since Berne immediately warned Charles Emmanuel against any new attempts, and since a treaty was signed
between Geneva and Henry IV of France in the following year,
no further attempts at reconquest were made.

The triumph of a pot over the enemies of the Reformation has
since been celebrated annually. It was fortunate for the people
of Geneva that the duke of Savoy should have made this attempt,
for in commemorating the event they were able to expend during
two days in the year their penned-up propensities for merry-
making.

The celebration involves a parade in the costumes of 1602, ending on the Cathedral square, where a huge bonfire is lit, the *Cé qu'é
laîno* is sung, and patriotic speeches are made. Boys and girls run
through the streets disguised as Savoyards or in nightshirts, singing derisive songs about their Savoyard neighbors, and all candy
stores and pastry shops are filled with *marmites*, varying in size
from miniature to gigantic, which are made of chocolate or a
special crunchy substance based on honey and contain sweet-
meats of all sorts. The *marmites*, of course, are consumed in
memory of *La Mère Royaume's* ambiguous container. There also
exists a patriotic society named *La Compagnie de 1602*, which
furnishes most of the paraders and behaves like most patriotic
societies.

The prestige which Geneva had gained under Calvin's rule
made the city the center of studies for students for the reformed
ministry from all parts of Europe and a refuge for persecuted
Protestants. It was the influx of these foreigners which made
Geneva what it is.

The first great influx came from Italy. Old Genevese names
such as Diodati and Turretini date from that time. From Paris
came Robert Estienne to establish his famous printing press.
Finally, when in 1697 Louis XIV revoked the Edict of Nantes
and thus ended the last vestiges of Protestant freedoms in France,
Geneva was swamped by Huguenot refugees.

It is a commonplace of historical writing that the Revocation of the Edict of Nantes ruined the economy of France and brought prosperity to the lands where the Huguenots took refuge. Nevertheless, it was with serious misgivings that the Genevese extended their hospitality to the persecuted. Not all Protestants adhered to the severe standards of morality of the Genevese; Calvin, for one, sensed the moral danger of too rapid an increase of the population and warned the newcomers that if they could not live an evangelic life "they might as well return to the dunghills whence they had come," a phrase which now has a somewhat familiar ring.

The greatest danger, however, was an economic one. In 1603 Geneva had lost its main agricultural hinterland, the Pays de Gex, to Henry IV of France, who openly admitted that he had no more right to it than he had to Castile. It was difficult to see how an overpopulated Geneva could find enough food to sustain life. And yet, within a century and a half, Geneva had become one of the wealthiest cities of Europe. The key to the success was foreign skill. A large segment of the French Huguenots were artisans, watchmakers and jewelers, merchants, and financiers. Bringing to Geneva both their knowledge and their capital, they made their new home a world center of their trades. By 1750, Voltaire tells us, there were five hundred gold and silver refineries in Geneva.

A new aristocracy, largely of refugee origin, had sprung up. It was a curious aristocracy, for it drew its prestige from its spiritual achievements as much as from its business acumen. In that respect it somewhat resembled the now vanishing type of Orthodox Jewish family, who labor for wealth and success mainly in order to support the one member of the family of whom they are proudest: the erudite, the student of the Bible. It is less surprising to find this Old-Testament quality in Calvinist Geneva than to miss it in other Protestant countries. Down to this very day the typical patrician family in Geneva is represented by two heads, one who takes care of the business with the accumulated shrewdness of generations, the other who pursues a career of studies and investigation, with the least possible amount of practical objectives in mind.

One of Calvin's main preoccupations was the education of children. Schooling was made compulsory, and the greatest luminaries of Protestantism, including Bayle, did not consider it beneath their dignity to instruct elementary classes. "It is in this," said Saint Francis of Sales, "that our miserable Geneva has caught us unawares." Mathurin Cordier, whose erudition might have made him one of the celebrated humanists of the sixteenth century, preferred to ask for the privilege of teaching only the youngest classes in the College of Geneva. To his old age the great Latinist cheerfully initiated ten-year-olds into the secrets of *amo, amas, amat.*

It is true that a brilliant star such as Casaubon preferred the more liberal air of England to that of his native Geneva, but his infidelity was more than made up by the presence of such imposing guests as Scaliger, Hotman, Henri Estienne, and, somewhat later, Agrippa d'Aubigné. As a training ground for ministers and theologians Lausanne rivaled, and perhaps even surpassed Geneva. As a center of humanities, Geneva could be rivaled only by England and Holland among the Protestant countries.

However, while the watchmakers were doubling their ingenuity and output and the bankers increasing their capital, the theologians became rutted in a sterile routine. It was science rather than theology that was to make so many Genevese names famous and respected from the eighteenth century to the present.

Secluded in their stern-faced houses in the Upper Town or rambling through the countryside in search of geological specimens, fossils, or butterflies, working quietly, unobtrusively, and conscientiously, the De Saussures, the Claparèdes, the Candolles, the Piagets, the Flournoys, the Diodatis, the Sismondis, the Bonnets, and countless others gained for themselves a peculiar type of anonymous international fame. So many excellent men of the same family name worked in so many different fields and in so unspectacular a manner that to mention them merely evokes a vague familiarity in the average educated person, implying a precise meaning only to specialists in their respective fields. Historians, entomologists, philologists, psychologists, botanists, they all preferred a discreet level of aristocratic scholarship to more resounding fame. Their world was small, yet the objects of their research were too vast for a lifetime.

This was the world into which, on a fine day in 1754, Voltaire was to drop like a billygoat into a watchmaker's shop. For nearly a quarter of a century he was to remain and to throw miniature monkey wrenches into the delicate machinery of the small republic. By the time he was through with Geneva it could never be quite the same again.

IV

The "Swiss Voltaire," as he now signed himself, purchased the property of Les Délices. He bought it through a proxy, for the acquisition of real estate was forbidden to Catholics. He quite literally began to cultivate his garden with passionate diligence, but he also set about to inject a little more life into the social habits of the Genevese. He charmed the ladies, flattered the pastors, and opened his house to the liberal-minded élite. Among Voltaire's intimates were the brothers Cramer, publishers and printers, who had printed many of Voltaire's works and Montesquieu's *Spirit of the Laws;* Pastor Vernes, a man of the world; and the astounding Dr. Tronchin, whose clinic rivaled Voltaire's wit when it came to attracting foreigners from all Europe to the shores of Lake Geneva.

Of Tronchin Grimm wrote: "Most of our doctors treat only illnesses; he treats the patient." A believer in inoculation, exercise, and fresh air, he startled the court of Versailles when he ordered, in the middle of winter, that all the windows of the hitherto hermetically closed palace should be opened at once. The Parisians shivered in the presence of so much genius, and Tronchin was immediately fashionable. Ladies began to take walks in the early morning hours, clad, for the sake of ventilation, in short skirts which became famed as *tronchines.* It was Tronchin who made it possible for Voltaire to proclaim himself on the threshold of death from the fifty-seventh to the eighty-first year of his life.

The relations of the perennial moribund with the Consistory were not quite as unruffled as they appeared on the surface. Within a year after Voltaire's appearance in Geneva the first clouds had begun to gather. It was not long before Europe was regaled with the spectacle of storm and lightning caused by the triple clash of Voltaire and d'Alembert with Geneva, of Rousseau with Voltaire and d'Alembert, and of Geneva with Rousseau.

Voltaire's estate had become a center of bustling and—to the Consistory—disquieting activities. Visitors and couriers would come and leave mysteriously; not very pious little pamphlets with pious titles were being circulated; and preparations were made which looked suspiciously like rehearsals for a play. Indeed, while Voltaire reassured the good pastor Vernet that he was "too old, too ill, and a little too stern for the young people," the young people kept flocking to his house, and the lines they spoke there were surely not taken from the prayerbook. One evening in 1755, the great actor Lekain, the French Garrick, chanced to be at Les Délices. A select society, including most of the members of the Little Council, also chanced to be there. The occasion was the reading, by Voltaire, Lekain, and Voltaire's niece, Mme Denis, of *Zaïre*. "Never saw I so many tears shed," Voltaire wrote; "never were the Calvinists so tender. . . . Geneva shall have a theater despite itself."

If the councilors were moved to tears, the Consistory was moved to something else, and informed Voltaire's budding actors accordingly. Voltaire, still cautious, decided to transfer his activities to Lausanne, where he also had an estate and the authorities were less severe. In Lausanne, several of Voltaire's pieces were privately performed by members of the town's most respectable families.

In 1756 Voltaire returned to Geneva, and events began to precipitate themselves. First there was the unobtrusive visit of Monsieur d'Alembert, coeditor with Diderot of the *Encyclopédie*, who had come to gather first-hand information for his article "Geneva." He established the most cordial relations with the pastors, tactfully engaging them in philosophic arguments, and no doubt the good pastors were animated by the desire to impress the great man as liberal and open-minded thinkers. They were considerably embarrassed when the seventh volume of the *Encyclopédie* appeared in the following year. Indeed, this is what they read: "Religion in Geneva is almost entirely reduced to the adoration of one only God . . . the respect for Jesus Christ and for the Scriptures is, perhaps, the only thing that distinguishes the Christian doctrine of Geneva from pure deism." In fact, the pastors of Geneva were Socinians.

Great was the shock in the church of Geneva. The pastors might be open-minded individually—but as a body they could hardly admit it. An ecclesiastical commission was appointed to answer the article, while Voltaire, who had inspired d'Alembert's article in the first place, denied even having read it. Secretly he wrote to its author: "Do not retract; your salvation, your conscience are at stake. . . . You do not need my holy exhortations. . . . The priests of Geneva will write to you . . . I assure you that I and my friends will give them a good time; they will drink the cup to the dregs."

Voltaire's war against the church was but one part of the trouble. He had also taken care to instruct d'Alembert to make a plea in his article for the establishment of a permanent theater so that Geneva could "unite the wisdom of Sparta with the polish of Athens." In their indignant uproar the pastors had overlooked the plea, but it did not escape the attention of Rousseau, who at the time was nursing a number of grudges at Montmorency as the guest of Marshal Luxembourg. Red hot with indignation, he seized the pen. The virtue of his fatherland was in danger, and Rousseau, who had begun his literary career by writing and composing a musical comedy, denounced the infernal project in his famous *Letter to d'Alembert on Spectacles*.

Dramatic representations, Rousseau explained, might be all right in large cities, which were already hopelessly corrupt. But in Geneva, the last refuge of purity—never. Tragedy after tragedy, comedy after comedy, are taken apart in that extraordinary work to demonstrate the subtle poison of immorality that pervades every one, even the most edifying of all plays ever written. After all the object of the theater is to paint life, life is immoral, *ergo* the theater is immoral—thus, in its broad outlines, runs the argument. This is not all: the austere Genevese, if a theater were established in their midst would begin by squandering money on their tickets; the next thing, they would buy expensive clothes for their wives, who would not be seen in public less fashionably dressed than their neighbors; from clothes to jewelry, from jewelry and fashion to indecency and luxury; and from luxury to levity, ruin, and perdition. "Elections will be held in actresses' dressing rooms and the leaders of a free people will be the creatures of a band of mountebanks."

The Genevese were surprised and flattered to learn how virtuous they were, and Rousseau became for a while very popular with his countrymen. But Voltaire was not one to be easily defeated. He began the next phase of his campaign by selling—at a great loss, he complained—his property in Geneva and acquiring the territories of Ferney and Tournay, just outside Genevese territory. In Tournay he built a small theater, which became a place of pilgrimage to the smart set of the Genevese, despite the long faces of the pastors. In Ferney he built a handsome Roman Catholic church, and over its entrance the traveler can behold, in huge letters, the astounding inscription:

DEO EREXIT VOLTAIRE

The controversy might have ended there had not Rousseau been busy in the meantime writing, besides the *Nouvelle Héloïse*, the *Social Contract* and *Emile*. The political implications of the *Social Contract* and the deism of *Emile*, as expressed in the "Profession of Faith of the Savoyard Vicar," the most hotly disputed section of the work, drew upon Rousseau the thunder and condemnation of both the Sorbonne and the Consistory. The works were burned by the executioner in Paris and in Geneva; Rousseau had to flee France for the canton of Berne; and Voltaire and the pastors of Geneva united to denounce him in poisonous pamphlets and ponderous tracts.

It is true that a little book called *Candide* had recently been published under a pseudonym, that it had been burnt by the Genevese executioner along with Rousseau's writings, and that certain evil tongues ascribed it to Monsieur de Voltaire, but Voltaire suavely brushed off such slander. Written it? He had not even read it. Finally he consented to look at it. "I have at last read *Candide*: one must have lost one's senses to ascribe it to me. I have, thank God, better things to do." But some did not quite believe him, and the Grand Council even had the cheek to enjoin the Genevese from acting in Voltaire's theater. Voltaire became belligerent: "I shall give orders to shoot the first Socinian priest that trespasses on my territory." But the Socinian priests had ceased to call on Voltaire long ago. No blood was shed.

Into this complicated struggle entered a new element: the people of Geneva, who had lost most of their political rights to the small aristocratic governing clique. Protesting against the condemnation of *Emile*, they also began to claim their democratic rights as Rousseau had set them forth. Their claims were answered by François Tronchin—not the physician, but the attorney general of Geneva—in a pamphlet entitled *Letters Written from the Countryside*. Rousseau, who in the meantime had been expelled from Berne and taken refuge at Motiers (which being in Neuchâtel was the territory of the king of Prussia), took violent issue with Tronchin in his *Letters Written from the Mountain*. The sovereignty of the people of Geneva, he thundered, was mere sham. "Your citizens cannot see the chains that are prepared for them until they feel their weight."

It was the overture to the French Revolution. On the heels of Rousseau's *Letters* came an open revolt of the workers and artisans of Geneva against their patrician rulers. No blood was shed, but confusion was considerable. According to Voltaire's description of the event in his burlesque *Guerre civile à Genève*, so many watchmakers had left their work that nobody knew any longer what time it was in Geneva. In 1767 the governments of Berne, Zurich, and France agreed to intervene militarily. They also sent special ambassadors to Geneva to settle the revolt.

It was now that Voltaire's hour of triumph had finally rung. No sooner had he heard the news that a French envoy was to appear, than he wrote to him with the suggestion that a company of actors would undoubtedly enliven the diplomatic proceedings. The government of Geneva had to accede to the envoy's wishes. Voltaire, exulting, cried: "Tout est perdu; Genève a du plaisir."

A few days after its installation the theater burned to the ground—but Voltaire had had his satisfaction, and now he could even accuse Rousseau of having instigated the fire.

Nothing illustrates more brilliantly the absurd paradox by which liberals and revolutionists were to join forces in the French

Revolution than the roles played by Voltaire and Rousseau in the civil troubles of Geneva. Rousseau, the true revolutionist, did not look forward, but backward. The ancient virtue had to be preserved, the lost freedom was to be regained, the moral authority of a state church was indispensable: in fact, Rousseau was the missing link between Calvin and Robespierre. Voltaire, on the other hand, looked only to the future: progress required more luxury, more entertainment, and, above all, more religious freedom—politics were secondary, and civil disturbance was the worst of all evils. It is not difficult to see why the two men, despite the many views they seemingly held in common, would have been irreconcilable enemies even if they had not been one a paranoiac and the other an imp.

v

On May 30, 1778, in the words of an unfriendly contemporary, "that godless arch-rascal Voltaire conked out at last." The contemporary was Mozart. Voltaire expired in Paris, where he had recently arrived from Geneva to see his latest play performed. Mozart wrote that he died like a dog; actually he died in an apotheosis. It was Rousseau who, barely five weeks later, was to die like a dog at Ermenonville, a few miles from Paris, after having been chased over the face of Europe both by persecution and by persecution mania. But with Voltaire's death, Voltaire's world was dead; with Rousseau's death, the age of Rousseau had barely begun. It was, fittingly enough, in Geneva that the first attempt was made, in 1782, to put Rousseau's theories into practice.

On the ninth of April that year the popular party overthrew the aristocratic rulers of Geneva and established a representative government. The experiment was short-lived. The aristocrats having appealed to France, Berne, and Sardinia, the three powers intervened, re-established the old regime more firmly than ever, and severely suppressed the revolutionists.

Among the Genevese who emigrated to Paris as a result of these events were three men of whom France was to hear considerably more within a short time. Jacques Mallet du Pan, who became the political editor of the *Mercure de France,* was one of the chief advocates, next to Mirabeau, of a constitutional monarchy in France. Entrusted with a confidential mission by Louis XVI in 1792, he failed, turned completely royalist, was sentenced to death in absentia by the Revolutionary Tribunal of Geneva in 1798, and died an exile in London in 1800.

Etienne Clavière, a prosperous banker, became the intimate of Brissot, the leader of the Girondists, and of Mirabeau, for whom he ghost-wrote numerous speeches on financial matters. Made minister of finance in 1792, he was denounced by Couthon the following year and committed suicide to escape the guillotine.

Luckier than these two was Pierre Etienne Louis Dumont, who had been pastor at the Huguenot church of St. Petersburg and tutor to Lord Shelburne's son in London. He went to Paris when the Revolution broke out, and he also joined the intimate circle of Mirabeau, but he knew when to leave. Back in England, he struck up a friendship with Jeremy Bentham, whom he translated. He finally returned to Geneva in 1814 and lived there to the happy age of seventy.

It may seem strange that these three men, who were important members of the highly articulate circle of French-speaking Swiss in revolutionary Paris should all have been moderates, with not one dogmatic Rousseauist among them.

In connection with the three-power intervention in Geneva in 1782, a theatrical company was once more allowed to visit Geneva. This time it was to stay for good, and it is regrettable that Voltaire was unable to witness his ultimate vindication. The name of the first director of the theater of Geneva was Fabre d'Eglantine—the same who a few years later, in the revolutionary Convention, was to devise the pretty names of the French Revolutionary calendar. His successor, another Frenchman, was to acquire an entirely different kind of notoriety. He was Collot d'Herbois, one of the leaders of the Great Terror, who in 1794 butchered the counterrevolutionists at Lyons. It was in Geneva that Collot, already addicted to hard liquor, claimed that he acquired his passion for the democratic liberties of the Swiss—which is difficult to understand in view of the thoroughly undemocratic character of the Genevese government of the time.

The aristocrats succeeded in maintaining themselves in power in Geneva until the end of 1792, but then the great wave from Paris engulfed the little republic. A revolutionary government was set up, and heads fell as they did everywhere else. However, the Genevese aristocrats did not have to go far to cross the border into Bernese territory, a definite advantage not shared by the French nobles. In 1798 at last Geneva was annexed to France as the Département du Léman, and it stayed under French rule until it was "liberated" by Austrian troops in 1814. Shortly afterward it was admitted as a canton (the last of the twenty-two) into the Swiss Confederation. The aristocrats returned, calm descended, and once more Geneva resumed its old character.

At the Congress of Vienna the Genevese representative, Pictet de Rochemont, might easily have won for his city a comparatively vast rural territory from neighboring Savoy. However, only small acquisitions were made, and even those were opposed by the advocates of a "Little Geneva," who were terrified at the idea of including into their state a vast Catholic rural population. Geneva was a fortress though its walls were to be razed, and a fortress it was to remain in spirit. Even if it was now a canton of Switzerland and no longer independent, its official title still was, and is, the "Republic and Canton of Geneva," a republic above all, and a canton only because it cannot be helped.

Before the peace treaties were signed, Léonard Sismondi, the great historian of the Italian republics, pled the cause of his native Geneva in a pamphlet addressed to the English. Geneva, he claimed, through its intellectual and religious ties was the outpost of Britain on the European continent. In this he was, perhaps, not entirely right, for nothing could be less English than to claim the glory of being the outpost of a foreign nation. Moreover, at the time Geneva was an outpost of Whiggism rather than of England.

However, the pamphlet was, perhaps, not without its effect—though not in the desired direction. In 1817 the British Isles paid off a long-standing debt to Geneva. England and Scotland had been evangelized long enough by Geneva; it was about time that Geneva, where morals, faith, and theology had somewhat lapsed, should be evangelized by England and Scotland. In the wake of Madame Krüdener, the Pietist lady from Riga and gray eminence of the Holy Alliance, arrived a number of English and Scottish missionaries who preached justification through Faith, a doctrine which had gradually fallen into discredit since Calvin's death. The movement gained ground, and Geneva once more was filled with the sound of hymns and psalms, composed mainly by the pastor César Malan. "Come ye all to hear the good tidings," says one of his hymns, "for today Salvation is being preached." As can be seen the cause for rejoicing was not so much Salvation in itself as the fact that it was preached; the thirst for instruction and improvement was greater than the thirst for bliss.

Meanwhile Sismondi could console himself with the presence in Geneva of Lord Byron, who did not preach salvation. Yet, libertarian though he was, Sismondi himself could not overcome the immense moral bias with which every Genevese is born. Composing his history of the Italian republics, in which he maintained the thesis that the greatness of a nation is in direct proportion to the amount of liberty it enjoys, he could not refrain from the most unjustifiable attacks on the role of the Catholic church in Italian history. Incredible though it may seem, he must have believed that Italy would have been greater had Raphael and Michael Angelo been Calvinists.

Though the patricians continued to govern, though the Turrettinis and the Pictets continued to be pastors, though the Candolles, the Colladons, the De la Rives, and the De Saussures continued to herborize, experiment, and investigate; though the watchmakers continued to make more and more watches and the bankers more and more money, and though Rodolphe Toepffer delighted the French-speaking world with his charming *Nouvelles genevoises* and *Voyages en zigzag,* in which the quiet and virginal gaiety of the younger bourgeoisie is brought to life, with Geneva and the Alps of Savoy as settings—despite all these self-perpetuating ivory towers which, working and existing side by side, characterized Geneva, times had changed imperceptibly, but significantly.

When Franz Liszt adulterously eloped from Paris with the Comtesse d'Agoult, he turned, of all places, to Geneva. There the couple, far from being pilloried or sewn into a sack and drowned, were welcomed with open arms by Genevese society, once the initial shock had worn off. The traditional right of asylum, once granted by Geneva to persecuted Protestants, had begun to attract a different category of men: Mazzini, Kropotkin, Bakunin, Lenin, Mussolini, Kamenev and a considerable number of other agitators of steadily diminishing respectability lived or stayed at Geneva at some time or another between 1830 and 1917.

In Geneva itself, thanks mainly to the efforts of James Fazy, an eminently respectable citizen who had espoused the Radical cause, the aristocratic government fell for good in 1846. At last, in 1907, the incredible happened: a referendum proposing the separation between church and state was carried by a majority. This was made possible by the tremendous increase of the Catholic population of Geneva (now more than 40 percent). The Catholics, mainly workers, farmers, and petty tradespeople of French, Italian or Valaisan origin, voted in favor of separation with as much fervor in Geneva as they had fought the same principle in France.

However, the worst was yet to come. In 1919 Geneva became the permanent seat of the League of Nations. The days of Bakunin and bespectacled female nihilist students from Russia began to appear in an almost rosy light of nostalgia. They somehow had belonged to the general picture of Switzerland, and tourists had come to stare at them as much as to view the Alps; but the influx of foreign bureaucrats, newspapermen, and general hangers-on met unqualified disapproval. The Turrettinis, the Pictets, and the De Saussures felt definitely crowded, and the old Genevese society, once hospitable to foreigners, closed their ranks and their houses hermetically. The foreigners, on the other hand, hardly aware of the existence of a Genevese patriciate, established their own ways. Night clubs were opened, money was spent lavishly (perhaps the most unforgivable crime), and for such pleasures as were too dangerous to pursue in Geneva there were hospitable institutions in France, just across the border.

It would be an exaggeration to pretend that these temptations met with uncompromising resistance on the part of all Genevese citizens (who, by the way, were now in a minority in their own canton). But discretion, at least, was the rule. As in all flocks, there were black sheep, and black sheep in white sheep's skin, and

occasionally a pastor would be found to be a wolf in disguise—
but such exceptions, even if frequent, were haughtily ignored. The
patriciate of Geneva remained essentially what it had been since
the eighteenth century: wealthy, unostentatious, frugal, narrow,
and extremely cultured. Though it lacks contact with the lesser
bourgeoisie and shuns foreign newcomers, it maintains intimate
connections with the elite of other capitals. Its cosmopolitanism
is not shared by the rest of the bourgeoisie. Indeed, the cosmopolitan character of the city is not due to the international or-
ganizations it houses, or to the profusion of foreigners which make
it a tower of Babel, or to the many splendid hotels and impressive
shops, or even to its commercial and financial importance. All this
would merely give it the character of a tourist center. The cosmopolitan nature of Geneva is entirely due to its most exclusive
and closed element, the patriciate, the spiritual elite.

VI

No example could elucidate this apparent paradox more clearly
than the life and the reputation of Frédéric Amiel, who lived in
total obscurity as a professor of esthetics in Geneva and after his
death, in 1881, at the age of sixty, became known to the world
as the author of one of the most extraordinary of intimate diaries.
Born in Geneva, educated largely in Germany, Amiel returned
to his native town to lead the most unobtrusive life ever recorded.
Timid to the extreme, more sensitive than the finest precision
instrument, at ease only in female company, but never in the company of a single female, an introvert par excellence, Amiel led
a bachelor's existence. He wrote a few poems and essays, gave
his courses, and in his solitary hours reflected on the nature of
action. In his diaries, of which the few published volumes represent only a part, he built the most complicated, the most ingenious, the most unassailable, and the most agonizingly exalted
ivory tower that was ever erected as a monument to impotence
and sterility. It is a life-long self-justification for never writing
the great work planned, for never taking the woman desired,
for never consummating the act contemplated, for never leaving
the dream he lived. Never? Well, almost never, for indeed there
was one thing that could make him leave his dreams.

Ce qui seul fait sortir du rêve,
C'est le devoir.

"The only thing that makes us leave our dreams is duty."

In Amiel the clinical observer cannot fail to detect the ultimate consequences of extreme Puritanism on an extremely emotional soul. To the non-Puritan the spectacle is, perhaps, tragically ludicrous. In Renan's words, "Amiel speaks of sin, of salvation, of redemption, of conversion, as if those things were realities. Sin, above all, is his chief preoccupation and saddens him—him, the best of men, who less than anybody else was in a condition to know what sin is. Here, indeed, is the great difference between a Catholic and a Protestant education."

As soon as it was published, Amiel's *Journal* made a sensation, and within a short time it was translated into all civilized languages. Here was not a disingenuous and exhibitionist record like the memoirs of Rousseau, the other great Genevese confessant. Aside from its great literary beauty, from its penetration and its culture, derived from the Latin as well as from the German civilization, the *Journal* is a unique document by all counts. The little provincial professor, from his modest grave, speaks to the world.

In an attenuated fashion, the story of Amiel was the story of all Genevese intellectuals, scientists, and artists. They could operate only in a vacuum. They achieved, in almost every case, excellence, but rarely greatness. Those among their countrymen who were truly great, such as Rousseau, or those who looked for worldly fame, like the financier Gallatin and the sculptor Pradier, could not remain in Geneva, which tolerated little activity. On the other hand the tradition which the Genevese intellectuals established, the respect they commanded, the control they exercised over their native city had a positive result: there were few towering peaks, but there also was almost no trash.

The Genevese eagerness for money has been the butt of many jokes, but the scoffers overlooked the fact that this eagerness was never transferred from the field of business to that of intellectual pursuits. Similarly, the local patriotism and the spirit of independence of the little republic have been laughed at more than they deserved.

If Geneva were to be annexed to France, it would become an

insignificant provincial town. If it should become any more Swiss than it is, it would be a tourist resort. Its present attitude may be anachronistic, and it probably is doomed. Yet the world would be a great deal poorer for its loss. Even to those who dislike Puritanism, the complete transformation of its traditional fortress into a Little Paris on Lake Geneva would be a saddening event.

V: The Rule of Bears

THE CURIOUS who might wish to form an idea of what Rome would have become had the advice of Cato the Censor prevailed should turn their eyes to Berne, and, *mutatis mutandis,* draw their own conclusions.

The trip by railroad from Geneva to Berne lasts only a few hours. But as one steps off the train one steps into another world, where each hour has one hundred and twenty minutes, where men lumber along rather than walk, where women look like the "Before" sections of "Before-and-After" advertisements, where all is solid deliberation, and where volatile impulsiveness, if at all present, is confined to raucous tavern songs. To the Bernese, Calvin's City of God is a Gomorrah. Indeed, Berne is probably the only capital in the world where honest married couples have been aroused from their sleep in a hotel room at three in the morning by the knocks of a policeman who wished to see their marriage license. It is also the only capital where night life ceases at eleven o'clock. In normal times, when food is plentiful everywhere, Berne is not a popular diplomatic assignment.

As a capital, Berne is unique in many other respects. For one thing, it has more embassies, legations, consulates-general, consulates, vice-consulates, missions, and international headquarters, ranging from that of the Universal Postal Union to some of extremely esoteric and obscure nature, than any other city can boast per head of its population—or so, at least, it would seem. It is the source of more false rumors than any other capital except Ankara and, perhaps, Stockholm. These rumors are often inspired by interested sources, but mostly they are merely the result of the desperate boredom of newspapermen. Above all,

however, Berne is the only civilized modern capital which does
not in the least look like a capital.

If Zurich gives the impression of a modern, bustling metropolis
despite its numerous medieval and baroque buildings, Berne on the
contrary looks like a town that fell asleep around the year 1650,
despite its many modern buildings and despite its activity. The
medieval character of the town is so striking that its modern
touches, such as the Federal Palace, are hardly noticeable. The
diplomatic activities do not, of course, appear on the surface. All
one sees are the stolid faces of the Bernese burghers.

Only on market days is some life injected into the picture.
Thousands of peasants fill the town, all stiff, substantial, and
ruddy, bearded or mustachioed, their black Sunday hats squarely
on their round heads, their shirts stiff and white, their black coats
and trousers awkward and well kept, their watch chains prominent, their curved and lidded pipes, held by ringed and meaty
hands, outlining sparse and deliberate gestures, and on their shirt
fronts, instead of ties, two red tassels hanging from an intricately
knotted silken cord. They are as likely as not to emerge from a
streamlined sedan, to have learned Latin in school, and to own
shares in Anaconda Copper.

The sense of permanency, prosperity, and rusticity that
emanates from these peasants is found again in the streets of the
town. Neither particularly narrow nor particularly crooked, they
remind one of a village rather than a city. The main streets are
lined by low arcades, where most of the shopping and promenad-
ing is done by the burghers, who do not bustle along, but rather
march in procession. It is, by the way, a mystery why arcades
have been abandoned as medieval, for they are the only practical
device found as yet to protect pedestrians from the rain; umbrel-
las are hardly more effective and certainly less esthetic. Surmount-
ing the arcades are the gabled houses of the merchants and patricians, dating mostly from the seventeenth and eighteenth centuries, when Berne was at its height.

The streets themselves are enlivened by a number of old foun-
tains, with wooden sculptures, such as the gaudily painted
"Ogre," represented in the process of devouring several little
children. One of them is disappearing into his throat, and another

is held by the ogre in readiness with his free hand. The sculpture is said to have been set up in memory of several Christian children who had been eaten for breakfast by some Jews—a dietary habit the historicity of which Julius Streicher has upheld as late as in 1944.

Another curiosity is the *Zeitglockenturm*, a very ancient clock tower on which the hours are announced not only on an enormous clock face, but also by a wooden rooster, a man in armor, a number of dancing bears, and a man seated on a throne, all of whom make an elaborate appearance each time the clock strikes a full hour. Swiss humor, which is sometimes peculiar, has found in the slowness of the Bernese one of the chief targets for its emphatic barbs. It is told that one day a painter was commissioned to repaint the face of the *Zeitglockenturm*; after five weeks the painter, who had begun with the "I," was still at work on that numeral when one of the city fathers happened by. Struck by the extreme leisureliness of the procedure (or perhaps by the expense connected with such slowness), he asked the painter what seemed to be holding him up. "I don't know, Your Honor," the man said in a puzzled way, "but each time I start applying the brush to the wall the minute hand comes swooping along and knocks it down onto the street."

Though slow, the Bernese were never addicted to idleness. Their proud history is a lesson in hard work, frugality, circumspection, and a wise and firm administration. Their fine churches, their imposing cathedral, their unobtrusively opulent guild houses, and their town hall, from which for centuries Their Excellencies of Berne have ruled a powerful and respected state, are all witnesses to the effect that turtles are almost always victorious over rabbits.

II

The association of Berne with bears is a hoary tradition. A bear has been its heraldic animal for seven centuries; bears have been kept by the city in a pit for hundreds of years and still are a major attraction to native and tourists alike; in fact, the Bernese themselves have more and more come to look, talk, and act like bears, and to pride themselves on the fact. No doubt the association is based on a mistaken derivation of the city's name. Berne, founded in 1109 as a military post by a duke of Zähringen, was actually named in honor of Verona in Italy. Similarly, the Dietrich of Berne in the *Nibelungen* epic actually is Theodoric, who resided in Verona. Subject at first to a feudal aristocratic regime, the burghers of the rapidly growing town revolted in 1294 and constituted themselves under a government which, in its basic features, and with some interruptions, lasted until 1831.

As a city government the Bernese system was, at first, democratic enough. It provided for a Grand Council, elected by the so-called College of Sixteen, who in turn were chosen by the sixteen districts of the city; and for a Little Council, appointed by the Grand Council. The Grand Council, moreover, won the right to have two of its members seated in the Little Council, where they exercised much the same function as the tribunes of the people in the Roman Senate. Two *avoyers*, or chief magistrates, constituted the executive power. This democratic appearance is delusive. In actual practice the ranks of the eligible citizens became closed to most of the inhabitants of the town. Besides, the government was not a city government at all, but the government of a large state.

A Free Imperial City since 1218, a member of the Swiss Confederation since 1353, Berne was by 1536 lord of one of the largest states within the Holy Roman Empire. Its handful of inhabitants (about 5,000 in 1500) ruled an area of about 4,000 square miles, reaching from the Rhine to the French Alps, which now would contain a population of more than a million. These lands, acquired by conquest, purchase, treaty, or bequest, did not include various bailiwicks jointly administered by Berne and other cantons, and associated territories where the power of Berne was paramount. The largest of the Bernese subject lands was the present canton of Vaud.

The economy of the large state was well balanced. Cheese and cattle were the products of the Bernese Alps, or *Oberland*, now the most visited part of the Swiss Alps, and of the Emmental, whence the characteristic Swiss cheese has taken its name. The Aar plateau, with Berne itself as its center, was rich in agriculture; Vaud provided wines, and the northwestern corner of the state,

SURRENDER OF THE TOWN OF ESTAVAYER TO THE
BERNESE AND THEIR ALLIES

Pen drawing from a chronicle, c. 1500

although it did not yet include the Bernese Jura, early began to develop watchmaking and other industries. Communication was greatly facilitated by the lakes of Thun and Spiez, separated only by the narrow strip of land at Interlaken, by the Aar River, and by the Lake of Geneva.

In addition to its natural wealth, Berne had another major source of riches: with the acceptance of the Reformation, in 1528, all church property was seized by the state, that is, by the city of Berne. This, of course, was the case in most Protestant countries, but whereas the heads of other nations lavished the newly acquired wealth on wars and other futile enterprises, the government of Berne held it in trust for its citizens, increased it by judicious use, and by the seventeenth century had invested a large part of it in foreign countries—with considerable profit.

The rule of city over country was not tyrannical. A large degree of democratic self-government was tolerated by the Bernese masters. No attempt was made to introduce the German language into the French-speaking districts; in fact, there was rather a tendency for French to take over in Berne itself. Nor was there, by and large, excessive economic exploitation. The Bernese knew better than to kill the goose that laid the golden eggs, and preferred even to take only part of the eggs and let the others hatch.

If the government of the city of Berne was originally democratic, it might best be characterized as paternalistic in relation to the state of Berne. However, by the seventeenth century, there was not a shred of democracy left in the government even of the city itself. Within the guild patriciate, which had replaced the former nobility of feudal origin, a small number of powerful families had emerged and gradually usurped all functions of government. The Grand Council was the only body, by the late fifteen hundreds, that was still open to all full citizens. However, since the bailiffs who administered the country districts were chosen from among the members of the Grand Council, and since the position of bailiff was quite remunerative, access to the Grand Council finally was restricted, too. Its electors, the College of Sixteen, based their vote on family considerations. Gradually the Council came to renew itself, and in 1649 the new procedure was officially confirmed. The exercise of sovereignty was transferred from the commune to the two councils, and elections were thenceforth held only if the membership of the Grand Council had sunk below two hundred. About seventy-five families formed the Bernese patriciate. Of these, only nine really counted. Their names run like a thread through three hundred years of Swiss history: Wattenwyl, Graffenried, Jenner, Stürler, May, Fischer, Tscharner, Steiger, and Sinner.

It is difficult not to draw a parallel between the history of Berne and that of Rome, great as the differences in many essential aspects may have been. There was the same division of the town into electoral districts, each of which had one voice in the election of the magistrates; the senatorial character of the councils; the existence of two *avoyers*, comparable to the two Roman consuls; the strict limitations of citizenship to the old families of the chief town; the administration of the subject districts by proconsular bailiffs; and, it might be added, the differences of status accorded to the various subject lands, allies, and associates.

Many of these similarities may have been due to the influence of the Italian republics, but some were purely fortuitous, arising, as in the case of the differences of status in the subject districts, directly from the previous feudal conditions. It must be added here that serfdom had been completely abolished in Berne, as in the rest of Switzerland, at a very early stage and that consequently, in contrast with Rome, all classes, no matter how underprivileged, were technically free. Intermarriage between the various classes, on the other hand, which was a frequent occurrence in Rome, was discouraged by legal limitations in Berne. But the essential parallel occurs with regard to the emergence of a patrician class, which gradually came to be trained for the specific jobs of ruling and commanding. To form an able governing class the Bernese resorted to an entirely original method, namely, that of creating a sort of practice-state within the state, the so-called External Estate.

The External Estate, which lasted from the fifteenth century till 1798, was a sort of club of young men who trained themselves for the art of government by forming a fictitious government of their own. They elected their own mayors, councils, and bailiffs, and they administered imaginary districts to which they gave the names of castles which had once existed. Originally, the External Estate was primarily a military and social organization, something between a cadet corps and a boys' gang. As Berne evolved from a military and dynamic to a prudent and static power, the External Estate became more and more political in its activities, and its importance gained by the fact that membership in it often opened the doors to the actual government. The club, which had its own town hall (it still stands), also had its peculiar festivals. On Easter Monday, for instance, it held a splendid procession, in which its members marched disguised as old Swiss warriors, William Tell, and the Bear of Berne. Part of the procession was also a tableau representing the heraldic emblem of the External Estate: a lobster walking backward, ridden by a monkey.

If the future rulers of Berne were encouraged to sow their wild oats in a spirit of virtuous prankishness and bearlike humor, the actual rulers forbade themselves any show of levity. Their sternness was not the result of theological considerations, as was the case with the Genevese patriciate. It was rather the sternness of a family father who will take no nonsense. The paternalistic spirit itself may well have been the fruit of the Reformation—but while the rulers of Geneva had only a city to govern, the Bernese were in charge of a large state. Administrators had no difficulty in superseding theologians. However, the Calvinist spirit, once implanted, made an admirable companion to the political interests of the city. It is to the combination of the two that Berne owed its Catonian character—for can there be any doubt that Cato, had he lived in the seventeenth century, would have been a Calvinist?

Like Cato, the Bernese government knew how to combine stern wisdom with considerable financial acumen. In 1648, at the close of the Thirty Years War, a depression swept the canton—a result of its immense prosperity during the war itself and of the export duties levied by the state to keep prices down. Angered against the government because of the low prices, the peasantry of Berne soon had another cause for complaint. In 1652 the government, without any warning, suddenly decreed a major depreciation of the currency—after having made sure that at the actual moment of the depreciation the larger part of the currency was not in the hands of the treasury. By this somewhat crude method the government had acquitted itself of all its debts without losing a single penny, leaving the peasants holding the bag. The result was the peasant revolt of 1653, which the government put down with the utmost severity. Such was the republic which was hailed by some enthusiastic eighteenth-century writers as an example of ancient democracy surrounded by an enslaved world.

III

One of these writers was Voltaire, who during his sojourn at Lausanne enjoyed Bernese hospitality. It is said that when Voltaire arrived, the Bernese bailiff of Lausanne gave him the following advice: "Monsieur de Voltaire, it is said that you have written against the Lord; that is bad, but He will forgive you. It is said that you have written against Our Lord Jesus Christ; that is very bad, but He will forgive you. Monsieur de Voltaire: be careful never to write anything against Their Excellencies of Berne: they will never forgive you." Voltaire heeded the advice, and the government of Berne was probably the only one with which he never had any trouble.

Foreign visitors were practically unanimous in praising the efficiency and authority of the Bernese government. There was one notable exception. It was Edward Gibbon, who spent major portions of his life in Lausanne, where he nearly married the future Madame Necker. In a letter (written in French) which he prudently ascribed to a Swedish gentleman Gibbon took up the cause of the people of Vaud, whom he cherished, against their Bernese oppressors. The Bernese, he found, allowed free speech, but only so long as no idea of action was connected with it. They kept down industry in their subject lands, and they deliberately kept down the standard of living, for they found that "poor and obedient subjects were preferable to rich and recalcitrant ones."

Gibbon, however, did not publish this criticism while in Bernese territory nor was he then known to be its author. Besides, he was remarkably little quarrelsome for an eighteenth-century writer. Unlike Voltaire in Geneva, Gibbon lived in peace and harmony with the society of Lausanne, including the Bernese bailiff. The upper bourgeoisie of Lausanne, like the Vaudois in general, were more easygoing than the Genevese, their neighbors, more intellectually agile than the Bernese, their rulers, more sedate than the French, their cousins. Gibbon felt thoroughly at home with them, and even Voltaire had nothing but good words for them. Indubitably, however, the Vaudois were, of all Bernese subjects, both the richest and the most recalcitrant. This was not apparent in Voltaire's time, but became very much so toward the end of Gibbon's sojourn, when the Vaudois colony in Paris, led by Frédéric César de La Harpe, the former tutor and life-long advisor of Alexander I, began to agitate for the liberation of Vaud from the Bernese yoke. It was due mainly to the efforts of La Harpe and to the sympathetic attitude of the Tsar that the canton of Vaud did not revert to Berne after the fall of Napoleon.

The Lake of Geneva had become a place of pilgrimage after the publication of Rousseau's *Nouvelle Héloïse* and *Emile*, where the scenes of both are laid, and Lausanne, the principal city on its shores next to Geneva, saw the passage of Europe's fashionable and famous. No doubt this contact contributed to the half-brilliant, half-provincial intellectual atmosphere of the town, which differed so radically from that of the Teutonic Berne. The revolution that separated Vaud from Berne in 1798 brought merely a political change. Socially and culturally, Vaud had been a separate entity for well over a century, a fact which speaks in favor of the Bernese method of administration. Its people have since then retained their highly original characteristics, notably a spirit of friendliness, unpretentiousness, and rich solidity, which may have something to do with their intimate bond with their fertile and wine-growing soil.

The good nature of the Vaudois has a charming example in the episode, related in Rousseau's *Confessions*, of Rousseau's experience as a music teacher in Lausanne, several years before he attained his international fame. The penniless Jean Jacques, who had just blown into Lausanne with the purpose of giving piano lessons without being able to read music, had taken it into his head—with the audacity of the desperate—to write a piece of chamber music and to have it performed in the house of a friendly patron.

As was frequent in the eighteenth century, the piece was performed without a previous rehearsal. Rousseau conducted the performers, though he really had not the slightest idea of what his composition would sound like. After the first few bars of catlike dissonances, the musicians were convulsed with laughter and the audience began to exchange remarks about the barbaric innovations of modern composers; but when the last movement was reached, in which Rousseau had simply transcribed a popular hit, hoping that the provincial Lausannois would fail to recognize it, the game was up, and the composer was clearly recognized as a fraud.

Anywhere else, in all likelihood, Rousseau would have been run out of town. Not so in Lausanne. The audience rather liked the young man, several gentlemen gave him money to pay his rent, and others confided their daughters to him for piano lessons. People who were capable of such a reaction showed that, though unsophisticated, they were nobody's fool. There is a sort of warmth shining through that episode that it would be hard to find in any other Swiss town.

In Berne itself the business of government allowed little time for an intellectual flowering. However, what there was of it was highly important. Béat Louis de Muralt (1665–1749), the scion of a patrician family of Italian origin, won enormous fame after his death through the publication of his *Lettres sur les Anglais et les Français*. This work anticipated and influenced the Anglophile fashion popularized throughout Europe by Montesquieu and by Voltaire, who acknowledged his debt to the "sage et ingénieux Monsieur de Muralt." Though Berne was in intimate economic relations with England, however, Muralt's enthusiasm for democracy as practiced in England did not impress it favorably. No sooner had the author of the *Lettres* returned from his extensive trip to Britain than he was banished from his homeland for his radical opinions. He died after a long exile in the territory of Neuchâtel.

Better known than Muralt was Albrecht von Haller (1708–77), who was equally distinguished and influential as a physician, a botanist, a poet, a political philosopher, and an administrator. Haller's poem *The Alps,* published in 1729, was written with a triple intention. First of all he wished to prove that one could be a Swiss and nevertheless a good poet, a combination which was held impossible by the critics of all civilized nations. In this he succeeded, at least in the estimation of his contemporaries. Second, he wanted to open the eyes of the public to the beauty of the Alpine landscape and the majesty of God's achievements. In this he was equally successful, to the point of creating a new poetic *genre* —the nature poem. Third, and perhaps most important to him, he aimed at preaching the return to a simpler, healthier, and more frugal way of life, exemplified by the pastoral population of the high Alps and threatened by the growing refinement and effeminacy of city ways. In this he anticipated Rousseau by a quarter century.

Unlike Rousseau, however, Haller did not round out his return-to-nature theories with such radical political suggestions as Rousseau's. He was a patrician in spirit; moreover, he was a high government official. The return which he advocated to the ideal simplicity of the past fitted very well into the scheme of things as contemplated by Their Excellencies. Lack of respect for authority he abhorred, and Voltaire he held in low esteem. It is told that when Casanova visited Voltaire in Ferney he informed him that he had just seen Haller. Voltaire thereupon began a long praise of that great man and his multiple achievements. "It is admirable of you," Casanova interrupted, "to speak so highly of Monsieur de Haller—the more so as he has spoken to me in quite the opposite sense about you." "*Que voulez-vous?*" Voltaire sadly replied; "probably we are both mistaken."

In his later age Haller published three political novels, in which he set forth his theories of good government. Their titles alone suffice to characterize the political ideals of Haller and the enlightened Bernese patriciate: *Usong,* which deals with China; *Alfred, King of the Anglo-Saxons;* and *Fabius and Cato.*

I V

The ghosts of the old heroes of the Roman Republic, who were remarkably active throughout the Age of Enlightenment, finally caught up with Berne, but not in the manner in which Haller had hoped. Not Fabius and Cato, but the Gracchi and

Brutus were invoked by the French Revolutionists who invaded Berne in 1798. Military resistance was heroic, but short, and the liberated Bernese soon were to watch the sad spectacle of the French carting away their savings of centuries, which were to be sunk into Bonaparte's mad Egyptian venture. When Their Excellencies, after lying low for sixteen years, came back into their own with the Restoration, they could to some extent re-establish the old order, but they could not regain the subject lands which Berne had lost. As a result Berne emerged from the French Revolution with considerably less sway over the other Swiss cantons than it had possessed before—though it still remained the most important single member of the Confederation. Some concessions also had to be made to the political rights of the rural districts: the Grand Council was so reorganized that it comprised 101 representatives for the city of Berne and 99 for the rest of the canton. In view of the fact that the city population represented only about one tenth of the total, this arrangement did not appear very equitable to the majority of the Bernese.

Radicalism had gained in the Swiss towns in the eighteen twenties, and the peasantry for its part had also become fully conscious of its importance and its contributions to the prosperity of the canton. By 1830 the patriciate had come to realize that even the use of force could not in the long run prevent the democratic forces from overthrowing the existing government. Grudgingly, but with infinitely more wisdom than the crowned heads of Europe, the patricians handed over the government to the Radicals in 1831. For a century not a single member of the once all-powerful families was trusted to serve as a high government official.

Such hostility on the part of the people was not caused by memories of mismanagement. Rarely did one class of citizens hand over the government of a country to another class in such excellent order and good condition as when the Bernese patricians yielded their rule to the people. The hostility was rather the result of the resentment, penned up for centuries, at the arrogance and pride of an urban aristocracy—a feeling somewhat comparable to the still existing hostility in the United States toward titles and traditions, expressed in the distrust of anything British.

Though the entire population of Berne has been democratically represented since 1831, there can be no question of a revolution, even a bloodless one, having taken place. The government of Berne remained cautious and slow. A major social change—the rise of the once depressed peasantry of the Bernese Oberland to wealth and independence—was marked by no violent convulsions. This change was faithfully described, in all its details, by a writer who of all Swiss authors was probably the most characteristically Swiss: Johann Bitzius, better known under his pen name, Jeremias Gotthelf.

A pastor in the Emmental, Bitzius was deeply aware of the economic as well as moral problems that the average peasant of the region was facing. To help the peasants find the road to economic independence, self-respect, and virtuous simplicity, he told, in two related novels, the rise of Uli the farmhand from servant to tenant farmer to landowner, without glossing over the difficulties that even Virtue Personified must encounter. Bitzius also dealt with more specific topics: among his writings, one finds such titles as *How Five Maidens Perished Miserably through Liquor*, and *Dursli, the Brandy Guzzler*.

The realism, the wit, and the language of Bitzius' books—they were largely written in the local dialect—gave them immediate popularity, and it cannot be doubted that they not only helped the peasants who read them but also pre-disposed the urban population in favor of the peasantry.

Yet Bitzius was a bitter enemy of liberalism, in which he saw but a threat to Christian virtue. The established order, on the whole, seemed to him a good one. In his lifetime his conservatism clashed sharply with the radicalism which was sweeping the Swiss and molding them into a unified nation, but since then the Swiss have come to recognize themselves in Bitzius. Their radicalism was a short-lived affair, and the spirit of the old village pastor survived. Nowhere in Switzerland has it survived as completely as in Berne.

v

Berne has been the Swiss capital for barely a century. From 1815 to 1848 Switzerland had had no less than three "capitals."

Berne, Zurich, and Lucerne, in their qualities as cantons, not as towns, alternately held the directorship over the Confederation for two-year periods. This system was found inconvenient, and the new constitution of 1848 made Berne—this time the city, not the canton—the seat of the federal government. Despite the numerous imposing government buildings erected since then, Berne, as the chief town of a largely agricultural canton, lacks the metropolitan character of some other Swiss cities. It is precisely for this reason, however, that Berne is more representative of Switzerland as a whole than the more cosmopolitan, commercial, and busy Zurich would be. There can be no doubt that the general atmosphere of calm and, sometimes, seemingly bovine deliberation of Berne has contributed to some extent to the formulation of Swiss policy, both foreign and domestic. Hysteria is not at home in Berne.

Nevertheless, there are few Swiss, and practically no French Swiss, who regard Berne with much affection. They deplore the lack of grace of its citizens, the austerity of its establishments, the inhuman slowness of its officialdom, and the magisterial sternness of its statesmen. Certainly, the Bernese lack color and are little given to the display of emotions. These negative qualities, many Swiss feel, have left their imprint on all Switzerland and given the Swiss the reputation of being narrowminded, humorless, materialistic, and preferring the security of neutrality between good and evil to the risk of taking sides for what they believe, or should believe, is right.

Yet it is doubtful that the same critics, if given the choice, would recommend any other course of action than that which they blame on the thick-skulled Bernese. Just as for hundreds of years Their Excellencies of Berne really knew best what was good for the people, so now does the Federal Council. The Federal Council, however, includes men from all the regions of Switzerland. Berne may be the collective name given to the federal government, but actually the Bernese do not exercise a disproportionate influence over it. They merely set a tradition, proved for generations, which has become the tradition of Switzerland in general. Lovable or not, it certainly has until now served the best interests of the country.

VI: Cows, Demons, and Wayside Crosses

When Charles the Bold of Burgundy was watching his troops lose the battle of Morat, he suddenly saw the approach of a new contingent of Swiss marching to the attack to the accompaniment of bleak sounds like the lowing of a gigantic bull and blowing into enormous horns that produced a blood-curdling music. Bold though he was, Charles felt uneasy. "Who are these men?" he asked one of his captains; "Are they Confederates too?" They were. The herdsmen of Uri, Schwyz, and Unterwalden had come to decide the battle.

It is not difficult to understand the fright which these men inspired. They were not like the burghers and peasants of Berne, of Zurich, of Basel—there was something savage and primitive about them that gave Western Europeans cold shivers, just as the Scottish "ladies from Hell," more than four centuries later, were to demoralize the German troops in the First World War. In the very heart of civilized Europe there was a race of men, just a few thousand, who perched, as it were, on the top of the great Alpine fortress, a corporation of robber barons who held sway over the great international trade roads, who descended at times to terrorize the fertile Lombard plains and towns, who spoke a rough and barbarously guttural tongue, and who regularly returned from their warlike expeditions to resume their pastoral pursuits and to sire children.

Admirers of Spartan ways, who believe that severe military discipline, frugality, poverty, and primitive simplicity are the best

SWISS WARRIORS DRIVING HOME CATTLE CAPTURED FROM THE BURGUNDIANS
Pen drawing from a chronicle, c. 1500

means to keep a nation from decay should ponder the history of the three primitive cantons of Switzerland. They will find that the sons of William Tell at an early stage began to prefer the relatively easy life of herdsmen to the hardships of tilling the soil, and the perhaps still easier life of soldiers and hirelings to that of herdsmen; that they had gained independence merely to sell generations of their manhood into foreign service for pensions doled out to them by Europe's tyrants; that they held entire districts in subjection, holding freedom dear only to themselves; that they came to be ridden by disease, beggary, and drunkenness to a most alarming extent; and that they recovered health, dignity, and orderliness only after they had given up their special privileges, their military ways, and their resistance to industrialization.

The three cantons of Uri, Schwyz, and Unterwalden, though by no means the only, or even the most, important of the Swiss pastoral regions, are nonetheless the most typical. For centuries their economy has been geared almost exclusively to the requirements imposed by a purely pastoral life, and in respect to political tradition, they have become typical of all Switzerland. Their government by direct democracy—or primitive democracy, as it is sometimes called—has shown the way to the more complex, but basically similar institution of popular initiative and referendum. It almost seems to have been their historical role to cling to their crude manner of government through popular assembly, a relic of the prehistoric past, until the time became ripe for its acceptance as the most advanced form of political democracy.

It will be remembered that the three cantons which by their alliance of 1291 laid the basis of the Swiss Confederation have ruled themselves by direct popular assemblies since times immemorial. It is a commonly held view that their Landsgemeinden can be traced to the Germanic popular assemblies which according to Tacitus decided on all vital questions of a tribe. Their revolt against the feudal encroachments of the Hapsburgs, which gave rise to the William Tell legend; their reputation of innocent rusticity, which gained wide credit when Rousseau's "Noble Savage" came into fashion; and their picturesque manner of self-government—all these facts and myths combined to make the three original cantons appear like a cradle of freedom in the eyes of the modern world. Late in the eighteenth century it became fashionable, both for foreigners and for the urban Swiss, to organize what a contemporary called "frequent excursions for the purpose of viewing the Alpine herdsmen in all their simplicity and of tasting pure joy in the lap af Nature." In the twentieth century the Swiss Federal Railroads run special trains during the meetings of the remaining Landsgemeinden, for much the same purpose.

After the outbreak of the French Revolution, tearful effusions in praise of Liberty knew no more limits. It was almost compulsory for travelers who visited the spurious Tell chapel "to fall on their knees and to kiss the soil on which a free man [William Tell] was the first to tread." The quoted words were written in 1796. It is probable that their author was surprised when, two years later, the descendents of William Tell took to poking pitch forks into the French soldiers who had come to bring Liberty, Equality, and Fraternity. Indeed, the soldiers had also come to deprive the mountaineers of their independence, which they cherished above all else. The three great gifts of the Revolution benefited exclusively the people of the mountaineers' subject lands and were scarcely appreciated by their former masters.

At the very moment when Schiller—who never set foot on Swiss soil—in his noble and idealized drama, gave lasting and final expression to the Tell legend and when Rossini, in his somewhat less lofty music, made it the standby of brassbands throughout the world, earnest historians began to doubt the authenticity of the account. The first to challenge the fact that there ever was a man named William Tell, or a bailiff named Gessler, was saved from national disgrace and possible lynching only by the fact that his books were so dull and unreadable that few people were aware of their existence. His research and theories were, however, taken up by other Swiss historians who bravely risked the accusation of treachery for the sake of truth. With the discovery of the original document of the Pact of 1291 (written in Latin, a language not commonly associated with the ways of Tell and his rustic confederates), the whole history of primitive Switzerland underwent a complete re-evaluation.

The birth of Swiss liberties, it is now generally conceded, was not the result of a spontaneous outbreak against Hapsburg tyranny (in fact, there was no tryanny), nor was it in any manner caused or helped by the isolation of the early Swiss from the rest of Europe. The text of the alliance of 1291 clearly implies the existence of earlier pacts among the same communities. As for the factor of isolation, it was non-existent: with the opening of the St. Gotthard road in the mid-thirteenth century, the early Swiss were anything but isolated.

Even before they founded the Confederation, Uri, Schwyz, and Unterwalden were primarily oriented toward the south, that is, Italy, and this remained their political and religious outlook for hundreds of years. The very idea of a league of free communities originated not in Switzerland, but in Italy, where the Lombard League was acknowledged in 1183 by Emperor Frederick Barbarossa, after he had vainly sought to subdue it. The Lombard League offered a tempting example to the Swiss mountaineers, with whom it entertained friendly relations.

Though these facts should be kept in mind they should not blind anyone to other facts. There is no reason to doubt that the lofty and rugged landscape of the three cantons had a profound influence on the inhabitants and their love of independence. If Rudolph of Hapsburg and his bailiffs went down in Swiss history and legend as tyrants and blackguards, although almost everywhere else their rule was regarded as mild and beneficent, the reason for this is not so much that Swiss chroniclers were exceptionally addicted to lying, but rather that the Swiss whom Tell symbolized were exceptionally sensitive to even the slightest interference in their affairs. Perched on their rocks, they developed the mentality of castle-owners rather than reasonable subjects. One might object that what applied to the citizens of the Forest Cantons should equally have applied to the peoples of their subject lands, who were also perched on rocks. The fact is that the subject peoples kept trying for centuries to gain equal rights from their masters. They lacked neither courage nor persistence, but, unfortunately for them, the masters against whom they rebeled were tougher adversaries than the Austrians.

All this being duly considered, there still remains a puzzle.

Granted that the possession of the three little cantons was valuable to the large neighboring powers for strategic reasons, and granted that they had in the first hundred years of their independent existence defended their freedom against several attempts at subjugation—it nevertheless is true that after 1388 no more such attempts were seriously made, that the sparsely populated and arid valleys offered little temptation to a conqueror, and that for the following two centuries it was the three Forest Cantons, not their neighbors, who showed the most aggressiveness. If their difficulties had been of a political nature, a struggle for the preservation of freedom, surely the reverse would have been the case. The fact is that it was nothing of the kind. Their troubles were almost exclusively economic, and their most implacable enemy was nature.

The facts are simple. At present, the three cantons, totaling 1,062 square miles, support a population of more than 131,000, or about 123 people per square mile. Only 70 percent of the area is capable of growing anything at all, and even in the lower valleys, where agriculture might be possible, it is rendered difficult in many places because of the swampiness of the terrain. What little industry exists is of relatively recent origin. There are no towns, only large villages, such as Altdorf, Stans, Einsiedeln, Schwyz. These conditions were essentially the same as far back as history goes.

Travelers who visited Switzerland in the eighteenth century nearly all commented on the fact that the scenery of these valleys consisted of an almost uninterrupted green. Hardly any cereals were grown, a few potato patches could be seen here and there, and perhaps an isolated patch of vegetables. All the rest was meadows, pastures, or forest. This is still the case. In Uri the total of the area devoted to the culture of cereals amounts to less than one square mile; almost half the surface is unproductive; the rest is divided between forests (about one third) and meadows and pastures (about two thirds).

At present, there is no reason why these essentially pastoral areas should not rely on other cantons and foreign countries for their supply of cereals and devote themselves entirely to the dairy and cattle industry. What is surprising is that they should have done so for the past six centuries, with complete disregard for the local self-sufficiency for which most other countries were striving. Agriculture is neither entirely impracticable in their valleys, nor had it always been neglected. Nevertheless, within the period between 1230 and 1386 it was completely abandoned in favor of cattle raising, dairying, soldiering, transportation of goods, the gathering of nuts and berries, beggary, and an early form of tourist trade, namely, the exploitation of pilgrims. The abbey of Einsiedeln, a favorite place of pilgrimage for many centuries, attracted 100,000 pilgrims in the single year of 1789, and there were other, if less popular, shrines.

Just why agriculture was completely abandoned is a difficult question to answer, for there are abundant contradictory reasons. For one thing, it was an arduous and ungrateful task. This difficulty, it is true, has not stopped agriculture in other, still more sterile regions of the world, but it might have done so had these other regions been suited for an alternative form of economy. Another cause frequently cited is that cattle raising and dairying offered a better outlook for profits than does agriculture. Indeed, the Swiss mountaineers soon discovered that "the products that can be obtained from milk and from cattle are the precious and divine minerals of our mountains and bring gold, silver, and much wealth into our country."

The chronicler of Lucerne who wrote this paean to the cow (in 1645) was exaggerating somewhat. The mountain districts of central Switzerland were always extremely poor. Their relative prosperity around 1645 was merely the result of the ruin into which the Thirty Years War had plunged the rest of Europe. In order to "mine" their cheese and to enable their cows to bring forth "gold and silver," the humans themselves had to undergo privations. Thus, in a less lyrical vein a traveler reported in 1781 that "country and people, everything seems to be created for the cattle, and everything is subordinated to their needs and comforts; humans come only in second place." Even so, dairying and cattle raising were found insufficient to sustain the population, as can be seen by the many other means to which it resorted in order to feed itself, and by the great number of emigrants that left the country for America in the nineteenth century.

Dairying with cows is a relatively advanced state of alpine economy. Before the Swiss of the pastoral regions discovered the beneficent properties of cows, which was approximately in the fourteenth century, their economy was based on goats and sheep. These had the advantage of not being difficult to feed during the winter months, but could not possibly bring in as much revenue as large cattle. As communications improved, the people of central Switzerland found markets for their surplus cattle and for their dairy products both in northern Italy, part of which they conquered and held in subjection, and in Lucerne, which came to be their principal trading post.

There came a time however, when their livestock had increased so that good prices could no longer be fetched in the fall and the fodder supply had become insufficient to keep the surplus animals fed through the winter. It was this dilemma which forced the peasants to choose between sacrificing their cattle or sacrificing what was left of their agriculture in order to increase their supply of winter fodder. They chose the latter, partly for the reason which has already been hinted, namely, that a pastoral economy involves less effort than an agricultural one; partly because the improvement of trade routes and the political power which Switzerland had gained seemed to insure an adequate supply of imported food; and partly because the craze for foreign enlistments which had just started created a permanent labor shortage. The larger part of the work which a pastoral economy involves can be done by women and children, while the men are left free to go off to wars.

The results of this transformation were not as rewarding as might have been hoped. The simplicity which came to be admired so much in these regions was not altogether voluntary, but rather the result of general misery. It is surprising, for instance, to find that in the eighteenth century, when Switzerland was generally prosperous, meat was eaten only on the principal feast-days in a region where cattle raising was the principal industry. Even those few families which had acquired wealth claimed that they were unable to profit from their position because they were afraid of offending the rest of the population, which was uniformly poor. To dispose of their superfluous capital, they lent it at high interest rates to the other peasants, who were nearly all in debt. Sober travelers reported on the unashamed beggary practiced by almost the entire population, on their unhealthy appearance, on their shiftlessness, and on their avarice.

With the loss, through the French Revolution, of their possessions south of the St. Gotthard Pass, and with the end of the mercenary service early in the nineteenth century, the position of the pastoral cantons became worse than ever. It was around this time that hard liquor began to replace beer and wine throughout Europe, and in central Switzerland alcoholism took on epidemic proportions. Poverty and inbreeding had already undermined the race. Liquor threatened to finish it.

That this did not happen was due to three main factors. In the first place, thousands of romantic-minded travelers, unaware of the vicissitudes which had befallen the home country of William Tell, began to invade its peaks and valleys from all parts of Europe with the unshakable purpose of admiring its scenery and delighting in the innocent virtue of its inhabitants. The tourist trade expanded with amazing rapidity, hotels sprang up everywhere, and gold began to pour into the pockets not only of the hotelowners, but of the whole population.

This phenomenon, taken by itself, might have done more harm than good, since easy money meant still more liquor and still less work. It was followed, however, by another, more important, development, namely, the intensive industrialization of Switzerland on a capitalist basis. As the production of cheese, chocolate, condensed milk, and other dairy products became a national mass industry, with a market which came to include the entire world, the economy of the Alpine districts became an integral part of a prosperous whole. On the other hand, the rise of the Swiss cities, due to the introduction of industry, drained the pastoral districts of the surplus population which formerly had depended on mercenary service or emigration abroad.

No doubt the unification of the country which followed the Sonderbund War was chiefly responsible both for the economic development of Switzerland and for the greater ease of population shifts. The Forest Cantons, which had been the most stubborn enemies of unification, derived only profit from their eventual defeat.

II

Switzerland's pastoral economy may have become part of a modern industry, but its methods have not essentially changed since the old times. Whether cheese is produced by an individual peasant or by a capitalist corporation, whether it is shipped on muleback or by steamboat, its source and its processing remain much the same. The major changes—changes in financing, ownership of the grazing land, middlemen, markets, and distribution—have not affected the lives of the pastoral population except inasmuch as they have raised their standard of living.

Though one might easily think of Switzerland as a land where the cows outnumber the people, statistics indicate that humans outnumber bovines by more than three to one. One and a half million cows still sounds like a goodly number, yet the ratio is less favorable to the cows in Switzerland than in the United States, where there is about one head of cattle for every two inhabitants. In money terms, the yearly produce of dairy cattle is twice as important in Switzerland as is that of slaughter cattle. It seems paradoxical that in the United States, where the feeding of cattle is less of a problem than in Switzerland, the primary use is for beef. Another apparent paradox is that in normal times Switzerland imports butter from Denmark, using up most of its milk for cheese, chocolate, and similar export products. In prewar times Danish butter, which was cheaper than Swiss butter, used to be a favorite contraband article.

Cheese, then, is the main dairy product of Switzerland—for chocolate, though its manufacture requires milk, can hardly be called a dairy product. Swiss cheese is known abroad chiefly as Gruyère and Emmental—names which took their origin from the Gruyère region in Fribourg and the valley of the Emme in the Bernese Oberland, but now serve to designate the brand rather than the origin of the product. Aside from these characteristic Swiss cheeses there are, of course, many other varieties, both soft and hard.

The chief aim in what might pompously be called the historical development of Swiss cheese was to increase its durability. It was a slow process, cheesemaking being something of an occult science painfully learned and improved by generation after generation. In the Forest Cantons Italian herdsmen were often called upon to teach their methods. The process itself is important, but it is not the only factor that determines the taste or the quality of a cheese. "Swiss" cheese manufactured in the United States, for instance, is processed exactly the same way as in Switzerland, but it lacks the flavor, due to the Alpine herbs which the cows eat on the high pastures during the summer months.

As for the inevitable question why Swiss cheese has holes in it, the answer is that in the process employed in the making of Gruyère and Emmental cheeses carbon dioxide is formed; as the cheese solidifies, the bubbles remain.

The age-old association of the ideas of Switzerland, Swiss cheese, mountains, and cows has produced the notion in most people's minds that somehow there is nothing more natural than a cow climbing over rocks and crossing snowfields in midsummer. Yet cows surely are not naturally fond of Alpinism, nor could they survive for long if they were left to themselves on the Swiss grazing lands, which represent only 27 percent of the country and can be used only for a short part of the year.

During the winter, when the cows are kept in barns in the valleys, they cannot get fresh fodder, and their productivity accordingly declines. Early in the summer they are driven first to the lower grazing lands, then higher up above the timber line, and by the end of August they begin their descent back into the valleys. Just how high the cattle are driven depends on their age groups. These migrations affect only a small fraction of the population—about 28,000—since a few herdsmen and cheesemakers suffice to take care of the work, but in some valleys, as in the Val d'Anniviers in the Valais, practically the whole population migrates during the summer months. In these cases villages tend to duplicate themselves, as it were, on different levels. Thus, village X in the valley, the winter village, has its counterpart, inhabited throughout the summer months, in the mountains.

It is unusual to think of the Alps as of anybody's property, yet property conditions have a profound effect on the details of Alpine economy. Originally the alps (as the Alpine grazing lands are called and of which there are about 10,800 in Switzerland) were the common property of the valleys above which they were situated. These "corporation alps" still constitute about 30 percent of the grazing lands.

In the case of the purely pastoral cantons they formed the basis not only of the economic, but also of the political life of the canton. Common ownership was restricted to the active citizens, newcomers being barred from free use of the grazing lands, just as in the towns they were barred from full citizenship. The political assemblies—the Landsgemeinden—were, in fact, nothing but conventions of the co-owners of the grazing lands.

In some cases ownership rights tended to narrow down to villages, parishes, and other smaller communities. A more recent phenomenon was the growth of private ownership, and still more recent the rise of co-operatives. The property status of the grazing lands affects, of course, the management of the cattle during the summer months, the methods of dairy production, and the quality of the products.

III

The summer grazing and the production of cheese which takes place during that period are as important in the lives of the herdsmen as harvesting is in the life of a farmer. Naturally, many hoary customs, some common to all alpine lands of Europe, some purely local, punctuate this most vital season of the year. The use of cowbells, which are often old and elaborately wrought and obviously fulfills the purely practical purpose of keeping the cattle from getting lost, is perhaps the best known. It is common to all Europe, and there is nothing particularly Swiss about it. More typical of Switzerland is the use of the alphorn, which has already been described, in order to gather in the cattle, and of vocal calls for the same purpose. These calls, set to traditional yodeling tunes which differ from valley to valley, are of extremely ancient origin. The words used are invariably something sounding like *Loba! Loba!*, a word which is presumed to have been part of an unknown language common to the prehistoric tribes of shepherds that once inhabited the Alpine chain.

The cattle are, of course, constantly threatened by maleficent forces, only vaguely named, by demons, witches, and by the Evil One. Sudden storms, avalanches, landslides, the weird shapes of mists and clouds, the threatening aspect of the rocks, the treachery of nature, and the immense solitude of man faced with the mountain have encouraged in all alpine countries beliefs which are called superstitious by those who have nothing to fear and nothing to lose. To those who have had intimate contact with the implacable enemies symbolized by these evil spirits, these superstitions are but realistic statements of an undeniable disproportion.

It is not necessary to be a cowherd to feel this—it is sufficient to be a mountain climber who has once found himself in a bad scrape. But the mountain climber, even though he may feel that suddenly all nature transforms herself into an army of demonic foes intent on the single purpose of destroying him, is unlikely to believe in his power of exorcising them. He will either pull himself together and fight them by denying their existence and taking practical action, or he will perish miserably. This is where the superstitious herdsman has a practical advantage, for he believes in exorcism.

Exorcism may be preventive or, more rarely, curative. In the Catholic regions (that is, practically all the Swiss Alps except the Bernese Oberland) the alps, and sometimes the cattle, are blessed by a priest before the yearly ascent. Another important rite— omission may be followed by dire consequences—is the so-called *Betruf* (prayer call) made every evening by the cowherds. The prayer is sung, in a sort of plain chant, as loudly as possible and is amplified by some such method as putting the hands to the mouth or using a milking funnel like a megaphone, for the blessing which is invoked from God, the Virgin, or the local saint is believed to be effective as far distant as the voice can carry. One of these invocations, which begins with the *Ave Maria* and continues with a litany to God the Father and God the Son, Saint George, Saint Martin, and Saint Gall, then addresses Saint Peter as follows:

Saint Peter, take your key firmly in your right hand,
Keep the bear from its prowling,
Lock the jaw of the wolf,
The throat of the lynx,
The beak of the raven,
The tail of the dragon,
The leap of the stone!
May God keep us from such evil hour,
May He keep such animals from threatening or biting. . . .
May God protect everything here within this circle,
And the dear Mother of God with her Child!
May God protect everything here in our valley,
Here and everywhere else,
May God protect us and may God will it and may God do it!
Ave Maria!

With the progress of what is called progress, customs like the blessing of the alps and the *Betruf* become increasingly rare and isolated. The knowledge of the different kinds of exorcism which have to be observed when the evil powers threaten the men or the cattle, now confined to the oldest among the herdsmen, may well be doomed in future generations. It is unlikely, though, that its extinction will come very soon. As long as men are directly exposed to nature they will find it very difficult to believe themselves its equals or its masters at all times.

The local customs which have been best preserved are, as might be expected, those that involve a certain amount of festivities and ceremonial. In the Val d'Anniviers the priest of the chief community, Vissoye, receives compensation in a rather spectacular manner for the blessings he gives to the valley's twenty-five alps. The chief cowherds collect the milk produce of the third grazing day, convert it into a gigantic cheese, and on the Sunday preceding Saint Bartholomew's Day (August 24, the day on which the cattle are driven back to the valley) the cheese is brought down to Vissoye and solemnly presented to the priest. Then the cowherds of the whole valley, led by the one who has made the largest cheese of the season, pass in procession before the altar, where the priest blesses their products.

Another tradition, especially common in the Valais, is the holding of annual cow fights. The Valaisan cows, the so-called Hérens breed, are small and highly pugnacious animals, as unbovine as can be, and fight each other with a gusto typical of female duelists. In some localities the victor of the year's cow fight is honored with the title "master cow" or "army cow" and leads the herd on its ascent to the alps in the following spring, carrying a milking stool between her horns.

The descent of the cattle in late August is impressive, even when no special ceremonies are connected with it. Cowbells fill the air all day long, and as the spectator looks up toward the mountain ridges he will see nothing but outlines of dark horns against the sky, like ancient Egyptian symbols. Converging from all sides, the herds become huge as they near the valley, and the noise of moos, bells, and human yells and chants becomes overpowering. To watch this is an unforgettable experience, but sometimes slightly risky, since cows insist adamantly on their right of way. During the night preceding the descent it is the custom, in the Bernese Oberland, for instance, to light fires on the mountain tops and to send burning blocks rolling down into the valley. In central Switzerland the descent is followed by all kinds of celebrations, involving wrestling matches, crude theatrical performances, flag juggling, dancing, and singing.

These no doubt were the occasions when travelers since the eighteenth century came to "view the Alpine herdsmen in all their simplicity," and it cannot be denied that, especially to sophisticated city dwellers, the spectacle offers an elating, or at least diverting, experience. They are likely to forget, however, that the festivities they have witnessed or heard of take place only during a few days in the year, which is otherwise filled either with dangers or drabness. Save for pondering the problem why Swiss cheese has holes in it, they give, pardonably enough, little thought to the difficulties of its production.

IV

The appearance of democracy that distinguishes the pastoral cantons of Switzerland—particularly Unterwalden, Glarus, and Appenzell—may seem deceiving to those who associate the concept of democracy with the concepts of progress and liberalism. This Association is especially common in countries where de-

mocracy is a relatively novel institution. Yet in those places where
democracy has its deepest and oldest roots it is usually based on
a spirit of conservatism, if not reaction.

There is logic in this. From Tacitus to Montesquieu, the best
political writers of the Continent have held that the rule by the
people, in all the most important questions affecting their lives,
was a peculiarly Germanic institution, and that in those countries
where political institutions rested on Germanic origins, freedom
had preceded tyranny and servitude. Rousseau proclaimed that
man, originally free, was now in chains, and the obvious inference was that to become free again, nations had to go backward,
rather than forward. The democratic cantons of Switzerland did
not have to go backward—they had never gone forward. Their
primitive democracy was much the same as that of their ancestors
in the time of Tacitus. It was their reluctance to change that
caused their fight for independence, their hostility toward the
Reformation, and their struggle against national unification.

Peasants are notoriously conservative, but not in the same sense
as pastoral peoples. They are loath to change their agricultural
methods, but against political changes they usually display merely
passive resistance. The pastoral communities of Switzerland, on
the contrary, were singularly bold when it came to adopting economic changes. Apart from the annual risk that every peasant
must incur, he shows no inclination for adventure. Mountaineers,
on the other hand, rather resemble seagoing nations. Adventure,
be it military or economic, is in their blood. The Swiss mountaineers, it would seem, never hesitated before taking the fateful
step of completely renouncing agriculture, and they enthusiastically left their little valleys to gain wealth or fame in every European quarrel, no matter how little it concerned them.

Yet, on the other hand, why should they have changed their
political system? Their states were, in a manner of speaking, closed
corporations. To extend their rights and privileges to others
would have needlessly diminished their own. Moreover, what
political changes were necessary in communities where for five
centuries there was almost no growth of population, no increase
of towns, no appreciable change in the means of gaining a livelihood?

The conservatism of the primitive democracies is equally strong
in the Catholic cantons and in the one Protestant half-canton
that still has a Landsgemeinde. A fine example is the canton of
Appenzell, which, though its total area is only 161 square miles,
and though it is entirely surrounded by the canton of Saint Gall,
found it necessary to split into one Catholic and one Protestant
half-canton in 1597. Appenzell-Inner-Rhoden, the Catholic half,
has its capital in the town of Appenzell, where the Landsgemeinde
meets. In Outer-Rhoden, matters are slightly more complicated.
The capital is Herisau, but the Landsgemeinde meets alternately
in Herisau and in the tiny village of Trogen. To attend the meeting, the citizens must carry swords as a sign of citizenship; if they
fail to vote, they are fined ten francs. The members of the government, which renders account to the assembly, wear top hats
in addition to their swords. Surely this democratic assembly yields
nothing in conservatism to the most elaborate court ceremonial in
England.

The feudal institutions against which the Swiss mountaineers
had fought in their own lands, they respected in the lands they
conquered. The people who inhabited the districts now known
as the Ticino were feudal subjects when the Swiss became their
masters, in the fifteenth and sixteenth centuries, and subjects they
remained, though their new lords were no longer counts and
barons, but cowherds and muleteers. Paradoxical as it may sound,
democratic rights in Switzerland were birthrights.

While Berne, Basel, Zurich, and Geneva were primarily
oriented toward the northwest, the pastoral cantons looked toward Rome and, to a lesser extent, toward Vienna. When the
Reformation came, they were deeply committed in Italy and solidly linked with the papacy. The lives led by their people were
austere enough without the introduction of Protestant austerity.
Their hostility to the cities, particularly to Zurich, caused them
to distrust the new doctrines, which had originated in the cities.
This, and reluctance to change in general, would have been sufficient cause to make the pastoral cantons reject the Reformation.
Since, moreover, the first point of the program of the Zwinglian
reform was the abolition of foreign military service, the very
existence of the Forest Cantons was at stake. It is not surprising

that they resisted the Reformation. That the Reformation succeeded in the Bernese Oberland was chiefly due to the fact that it was imposed there by Berne.

The traveler who believes that Switzerland is uniformly clean and tidy will be surprised by the contrast, in that respect, between the Protestant and the Catholic cantons. In the Bernese Oberland he will find everything so neat that it is impossible to tell whether a house is old or new. In the Valais, in Fribourg, and in other Catholic cantons, he will find signs of dirt, poverty, and neglect, and a generally lower level of education. Even in architecture there are striking differences. In the Oberland, he will find prosperous isolated farms and the typical Alpine chalets with whitewashed stone facings at the base and elaborate carvings in the wooden upper part. In the Valais, he will find villages rather than farms, with houses of a far more primitive appearance.

It is, perhaps, no less characteristic that a disproportionately large part of domestic help in Switzerland comes from the Catholic cantons, surely a sign of their economic inferiority to the Protestant ones. Servant girls from the Valais and Fribourg are cheapest and consequently most popular, despite their reputation for dimwittedness and negligence. Since housecleaning in some villages of the Valais consists of the simple process of hanging all washable objects into the nearest brook once a year, one can easily imagine that Swiss housewives occasionally have a difficult time "breaking in" their help.

v

As for cultural achievements of the Catholic cantons, their development was almost entirely confined to two or three towns: Fribourg, Lucerne, and Einsiedeln.

Lucerne indubitably was and still is the Catholic center. Though not properly a part of the pastoral region, it always was its main economic outlet and its spiritual and political leader. This was only natural, since Uri, Schwyz, and Unterwalden all three abut on the Lake of Lucerne (which for this reason is also called the Lake of the Four Forest Cantons). Lucerne was something of a Catholic Berne, governed by an aristocracy of twenty-nine families, a rival capital where foreign ambassadors used to curry the favor of the Catholic cantons, and a center of Jesuit activities till the final suppression of the order in Switzerland in 1848.

In its Alpine setting, its mixture of Gothic and Baroque, its wooden covered bridges, all gay outside and painted inside with representations of such subjects as the Dance of Death, it certainly is a handsome synthesis of the culture which it represents. Yet even here intellectual life was almost entirely limited to the activities of the Jesuits; the main preoccupation of the aristocracy was with politics and with leading armies for the kings of France.

The same was true of the aristocracy of Fribourg. As for St. Gall, it had ceased to be a center of learning after the late Middle Ages. The town itself accepted the Reformation, but the abbey has retained outward splendor, thanks to the ambitious prince-abbots of the seventeenth and eighteenth centuries, who were great builders. It is generally characteristic of Catholic central Switzerland that the modest, if often handsome, houses of its towns and villages contrast sharply with the magnificence of many of its churches. The abbey of the little town of Einsiedeln, for instance, modeled on the palace of the Escorial and dominating a square that might easily rival the most famous, is a unique example of Spanish Baroque in that part of Europe, and certainly something of a surprise to the unprepared traveler.

The urge to create with one's hands, which in the Protestant regions was suppressed in favor of creation through the pure mind, has produced a rich and original peasant art in Catholic Switzerland. In the idleness and isolation of the long winter months, many an anonymous peasant or herdsman had the idea of picking up a piece of wood and of carving it in the image of the Virgin or of a patron saint. The Valais is particularly rich in carved images which decorate village churches or wayside chapels and which are often strikingly different from similar works in the Austrian, Bavarian, and Italian Alps. There is a certain sternness about them, an almost Grecoesque haggardness and asceticism that reflects the austere state of mind of nearly all Swiss, Calvinists and Catholics alike.

Woodcarving has also flourished in the Protestant Bernese Oberland, but somehow the subject matter has been limited there to practically only one theme: a bear. Sitting bears, walking bears, standing bears, dancing bears, bears in the shape of paperweights, book ends, clocks, inkstands, watch charms, and even armchairs (you sit in the bear's lap and put your arms on his) are on sale in every Swiss souvenir shop. In other words, peasant art in Berne has been one hundred percent standardized and commercialized. Not so, thank God, in the Valais.

Another specialty of the pastoral cantons, particularly of the Ticino, is the outward decoration of their houses. Vivid *al fresco* paintings, usually representing religious subjects, often cover entire walls of the whitewashed farm houses and barns. In the Bernese Oberland, since saints were forbidden and bears were monotonous, the peasants took to whittling their houses away. Carved gables are common throughout the European Alps, but hardly anywhere do they attain such extravagantly elaborate treatment as in Berne. Often they take on the shapes of real or fancied animals, or they may be simply decorative curlicues. It is curious to think, in this connection, of the whittling propensities of New Englanders. Is there possibly any logic in the gradation from Catholic amateur sculptors of saints to Puritans who are ascetically content with slicing chips off a stick?

There is a great temptation to credit the general neatness, prosperity, and high level of education prevailing in Protestant Switzerland to the influence of its religion and to blame Catholicism for the dirt of the Catholic cantons, for the contrast between their opulent churches and their poverty-stricken populations, and for the ignorance and lack of intellectual achievements prevailing in them. To some extent such conclusions are correct. Certainly the Catholic church in Switzerland failed to rival the great educational effort of Calvinist Switzerland. Certainly it laid less stress on the next-to-godliness of cleanliness, and certainly it did not believe that churches should look like barns, an architectural ideal favored by a great many followers of Calvin.

Such comparisons, however, are essentially irrelevant. One cannot expect universities to rise in pastoral villages, nor can one expect much opulence. The only fair comparison between Catholic and Protestant Switzerland would be between the Catholic cantons and the Bernese Oberland. The neat and peeled aspect of the latter is easily explained if one considers that nearly every village and valley of the Oberland is tourist territory and accordingly spruced up. Contrariwise, many parts of, for example, the Valais, though no less beautiful, are visited chiefly by Swiss tourists and consequently have retained a somewhat more human and ingenuous character.

The Bernese Oberland, until the end of the eighteenth century, was just as poor as the rest of the pastoral districts and, in contrast to them, was not even governing itself. In the nineteenth century alcoholism was no less epidemic in the Protestant than in the Catholic cantons. It is true that it was chiefly the growth of capitalism emanating from the Protestant cantons that since then has raised the entire pastoral area to higher standards of living. Yet it was certainly not from the Bernese Oberland that capitalism emanated. Moreover, it would be difficult to convince a reasonable person that a people's choice of its religion should rest on economic considerations. Geneva's Calvinism suited its watchmakers and bankers who lived behind walls. To the herdsmen, the guides, and the adventurers of Alpine Switzerland, Catholicism seems to have given more happiness and greater strength in facing nature in the open.

Finally, although the Catholic cantons resisted the nationalist movement for Swiss unification with all the firmness of character that their mules and cows had taught them throughout generations, it was precisely their stubborn tradition that has left the deepest imprint on Swiss nationalist feeling. Through the pastoral cantons, unchanged for centuries, the Swiss as a whole have preserved a direct link with their very origins. The Tell legend may have been exploded as a myth, it remains nevertheless a most vital factor in the national consciousness of Switzerland—and for a nationalist myth, it must be admitted that it remains one of the best ever invented.

VII: The Brawny Mystics

WHAT MAKES a Swiss feel Swiss? Why should he not rather see himself as a Bernese, a Vaudois, a Genevese? Or a German Swiss, a French Swiss, an Italian Swiss, a Catholic Swiss, a Protestant Swiss? Or even a German, a Frenchman, an Italian? Several pat answers come to one's mind before one even has time to ask the obvious question: Does he really feel Swiss?

One of these all-explanatory magic formulas consists of mumbling some words about nineteenth-century romanticism, liberalism, nationalism, industrial revolution, and national unification. These words, which commonly pass for historical explanations, may do well enough for Germany or Italy, but in the case of Switzerland they would apply only if Switzerland had broken up and been absorbed by Germany, Italy, and France. Yet, far from breaking up, Switzerland underwent its unification precisely at the time when, by all logic, its constituent language groups should have joined their long-lost brothers across the borders.

A more plausible explanation could be summed up approximately as follows: It always has been in the economic and political interest of the Swiss to remain a nation. Until the mid-nineteenth century they had been able to afford to live in disunity and yet retain their independence. Such luxury was no longer possible in the nationalist maelstrom of which they were the vortex. To keep the advantages of independence, they were obliged to invent a nationalism of their own.

Surely, this necessity was a contributing cause, but it is difficult to believe that a nation should suddenly reform its habits merely because such action would be to its best advantage. And even if the Swiss were wise enough to mend their errors in the nick of time, it still would be interesting to know why they were so wise, while other nations, hardened in their sins despite their better knowledge, have foundered.

Yet, does a Swiss really feel Swiss? The question cannot be answered simply, but in the answer there also lies a partial explanation of the problem why the Swiss feel Swiss.

A Swiss feels more Swiss on certain days than on others. He feels very Swiss when he stands on a mountain top and looks upon his land; he feels very Swiss when he serves in his army, when he commemorates old battles, when he compares his country with the rest of the world—in other words, he is eminently Swiss on special and important occasions. In his everyday life, he is more likely to feel Argovian, Neuchâtelois, or whatever he may be. In his intellectual life, he may feel more affinities with the French, the Germans, or the Italians than with those among his fellow-Swiss who speak a tongue different from his. At other times, he may even like to think of himself as a citizen of the world. Which is more important: the attitude of every day or the attitude of special occasions? It would seem that in everyday life the every-day attitude is what counts, and that for special occasions it is good to have a special attitude.

Now anyone who unites so many levels of loyalty within his person is unlikely to be swayed overmuch by any particular loyalty. A German Swiss, for instance, will sympathize with Germany—but only culturally, as it were. He will sympathize with humanity, in a humanitarian way. He will feel strongly for his canton most of the time. But when the question of his being Swiss is involved—well, he is a Swiss, and he intends to stay one. What is more, on all levels of loyalty he is equally faithful to his national traditions.

Let us consider the Swiss as he likes to consider himself in his various moods: as a leaf of grass in the democratic community; as the patient educator of mankind; as the disinterested scholar and humanist; as the soil-bound lover of his native region; as the brawny champion of individual freedom; and as the mystic wrestler with nature. And for this purpose let us not consider the nameless and nonexistent "typical Swiss," but some representatives of each of these manifestations of the national spirit.

A national tradition, in every country, is based to some extent on fancies and myths. To become real, it merely needs to be imagined. Just how much of it is myth, how much the genuine product of a nation's environment, condition, and heredity, it is very difficult to tell. In the particular case of Switzerland the central factor of the national tradition seems to be the rather elementary fact that Swizerland is crammed with mountains.

There is nothing mythical about the existence of the mountains. They are definitely tangible. The myth begins with the characteristics which the Swiss instinctively feel they have derived from their mountainous environment. By dint of believing that the mountains have produced the Swiss, the Swiss have come pretty near to hinting that they have produced their mountains. It was, no doubt, in an effort to offset such hints that an Englishman, John Lubbock, 1st baron Avebury (1834–1913), wrote a book entitled, *The Scenery of Switzerland and the Causes to Which It Is Due.*

At present the mountains are considered the cradle of Swiss liberties, as they were indeed, since it was in the central Swiss Alps that the Confederation had its origin and since it is there that one can still observe the oldest traditions of Swiss democracy. Even the federal flag of modern Switzerland, the white cross on a red background, was the distinguishing mark of the earliest Confederate warriors. The birth of Swiss liberties is celebrated every first of August by lighting fires on every mountain top or hill top of the country. In short, the mountain has become a sort of national symbol, just as the plain seems to have taken on a symbolic meaning to Americans. This has by no means always been so.

Like electricity, the Alps were known to the Swiss before the eighteenth century, but nothing much was made of it. Like that of electricity, their real discovery occurred by chance. It was the result of the awakening of science in early eighteenth-century Switzerland.

Interest in science became general throughout Europe at that time, but in Switzerland it took on special characteristics. While Newton gave the universe a law, while the French *philosophes* were trying to reduce all human problems to some Newtonian formula, the more cautious Swiss left human problems and universal laws to their pastors, preferring to investigate nature modestly and meticulously and, as it were, from the bottom up. While looking for specimens of rocks, fossils, plants, and insects, the Swiss scientists accidentally discovered the existence of the Alps. It would have been easy to overlook such things. In an objective way, they had been aware of their mountains all along, but what was needed was a subjective "double-take." Climbing them with the original purpose of investigating the origin of the Alps, they suddenly looked up from their specimens, blinked, and stood struck in admiration. Let us give their due to the scientists of a past age, for it is extremely doubtful that those of the present century would ever have made the discovery.

It is almost a commonplace that before the eighteenth century Nature with a capital N was unknown. The fact that the Alpine landscape had been invariably described as horrible and desolate is usually adduced as the clinching proof. This belief springs from another, no less general, conviction, namely, that nothing existed in the past except what has been recorded black on white. Racine mentioned no trees, *ergo* seventeenth-century Paris was unaware of Nature. The same rule might be applied to the appreciation of the Alps: utterly ignored by all men until a certain day in 1729, they suddenly came into their own when Albrecht von Haller published his poem devoted to their glorification. That millions of less articulate humans may have entertained, in their own muddled manner, similar sentiments long before they became fashionable, is generally discounted as a theory. That words such as "awful," "terrible," and "desolate" were perhaps more truly descriptive of the high Alps than the more recent epithets "picturesque," "lovely," and "romantic" is, however, a possibility that might be pondered. Life had discovered Nature somewhat earlier than literature did. Yet, in our modern nationalist civilization, life has to some extent become a product of literature, and thus the literary discovery of the Alps was to play an important role in the formation of Swiss national consciousness.

Since Haller was Bernese, it might be expected that the particular Alps he celebrated were the Bernese Alps. But Haller was not overly concerned with the Alps *per se*. He described them as beautiful, and that was an important step; but their greatest significance to him was moral and sociological. It was the freedom of the Alpine dwellers, their simplicity, their patriotic meaning to the Swiss that Haller really meant to sing. In his youth he had written an epic poem celebrating the origin of Switzerland, and though he burned the manuscript, his *Alps* really were the realization of his first project, with the only difference that he had chosen the lyrical form, whereas he had at first meant to be epic. The Alps described by Haller were primarily the Central Alps, the home of William Tell. In his eyes the solid and scarcely frivolous burghers of his Berne were on the road to luxury and perdition like the citizens of imperial Rome. He was to be their Tacitus, seeking to mend their ways by praising their ancestors,

> Whose fists held lightning, and whose hearts held God.

Haller's words fell on fertile ground, for at the time of the publication of his poem a conscious quickening of the Swiss intellect was taking place.

Swiss writers had begun to chafe under their reputation abroad as lacking wit and grace; they now were rallying in small groups and asserting their equality with the rest of Europe in a number of pamphlets and periodicals. One such periodical, the *Mercure Suisse*, founded in Neuchâtel in 1732 and later known as the *Journal Helvétique*, greeted Haller's poem with a defiant accolade. "Until now," its editors remarked, "Switzerland has been regarded as unenlightened and incapable of producing poets. Especially the French were of that opinion. For them a thinking Swiss was not only a rare, but even an incredible phenomenon. M. Haller teaches . . . them that a Swiss can think, write verse, and measure himself with the best poets."

Haller's poetic success was nothing compared to his influence on patriotic thinking. At the very time when Switzerland had practically ceased to exist as a political concept, minds seemed to have become receptive to patriotic myths. The notion that Switzerland's golden age lay in the past, that its greatness was to be found in the Spartan simplicity of the primitive cantons, and that a return to natural simplicity would revive the nation from its torpor, all this was already contained in Haller's writings. With Rousseau's sudden fame, the same ideas gained still wider acceptance. In 1762, at last, the movement crystallized itself through the foundation of the Helvetic Society.

One of its founders, Johann Jakob Bodmer, who is best known for his part in the birth of a national German literature, inspired a whole crop of reformers, among them Lavater and Pestalozzi. The ambitious program of the group was nothing less than to bring about the regeneration of Switzerland and the re-establishment of lost liberties. The cantonal governments frowned on such libertarian ideas from the very beginning; they continued to frown when after the Restoration of 1815 the revived Society resumed its activities.

By that time all liberal and romantic Europe had come to hold pretty much the same ideas. Even if one concedes that the success of these ideas in Switzerland after 1848 did not altogether measure up to the expectations, one also must admit that in comparison with their ultimate fate in the rest of Europe, they fared not too badly.

The monument to the Swiss patriotic awakening of the eighteenth century was, no doubt, the *History of Switzerland*, written by Johannes von Müller, a citizen of Schaffhausen. Swiss patriot though he was, Müller spent the larger part of his creative years in the services of the elector of Mainz, the emperor, the king of Prussia, and, finally, King Jerome of Westphalia. His *History*, which began to appear shortly before the outbreak of the French Revolution, was hailed throughout Europe. Müller's account of the Tell legend and the Rütli Oath, which he accepted unquestioningly, inspired Schiller's drama and popularized the myth so thoroughly that a critical appraisal of its authenticity was burned by the executioner in Altdorf as being harmful to the state.

The fact that the Tell legend was ultimately proved, to nearly everybody's dissatisfaction, to be apocryphal, did not perturb the Swiss for long. Tell may never have been an actual person, but, they felt, he was much more than that—he was the very personification of the Swiss people. In fact, once the initial "debunking" process was completed, it was discovered that a fictitious Tell was worth a thousand historical ones. Where once the necessity of adhering to facts had resulted in stale repetitiveness, unbridled fantasy was suddenly allowed to run amok. A whole new crop of Tell dramas and poems burst forth from the rocky soil of patriotic imagination, and instead of one Tell, there were dozens, each one a monumental symbol slightly taller than the Jungfrau. As the twentieth century progresses, bigger and taller Tells continue to be produced. The final consecration of Tell as a national symbol, however, probably took place when Tell's crossbow became the official trade mark of all Swiss products, taking the place of the words, "Made in Switzerland."

Maurice Barrès, who was no fool, remarked somewhere that everything about the civilization of Wilhelminian Germany had to be colossal—or rather *kolossal*—and that it mattered little to the Germans whether a cathedral was built of marble or of *papier-mâché*, as long as the proportions were duly *kolossal*. In Switzerland, the emphasis is rather on the word "monumental."

There is quite a difference between the two adjectives. People who like things to be *kolossal* are a bit disquieting. Colossi have the dangerous habit of moving about in steamroller fashion. Monuments always stay in their places, no matter how much they may seem to be ready to pounce on you. It is, in substance, the difference between threat and defiance. When the patriotic mood is upon them, the Swiss like to gather in monumental groups and to display considerable defiance—against nobody in particular.

The Swiss think little of political conventions, in the American style, for political conventions markedly lack that cohesion and dignity which monumentality requires. Sharpshooters' conventions, on the other hand, come closer to the ideal. Neglected during the seventeenth and eighteenth centuries, these manifestations of the Old Swiss spirit were consequently revived. They are, however, by no means the only Federal or intercantonal patriotic manifestations. Federal athletic festivals have been held, usually at three-year intervals, ever since 1832. Wrestling is a fine monumental activity, especially when practiced in mass contests, as has been the case in Switzerland since 1894. The Swiss Alpine variety of wrestling, by the way, is a special brand called *Schwingen* and is very spectacular.

Of greater interest to Americans is probably the sport called *Hornussen*, a batting game in which one team is to propel through the air a small disk by means of flail-like bats, and the other team is to keep the disk (called *Hornuss*) from falling into their goal by intercepting it with wooden shingles which they throw into the trajectory of the *Hornuss*. This peculiar game also serves as an occasion for great Federal feasts.

In addition to such sportive conventions, the Swiss hold innumerable singfests, outdoor commemorations involving open-air theatrical performance on gigantic scale, brass band contests, harvests and vintage feasts, and just plain festivals for no particular reason at all. No matter what the nature of the celebration, it is always colorful, it always serves as an excuse for displaying medieval costumes, and it always is somehow stylized.

Of course, only a small number of Swiss actually participate in these activities, and a large number lack interest in them. Primarily vocal and athletic gatherings are popular almost exclusively in the German-speaking part of the country. However, where general taste is concerned, the robust monumentality of the Swiss ideal is common to almost all Swiss. The ideal, no doubt, is derived from the features of the mountains. Their rugged, angular symmetry has influenced the Swiss esthetic sense so deeply that it would be no exaggeration to say that even the concept of human beauty has become monumental. That this is no mere fancy can be readily seen by even a cursory examination of Swiss art, particularly modern art.

III

What is surprising even in the earliest of the great Swiss artists, Urs Graf, is the supreme ease with which he combines movement with statuesqueness. Compared to his woodcuts, Dürer's seem almost stiff. Though he represented his characteristic subject, the Swiss warriors of the Italian campaigns, with great realism (he was one of the warriors himself), Graf gave them a sweep, a stylized vigor, which transfigured them into heroic symbols—the very symbols that still figure most prominently in Swiss art. This theatrical tendency is present to some extent even in much of the work of Holbein, who may be called a Swiss artist, since he spent a major part of his life in Lucerne and Basel and was even a citizen of Basel.

The eighteenth century softened, but did not eradicate, these stern characteristics. At the same time, it gave a great stimulus to landscape painting. Solomon Gessner, who gained equal fame as a poet and as an engraver, was more inspired by the classical calmness of Poussin and Claude Lorrain than by the French rococo painters. His Swiss landscapes, though pleasing to the taste of his day, were meant to express a patriotic as well as an idyllic ideal. Indeed, while the French thought of idylls as existing only in dreams, the Swiss considered that idylls, nature, and reality were synonymous. Hence the Rousseauan ideal was a mere fad in France and a lasting influence in Switzerland.

Among the other Swiss painters of the eighteenth century was the Genevese Liotard. Unfortunately, he is best known for his least typical canvas, the *Belle Chocolatière*, one of his rare concessions to the rococo taste. His portrait of Madame d'Epinay, on the other hand, though by no means monumental, is remarkable for its unflattering realism.

Henry Fuseli, who was born as Johann Heinrich Fuessli, in Zurich, made no concessions to his time whatever. His illustrations of Dante, Shakespeare, Milton, and the Nibelungen show traces of stylization which were carried to extremes by his pupil, William Blake. While symbolism as expressed in human groupings was already present in Fuseli, it took a longer time to be applied to landscapes. Alexandre Calame, a Vaudois, probably still remains the greatest technician among Alpine painters, Swiss or non-Swiss. But Calame was essentially a realist. No matter how dramatic his peaks and glaciers may be—and he almost always showed them in the illumination of violent lightning, or obscured by menacing clouds, or traversed by tempestous torrents—his art consisted in his utmost skill of creating the illusion of material reality. This was, perhaps, all to the good, if one considers the results of symbolism in the Victorian age—if one considers, for instance, the work of Arnold Böcklin.

It is a most distressing thought that Böcklin is still enjoying the reputation of having been the foremost representative of Swiss art—or even German art—of the nineteenth century. Böcklin, who was born in Basel in 1827, spent his life traveling between Switzerland, Germany, France, and Italy. In each of these countries he developed an admiration for its particular brand of ham. The ultimate results were some of the most monumental hams in the history of art: the *Elysian Fields*, the *Sacred Grove*, and, last but not least, the *Isle of the Dead*, which received adequate symphonic treatment by a kindred master, Rachmaninoff.

In Böcklin one can observe the worst feature of monumental symbolism, for the simple reason that his monumentality and symbolism were essentially affected. These naked masses of writhing flesh, these lurid lights, this made-to-order mysteriousness, these profound statements of adolescent nightmares—were they not really colossal where they intended to be monumental? And do they not remind one uncomfortably of something or other— possibly of the gigantic expressions of impotence that Richard Wagner was trying to produce on the stage of Zurich while Böcklin was wielding his brush in Basel?

Where Wagner, with all his genius, only barely succeeded, Böcklin, a lesser genius, merely uncovered his inherent weaknesses. Possibly the Switzerland of the late nineteenth century, especially German-speaking Switzerland, was too much under the spell of the newly risen German Empire to distinguish the monumental from the colossal. The twentieth century marked a conscious return to earlier traditions. It was in Ferdinand Hodler that Swiss art found its real soul.

Hodler, who was born in Berne in 1853, but spent the later part of his life in Geneva, reflected in many ways the influence of the *Jugendstil*, which began to flourish around the turn of the century. His purely allegorical compositions, though simpler and better balanced than Böcklin's, probably show Hodler in his least original and least successful vein. These, unfortunately, include Hodler's best-known works—such as *Night*, *Truth*, and *Love*— for the simple reason that they hang in museums. His strongest and most original paintings, those inspired by the Swiss landscape and the Swiss past, are undeservedly ignored in the United States, possibly because they are largely hidden away in European private collections.

Hodler's originality lay in his realization that monumentality is always enhanced by simplicity. Now there is nothing more monumental, and at the same time nothing more simple, than a naked mountain—that is, if the mountain is seen through a Puritan rather than a romantic eye. Calame's landscapes were romantic; Hodler was a Puritan, seeing the mountains in the abstract, as it were. Where Calame saw a thousand bizarre details, Hodler saw a juxtaposition of three-dimensional geometric patterns, stern, uncompromising lines, and hard, unfeeling surfaces. Where Calame saw infinite varieties of color and gradations, Hodler saw but a few, pure colors and no gradations. His Alps are as pitiless in their rectitude, as intolerant of mitigation, as inhospitable to human weakness as were Calvin's *Institutions*—and just as sublime in their refusal to admit of any mediation. Here Rousseau's concept of nature no longer has meaning, for Rousseau's nature was kind and good. Hodler's nature was the cold and unforgiving law, a law as strict and as immovable as the geometric patterns to which it has been reduced.

The beholder of Calame's landscapes might feel tempted to visit the places which Calame has painted—though possibly in more favorable meteorological circumstances. The beholder of an Alpine painting by Hodler feels no such desire, unless he knows that he is chosen. Good intentions are no excuse for failure in Hodler's Alps; the Alpinist who tries to scale his walls might be an expert, he might do exactly the right thing at exactly the right time—but little would this avail him if he were not chosen, if he were not *predestined*, if he were not as pure and uncompromising as the rock itself.

It is very hard to convince oneself that these monuments of divine inaccessibility are, in actual fact, the scenic features of tourist resorts. Here, indeed, is perhaps the true reason why Hodler met little understanding in countries where mysticism is considered a form of insanity and people satisfy their extroversion by flocking to foreign tourist centers.

The Swiss despise the mass of foreign tourists. The reason for this is not so much that tourists are thought of in terms of the amount of money they yield, or because they are vulgar and noisy—Swiss tourists abroad are likely to be vulgar and noisy too

SELF-PORTRAIT

Sketch by Ferdinand Hodler

—or even because they are foreigners. All these are contributing reasons, but the real reason lies deeper: tourists desecrate Switzerland. It might be said that the Swiss have spared no efforts to attract as many desecrators into their country as they can possibly accommodate, but this is only one more motive for the Swiss to despise them, as any student of psychology will admit. The Swiss see in their Alps what Hodler saw in them: monuments which were the cradle of a monumental people. The ordinary run of tourists sees but a picturesque landscape inhabited by a quaint people.

The Swiss may be prejudiced, but it would seem that their feelings are less superficial than those of casual visitors, and thus are probably nearer the truth. Only the vulgar and the shallow have a better eye for quaint details than for essential contours. However, even sublimeness can be carried, at times, too far. In painting, especially, there is but one step from sublime monumentality to effective poster art.

There is nothing wrong with poster art, except when it was not intended as such. Hodler had genius enough to avoid the final step. Even his battle scenes, the *Retreat from Marignano* (it can be seen at Basel), for instance, in which every detail would make an excellent patriotic poster, avoid the effect of poster art in their ensemble. Like Hodler's mountains, Hodler's warriors are uncompromisingly stylized. Each one is a monumental projection of a patriotic ideal type, and each group is a monumental projection of a vaster patriotic concept.

In his vigorous sweep Hodler was indubitably indebted to Urs Graf, yet Urs Graf's men did not look as though carved out of rock; they looked like the Renaissance men they were, despite all their barbarous crudity. Hodler, to bring the Swiss ideal up to date, was obliged to falsify history. His heroes are, indeed, carved out of rock, despite all their dynamic animation. They are as sublimely righteous as mountain peaks, whereas Graf's were lusty and brutal.

Hodler's unconscious Puritanism was unconquerable. His inhibitions are evidenced in their full crudity in his nudes. They are entirely sublimated in his battle scenes, where they merely idealize the national characteristics. Indeed, whether Catholic or Calvinist, the Swiss all have come under the spell of Puritanism. To paint a Swiss warrior animated by sensuous instinct rather than holy wrath would have been an insult to the Swiss national ideal.

Hodler had a profound and lasting influence on Swiss painting. Since his death, in 1918, his monumental style has become the national style. If it is a trifle wearing when applied by a lesser genius, it is, at least, never vulgar. In the field of commercial art it probably has helped to set a level higher than almost anywhere else in the world.

Where American advertising posters tend to crowd as many desirable objects as possible into one composition—preferably a father, a mother, a boy, a girl, a dog, a car, a house, an electric kitchen, and a radio-phonograph, all representing what in the advertiser's mind constitutes the basic ingredients of the American way—the Swiss like to have their posters clean, uncluttered, striking, and soberly monumental. An American advertisement for chocolate is likely to show a whole family, all eagerly smiling and stretching their hands across the table with utter disregard for good manners, with endless quotations flowing from their mouths in praise of the product. In such profusion, one is apt to overlook the article which is actually advertised. The Swiss order these things differently, if not better. All the poster would show is the name of the product, in clear and bold lettering, and a monumentally idealized bar of chocolate, symbol of God's profusion and Man's ingeniousness.

IV

It is a long way from the esthetic influence of the Alps to the advertising of chocolate bars. Yet it is obvious that any genuinely deep influence is likely to show its effects in trivial as well as sublime matters. Perhaps, even, this is the only proof of its genuineness. However, the mystic and personal relationship of the Swiss with their mountains has resulted not only in a slightly boastful patriotism, monumental art, and effective advertising method, but also in their active demonstration of their love of their country.

Some nations love their country in the manner in which some parents dote on their plain children. The Swiss are extremely privileged in that they live in one of the most beautiful spots in the world. There are a great many Swiss who would rather do without their countrymen—but if there is such a phenomenon as a Swiss who does not love his country he has not revealed himself yet.

The Swiss possess another advantage over many other nations. Their contact with their own country is probably more reciprocal than anywhere else. To the Parisian, for instance, the French countryside is a sort of a mistress: he likes to admire its charms, forget his daily cares in its company, enjoy its bounties, or explore its varied features. To the Swiss, his country is a lifelong challenger to athletic contests. To a mistress, one sooner or later becomes used or indifferent, and affection becomes mechanical; to an unconquerable challenger one never becomes used, for he always reserves new surprises and new mysteries. The Swiss loves his country as a warrior loves an honest but pitiless adversary.

Four fifths of all Swiss are of peasant stock. Though they have in the past hundred years swelled the ranks of the urban population to the point where there are now ten times more city dwellers than in 1850, they have retained their rustic characteristics to an amazing degree. They have not forgotten the challenge that nature had flung at generations of their ancestors, nor have they cast aside the qualities of caution, persistence, and thrift that enabled their fathers to counter the challenge. For though nature in Switzerland is beautiful, it certainly is not bountiful; though it attracts, it attracts only to repel.

The larger part of the Swiss no longer feel the direct challenge of nature in their pursuit of a livelihood. Yet nature has remained a challenge to them, and they continue to give it battle. Nowhere can there be found as complete a fusion of patriotism and sport as in Switzerland. To the Swiss Alpinist, the adversary is at the same time a manifestation of divine power and the symbol of his fatherland. He never conquers a mountain as one conquers a woman; even when he has reached the peak, he is left humble. The challenger has let him have his way—but only to make him feel more intensely the unconquerable discrepancy dividing them.

Obviously not all the Swiss are Alpinists—though even from a statistical point of view mountain climbing and skiing are national sports in the same sense as baseball is in the United States. Even those whose Alpinistic exploits remain confined to easy and unspectacular ascensions, even those who for some reason never practice the sport at all, somehow have a taste of its experiences and vaguely know what feelings stir in the breasts of their more ambitious countrymen. To the most ardent, Alpinism is a mystic experience; the uninitiated do not share it, but they guess at it and to some extent can imagine it vicariously.

Alpinism in Switzerland is not only a mystic and patriotic religion, it is also an ultimate expression of individualism and equalitarianism, which it reconciles and fuses.

In a sport like baseball, the competition takes place between men. In Alpinism, it takes place first of all inside man—for he must conquer his own weakness and fear before he can conquer anything else—and then between man and nature. For technical reasons it is impossible for a single man to undertake a difficult ascension. Thus, as in any competitive sport, there are a team, in which every one has his distinct functions and responsibility, and a leader, the guide, who must be implicitly obeyed.

But there is only one team, not two. There is no trace of competition between humans, only co-operation. Anyone who likes to excel the members of his party in anything but mutual subordination will never make an Alpinist. The way is shown by the strongest and the most experienced, but the pace is set by the weakest and the least competent. The ethical code of Alpinism is simple and trite: one for all and all for one. In theory this holds of any teamwork; in practice, however, only the first half is usually insisted on.

As soon as an ascension is planned, social differences cease to exist. The guide, usually a professional, often is socially inferior to the other members of his team, but the ethics of Swiss Alpinism have done away with the most rigid conventions. Dukes and kings have subordinated themselves to the commands of hired peasants —not so much because their lives depended on his instructions, but because they sensed that in their common naked struggle he was their equal or even their superior. From the economic point of view a guide is a well-paid servant—yet few men have been as highly regarded and respected as some of the great guides. Even millionaires have been known to feel inferiors to them.

In the matter of discipline the spirit is democratic rather than military. The leader is servant, not master; the followers obey because each of them owes discipline to the rest, not because they are drilled into obedience. Thus, the experience of Alpinism makes possible on a small scale what seems to be impracticable on a large one: a society of distinct individuals acting as one for their mutual benefit. An ideal ascension is the symbolic acting out of a philosophy of life. This may sound grandiloquent but it should be possible to show the simplicity of the statement.

The ultimate object of the ascension is the self-fulfillment of the individual. It is for his own sake, not for anyone else, that he seeks the danger, vanquishes the difficulties, and ultimately obtains the feeling of release and mystic union upon reaching the goal. Yet as a lone individual he would never be able to experience this self-fulfillment, but would stray and perish on the way. Therefore he renounces his individuality in whatever regards the means toward obtaining self-fulfillment, reserving to himself only the ultimate experience. The philosophy might be summed up in five words: work together and enjoy separately.

It is a noble philosophy, and it is a noble sport that embodies it. In the United States Alpinism is, unfortunately, frequently regarded as an incomprehensible hobby of madmen—though it is considered altogether reasonable to join a crowd of fifty thousand in order to watch two dozen people kick a ball around and though it is thought heroic for a thinking human being to flit through space as though he were a robot bomb.

Mountain climbers, of course, rarely obtain fat contracts with national Alpinist leagues, and they are in the habit of making the headlines only if they fall or freeze to death. Perhaps this is to be regretted, because it keeps the sport from becoming popular in some parts of the world. On the other hand, there is comfort in the thought that there are two sports—mountain climbing and just plain walking—which will never have well-paid stars and champions, which will never be broadcast over national networks, in which bets will be bets of honor, and which have to be practiced in person, since no spectator tickets are on sale. At any rate, people who like to work for themselves and to take their enjoyments *en masse* will never understand what makes Alpinists climb mountains.

It would be unjust to accuse Americans in general of working selfishly and employing their leisure sheepishly, and it would be too complimentary to praise the Swiss for working only for the common good and for enjoying things as individuals. The Swiss believe just as firmly in free individual enterprise and are just as likely to gather in herds for their pleasures as Americans are. But in their most typical manifestations Americans certainly incline rather to the one side, and the Swiss to the other. Through their favorite sports nations seem to express their fundamental approach to life.

v

Alpinism is not an old sport, not even in Switzerland. It may be said that, in the national consciousness of the Swiss, Haller discovered the Alps, Rousseau formulated the relationship of patriotism and nature, and De Saussure, a fellow-Genevese, invented Alpinism.

In the case of Horace Bénédict de Saussure it is particularly true to say that he discovered the Alps by stumbling over them. Born in Geneva in 1740, the son of a distinguished family, De Saussure met Haller while still a young man, became his disciple and companion, and began to share his scientific interests. At the age of twenty-three he became professor of philosophy at the Academy of Geneva, and he promptly set about to prove the immortality of the soul and the existence of God. As was typical of his age, he was intent on proving, in the words of Beethoven's song, *die Ehre Gottes aus der Natur*. In 1760 he had begun to explore the Alpine chain in order to study its geological structure, and in the course of his lifetime he crossed the Alps no less than fourteen times, on foot, besides paying little side visits to the mountains of France, Germany, Great Britain, and Sicily. His scientific ardor disquieted his wife, but she merely elicited the somewhat un-chivalrous reply; "How can I give up a vocation which is my entire existence?"

All this was mere exploration. Exploration, though often involving Alpinism, should never be confused with it. Alpinism for Alpinism's sake began when De Saussure suddenly felt that he had to climb atop Mont Blanc. Mont Blanc, it is true, lies not in Switzerland, but on the French-Italian border. But it is part of the Swiss landscape, and there was nothing really unpatriotic about De Saussure's choosing a foreign mountain to launch a national sport. For twenty-seven years De Saussure carried on a one-sided love affair with Mont Blanc. His failures in his successive attempts to vanquish, to possess it, made him physically ill. "This had become a sort of sickness with me," he wrote after his final triumph. "My eyes could not meet Mont Blanc, which is visible from so many places of our countryside, without experiencing something like a painful spasm."

Even when, in 1787, he had attained the goal of his desires, his first reaction was that of a sensitive lover. "The arrival [at the peak] did not at first give me the pleasure that one might think. My strongest and sweetest sensation was the thought that my restlessness had ceased; for the length of my struggle, the memory —and the sensation which even then was still strangling me—of the suffering that my victory had cost me, produced in me a kind of irritation. The instant in which I reached the highest point of the snow that crowns the peak, I stamped on it in rage rather than with a pleasurable sensation."

However, once he had become used to the thought of his victory, his sentiment betrayed the satisfied lover: "I saw Mont Blanc again with true pleasure and without experiencing that troubled and painful feeling which it used to cause me before."

The parallel is not meant to be frivolous. De Saussure was not merely the founder of a new sport. Unwittingly he had from the very first found words for the mystical passion that binds the mountain climber and the mountain and for its ambivalent feelings of hatred and love. Earlier in this chapter it has been said that the true mystic Alpinist feels humility rather than triumph upon reaching his goal. Perhaps De Saussure may be excused if after a courtship of twenty-seven years he indulged in a little boasting. That he did not lack humility toward his challenger can be seen in many other utterances of his.

Haller, who tried to be a poet, has written some indifferent verse on the Alps, a theme which deserved better treatment. De Saussure, who never pretended to be poet and who wrote in prose, left passages which remain unsurpassed in the field of Alpine poetry. Unlike Haller, he did not seek to instruct or to please and unlike most Alpinists of later ages, he was highly articulate. His poetry was the involuntary outpouring of a passionate yet articulate man. When he naïvely revealed his relationship with Mont Blanc in terms which describe what is commonly known as love sickness, he created a poetry which, though exploited to surfeit in the erotic field, had rarely been applied to man's relationship with the universe. When he took a humbler view of his position with regard to nature, his poetry became still more compelling. Few poets have done greater justice to the subject than De Saussure in the following passage.

"The sky was perfectly pure and cloudless; the mists were visible only at the bottom of the valleys; the brilliant stars, without any kind of scintillation, spread an extremely weak and pale light over the mountain tops, yet sufficient to distinguish shapes and distances. The repose and the profound silence that ruled over the vast expanse, enlarged by my imagination, inspired me with something like terror. It seemed to me that I alone had survived the universe and that I was seeing its corpse spread out beneath my feet."

VIII: State and Man

For centuries the word "state" was to the Swiss synonymous with the word "canton." When the Swiss united their cantons in a national state, in 1848, their political habits of thought, at least as far as the inner structure of the state was concerned, were entirely based on their experience with cantonal government. The forms of cantonal government differed widely, yet in every canton the liberal elements which brought about the change were imbued with the notion that there once had been a primitive Swiss democracy, a notion on which their very consciousness as a nation was largely based. The old freedom had been corrupted and lost, but not forgotten, and it could be regained. Of the three great political theorists who held that natural law entitled nations to revolt, one—Locke—was English, and two—Vattel and Rousseau—were Swiss.

Thus, the main political object of the national unification was to guarantee free and democratic governments in all cantons rather than to establish anything new like a superstate. Except in times of crisis, the canton still is the working unit of Swiss political life. This does not necessarily mean that the cantonal governments possess wider scope or greater power than the federal government; it merely means that in normal times cantonal affairs arouse considerable political passion, whereas the somewhat impersonal and colorless government in Berne merely looms in the background.

The Swiss have a word of their own for their approach to politics: *Kantönligeist*, which literally translated means "little-canton-mindedness." The situation is perhaps best understood if one imagines a United States of America where every state feels and behaves in the manner of Texas. Americans—including Texans—tend to take a humorous view of such manifestations of local patriotism; in Switzerland, which is about one sixteenth the size of Texas, *Kantönligeist* has been earnestly criticized or gravely extolled, but rarely laughed at. Moreover, in the United States local patriotism finds expression chiefly in the assertion of states' rights against the federal government, whereas in Switzerland there exists, besides that particular form of rivalry, the additional rivalry between the individual cantons.

This stubborn loyalty to one's original canton often goes to great lengths. One can live for years in Geneva without ever hearing the Swiss national anthem sung, but one can hardly escape the Genevese hymn, *Cé qué laîno*. This phenomenon should not be interpreted as an indication of lukewarm patriotism or as an absence of national consciousness. On the contrary, the preoccupation with one's own canton is probably one of the main elements of the national tradition. It is, as it were, a national virtue to be concerned only with local affairs.

There is a great deal to be said for this attitude, for it encourages active participation of all citizens in the democratic process and a healthy interest in keeping one's own doorstep clean. The unification of Switzerland which followed the Sonderbund War put an end to the excesses of that local spirit, but left alive its positive potentialities.

The Swiss are an intensely political nation, though on the surface they may appear to be more concerned with economic pursuits than with taking sides in ideological issues. The reason for this seeming contradiction between reality and appearance is precisely the fact that political passion has but the canton as its theater, and thus causes little stir in the outside world, while the qualities of cautious neutrality and economic astuteness reflect the political philosophy of the nation as a whole. This kind of double nature is no recent phenomenon: as early as in the sixteenth and the seventeenth centuries the Swiss were fighting violently among themselves about religious issues, and at the same time observed strict neutrality in the international wars that were being fought over the same issues.

Despite their appearance of calmness, then, the Swiss are in a chronic state of political excitement. That this has not prevented them from being the most stable nation of the Continent is a rather interesting fact, which will be examined at another place. It is sufficient here to stress the intimate relationship, in Switzerland, between practical and theoretical politics on the one hand, and almost all cultural and social life on the other. In this the Swiss contrast sharply with the Germans, whose politics and cultural pursuits were traditionally divorced, and show close affinities to the Italian tradition of the Middle Ages and the Renaissance.

With politics holding so vital and honorable a place in Swiss traditions, it is surprising that the Swiss in all their long and eventful history have produced not a single truly exceptional political figure. In as narrow a field of action as theirs it was, perhaps, difficult to attain the first magnitude, but the primary cause for Switzerland's lack of great statesmen must be sought elsewhere.

It will be found that nearly all those Swiss who attained international fame—Zwingli, Rousseau, Pestalozzi, to name but the three greatest—were deeply concerned with politics. In a manner of speaking, they were Switzerland's true statesmen. Possibly it was, again, the narrowness of the field of political action that made these men reach the decision to guide mankind through the spirit rather than through statesmanship. This explanation would be only partly correct in the case of Zwingli who was, perhaps, a mediocre statesman, but nonetheless a statesman. As for the others, there was nothing to keep them from obtaining high political posts abroad, as many other Swiss had done.

It seems more reasonable to suppose, despite all possible objections, that it is peculiar to the Swiss genius to be conservative, wise, and mediocre in the field of practical government and to be revolutionary, sometimes a trifle foolish, and often brilliant, in approaching political problems in their spiritual and cultural contexts.

II

The palm for brilliance and foolishness undoubtedly belongs to Jean Jacques Rousseau. The proletarian Jean Jacques was no

ANNO AETATIS EIVS XLVIII.

ULRICH ZWINGLI

Woodcut made in 1539

less typical a product of eighteenth-century Switzerland than the patrician Haller. The son of a somewhat footloose watchmaker and of a mother who died when she gave him birth, Rousseau was born, as it were, "on the wrong side of the river," in the poorer section of Geneva. True, he bore the treasured title, Citizen of Geneva, which set him above the major part of his city's artisans and workers—but this did him little good abroad, where he spent the larger part of his life. A flunkey in Turin, an unknown in Paris, where he was once asked to eat at the servant's table, a much sat-upon secretary to the French ambassador to Venice, and a parasite during the rest of his life, even after he had reached fame, Rousseau accumulated in the course of his chequered career an ineradicable resentment against anybody who found life enjoyable. This attitude was caused, in part, by his Calvinist upbringing, which may also have been partially responsible for his masochistic tendencies, of which he boasts in his *Confessions*.

With a predisposition like his he was bound to be deeply scarred by the humiliating experiences that he had to undergo on account of his social inferiority. Rousseau never quite got over the fact that he had been the house guest of dukes and that he once had declined an invitation from the king of France. In his ambivalent attitude toward the great and powerful he was a thorough proletarian who never could adjust himself to the polite world. Few men ever felt more flattered by attention from high places and at the same time were readier to insult their flatterers. Even his paranoia, the final result of his ambivalence, was somehow proletarian.

There was something new in Rousseau's rumblings that jarred with the spirit of his time. Neurotic, physically handicapped, somber, and resentful, Rousseau represented a new and dangerous type of social reformer, a type which was to become more and more frequent in the maladjusted century and a half that followed.

The *Social Contract* is required reading in several American colleges, yet there seems to be an almost universal misconception as to its contents. This misconception seems to stem from the ineradicable notion that Rousseau merely repeated what Locke had said before him. From this misconception one must also trace the widespread idea that the American or English forms of democracy represent a fulfillment of Rousseau's ideas. Nothing could be wider of the mark.

In the first place, Rousseau scarcely ever thought that the world could be changed for the better; he merely hoped that in some parts of the world it might take longer than in others to change it for the worse. His philosophy was intrinsically pessimistic. There could be nothing more optimistic than the philosophy of American democracy. To Rousseau, history was a progressive change from freedom to slavery. To the American optimist, it is the contrary. Rousseau did not seem to feel that this "progress" could be stopped. When the king of Poland requested him to draw up a constitution for the Polish people, Rousseau did not even suggest the abolition of serfdom. While he may have held some hope that in fields like hygiene, infant care, or education some return might be made toward natural practices, this hardly applied to political institutions.

Rather than advocate political changes, Rousseau was of the opinion that the best should be made of the worst. He warmly recommended revolution to oppressed peoples to recover lost liberties, yet at the same time he believed that true democracy could exist only within a "nation of gods." Short of revolution, at any rate, he did not seem to see any possibility of improving a political or social system.

Sovereignty was held exclusively by the people, that is, by a group of individuals who by a social contract had decided to live together as a society. Sovereignty could not be delegated, divided, alienated, or restricted. No laws could be made except by consent of the sovereign—hence, "few nations really have laws." The government of a nation could be nothing more than its executive and judiciary power, since legislation was not in the hands of the government, but of the sovereign. Finally, legislation had only two objects: liberty and equality. Liberty, "because any individual restriction of freedom means a corresponding diminution of the power of the state; equality, because liberty cannot exist without it." Equality Rousseau defined politically and economically. Politically, it exists as long as "power is never exerted except as rank and laws permit it"; economically, "no citizen must be rich enough to buy another, or poor enough to be obliged to sell himself."

Like most political writers of his time, Rousseau divided the prevalent forms of government into three general types: democracy, aristocracy, and monarchy. However, where Rousseau differed from other writers was in his thesis that in *all* forms of government, sovereignty, and consequently the right to legislate, belonged by right to the people. The differences among the three forms lay merely in the nature of the executive: if it was shared by all, or at least more than half, the people, the state was democratic; if by less than half, aristocratic; if held by one person (or corporate person) alone, it was monarchic. Of all forms of government a hereditary aristocracy based on wealth was the worst.

No particular form of government was suitable for all nations or climes. Now the criterion used by Rousseau to determine what form suits a country best is highly original, and has been unduly disregarded. The criterion is economic. It is a commonplace today that democracy is preferred by rich nations, while authoritarianism is inevitable in poor countries. Rousseau held exactly the opposite point of view. Government subsists on taxes. Taxes are levied on the surplus production of labor. The less a people consumes, the more surplus it produces; and the deeper the cleavage between the people and its government, the heavier becomes the onus of taxation. Hence the paradox that the country with the lowest living standards and the highest tax burden is also the most opulent; only in such a country can monarchy or despotism work. Aristocracy is best suited for medium-sized and moderately wealthy states. Democracy is possible only in very small and poor countries.

It is evident that Rousseau's argument would be meaningless unless by wealth he understood, not a people's living standard, but its natural resources.

Rousseau believed that Switzerland, being a small state, poor in natural resources, and situated in a moderate climate, was ideally suited for democracy. Misinterpreting the constitution of his own home canton, which was as plainly an aristocracy as anyone could wish, he felt that he was a citizen "of a free state and member of the sovereign body." It is indubitably true, how-

ever, that in the Swiss cantons which were governed by Landsgemeinden the citizens constituted a democratic state as nearly as
was possible. They were, indeed, small and poor; their governments were merely the executive and the judiciary, while the
legislative was in the hands of all citizens. Yet Rousseau would
probably have thought that even Switzerland was too large a
state to permit this type of pure democracy on a national basis.
He would have been wrong, for though the framers of the Swiss
constitution of 1848 intended to model it on that of the United
States, the final result was a democracy *à la* Rousseau.

III

On the face of it, the Swiss constitution provides for legislation by representatives. Rousseau disapproved of nations which
delegated their sovereignty to representatives. "By dint of in-
ertia and money," he wrote, "they finally get soldiers to enslave
the fatherland, and representatives to sell it." As for the English,
"they think they are free, but they are much mistaken. They are
free only while they are electing the members of Parliament; as
soon as those are elected, they again become slaves, nothing. The
use which they make of their brief moments of freedom [shows
that] they deserve to lose it."

The Swiss thought along similar lines. Not that they were particularly influenced by Rousseau's writings—it was rather that
Rousseau had been writing from a sentiment shared by all Swiss.
Karamzin, the Russian historian, wrote of the citizens of Zurich, in
1789, that they were "as proud of their title [of citizen] as a
king of his crown. For more than a hundred and fifty years no
foreigner has obtained the right of citizenship." These citizens,
and those of the other cantons, all felt like Rousseau that they
were sovereigns—not in legal theory only, but in actual fact. That
a few families among them had arrogated to themselves the functions of sovereignty did not change the feeling, but merely resulted in the eventual downfall of the aristocratic families.

This change occurred in the eighteen thirties. Were the sovereign Swiss, now that they had actually come into their own
again, to renounce the direct exercise of their privileges? Or
were those citizens who, after centuries of subjection, had at last

become the equals of their former masters and part of the sovereign body themselves, to countenance the elimination of privileges to which they had so long aspired?

They certainly were not, and it took little time before the legislative bodies were made virtually powerless through the extension of the citizens' inherent rights as direct lawgivers. The true legislative body of Switzerland is the people, and legislation is not transacted by any representatives in any halls, but through the referendum and the initiative in the voting booths. This was, indeed, the triumph of the primitive freedom of the three original cantons. Initiative and referendum more than adequately replaced the practice of popular assemblies, which is clumsy even in the smallest communities.

Rousseau, who thought of the institution of government exclusively as of an executive and judiciary apparatus, was not particularly concerned with the methods of choosing magistrates. In fact, he felt that in a democracy the most adequate method of electing the chief executive is by lot. One might easily be tempted to concur, but not for the reasons advanced by Rousseau. In his opinion, to hold a government post was a burden rather than an advantage. Besides, in a true democracy one man should be as good as another, especially where no particular qualities save common sense, justice, and integrity are required. Choice by election was preferable only for posts which demanded some special knowledge, such as military commands. In other words, in Rousseau's opinion the people of the United States would be just as well, if not better, off if they chose their president by tossing a coin and elected their chief of staff by ballot.

Curiously enough, in this point the Swiss attitude again seems to coincide with Rousseau's. The choice of their supreme executive, the Federal Council, is made by the two legislative chambers, not by direct election. Few Swiss even know the names of all seven members of the Federal Council or that of the president. On the other hand, on the lower echelons of government the election of magistrates is taken very seriously, and the designation of a commanding general in wartime is not in the hands of the executive, but in those of the legislature.

Even when the method of electing the legislature was concerned, the Swiss shunned the Anglo-Saxon party system, which is based on an extreme theory of government by representation. In that extreme theory an elected official represents his district as a whole rather than those particular constituents who chose to vote for him. According to Rousseau, he represents only himself. However, Rousseau indubitably would have found that the next best thing to no representation at all would be as exact a representation as possible of the various shades of opinion and interest that exist within a constituency. This can be obtained only through proportional representation.

Those Americans who maintain that proportional representation is contrary to the American tradition of democracy, which is based on a two-party system, are probably eminently right. Moreover, most of the democracies of western Continental Europe do not seem to have apprehended the fact that representative government cannot exist along with a multi-party system. They are somehow wavering between the two extremes of the Anglo-Saxon concept of legislation by representatives and the Rousseauan ideal of legislation by the people. The Swiss reflect Rousseau's preferences: they fundamentally do not believe in government by representation; they have a seeming multi-party system which actually is no party system at all; and they have introduced proportional representation as the least evil wherever representation was inevitable.

Such a system cannot work without unanimity on all essential matters. This again was realized by Rousseau. In his concept, only gods could achieve perfect democracy, for only gods always know what is best for them and can achieve unanimity. In routine matters, an absolute majority might be deemed satisfactory; but in vital questions (unless they require great urgency), the common will should be expressed *quasi* unanimously. In a true democracy, where freedom and equality are actual facts, the common will, according to Rousseau, invariably is held by an overwhelming majority, because the same interests are shared by all. The introduction of political parties transforms all questions which should be judged in the light of the common interest into matters of controversy. In such a case, to decide the issue by taking a vote is not only absurd, since the outcome of the vote reflects merely the "conclusion of one of the parties" rather than the "general will," but it is, moreover, the negation of democracy. "What makes the will general is not so much the number of votes as common interest."

It will be seen elsewhere that the Swiss have, on all essential points, come very close to unanimity, for the simple reason that their interests are, indeed, by and large, shared by all citizens. Whether such stability can be maintained in the midst of a world torn by class strife is another question. Rousseau's principles required what amounts to a classless society, what he called a society of gods. Admittedly the Swiss are far from classless and still farther from godlike. Yet in a comparatively small community this weakness is remedied by the fact that its common interests are more clearly and more immediately before its eyes than is the case with a large nation, where particular interests are more likely to be confused with the general interest.

It cannot be repeated often enough that Rousseau had little, if any, influence on the political development of nineteenth-century Switzerland and that his analysis of the various forms of government merely reflected, as far as it coincided with the general sentiment of the Swiss, the tradition in which he had been brought up during his most impressionable years. His political influence was probably greatest in countries which had few or no democratic traditions: France, Germany, and Russia. In his own country his influence was little needed: to adhere to his views was an act of conservatism. But in France or in Russia, where his theories would have to be applied from above, they took on an entirely different hue and became extremely noticeable.

Though orthodox Communists would—probably rightly so— raise their hands in horror if told that they derived anything from Rousseau, it still remains true that in several respects they follow his doctrine. The identification of a classless society, where community of interests insures community of opinion, with the only true form of democracy is one of them. Another is Rousseau's statement that the term "Christian republic" is a contradiction in itself, because "Christianity preaches only servitude and dependence," because "its spirit is too favorable to tyranny to prevent it from always profiting from tyranny," and because "true

Christians are made to be slaves." A curious view to be taken by one so fond of the liberties of Calvin's Geneva! But then, was Rousseau entirely emancipated from the Calvinist concept of the City of God?

Certainly not, for he believed that it was impossible to be a good citizen of a democratic community without believing in a civil religion which includes the following dogmas: the existence of a powerful, intelligent, beneficent, foreseeing, and provident divinity; life after death, recompense of the just, and punishment of the evil; the sanctity of the social contract and of the laws; and the necessity of suppressing intolerance of any kind. To these dogmas every citizen should be made to swear, and if his deeds contradict his oath, he should be punished by death.

Such a program obviously was purely doctrinaire and unrealistic. Robespierre, to whom intellectual schemes were more real than live human beings, tried to apply it textually—every one knows with what results. Yet Rousseau's suggestion was not entirely unreasonable. If between the ultimate goal of classless democracy and the present stage of society one inserts, as later doctrinaires were to do, the intermediate stage of a dictatorship of the proletariat, it becomes not only reasonable but even necessary to exact a profession of faith from those who exercise the dictatorial power and to punish them with death or exile if they fail to abide by it.

It might be said that in his affinities with utopian communism Rousseau was essentially un-Swiss. This is true in the sense that the Swiss never tolerated any form of communism in their society. At the same time their preoccupation with Evangelism encouraged some curious theological doctrines, especially among the poorer classes. The Anabaptists, the Swiss Brethren (known in the United States as the Amish), and similar sects were extremely strong in sixteenth-century Switzerland, where they largely originated. They were forced into exile, just as the Puritans were in England, but this does not invalidate the fact that their brand of utopian communism was as typically Swiss as Puritanism was typically English. Ideologically, it is a long way from the Amish to the *Social Contract*—but in practice there is really very little difference between the peculiarity of an Amishman and the peculiarity that characterized Rousseau, especially in his later years.

I V

The *Social Contract* owed a great deal to Swiss institutions and traditions, but Swiss institutions and traditions owe little to the *Social Contract*. Outside Switzerland, Rousseau is above all the author of the *Social Contract*. To the Swiss he is above all the author of *Emile*. They were not interested in learning from him how their country should be run, but they were very much interested in learning how to form citizens that could run their country.

It has often been said that *Emile* contradicted everything Rousseau had said in the *Social Contract*. This is unlikely, erratic and incoherent though Rousseau may have been, since he wrote the two works in close succession. The belief in Rousseau's self-contradiction seems justified by his statement that "one must choose between making a man and making a citizen, for one cannot do both things at the same time." But, in truth, there was no contradiction. It would be impossible to create a community of free and equal citizens, willing to exchange—as the *Social Contract* specified—their natural and anarchical freedom for social freedom, unless the members of that community have some natural freedom to exchange. The basic material had to be unspoiled, and Rousseau tried to show, in *Emile*, how such basic material could be obtained.

The theory underlying *Emile* is ridiculously simple; it probably is the best known and the best understood of all of Rousseau's theories. A child, at its birth, is entirely natural and unspoiled; its education should consist of nothing but the opportunity to develop its natural gifts unhampered and to shield it from the corrupting influences of civilization. It should not be taught anything it neither needs to know nor understands. Everything it learns should come from an inner realization, not from without. "A child's earliest teachers are its feet, its hands." The ultimate object of its education should be to teach it to live, not to train it for anything special.

The theoretical part of such an education breaks down entirely because of the simple fact that a child, at its birth, is neither un-spoiled nor in a pure state of nature. A century before Freud, Rousseau's erstwhile friend, Diderot, observed that a boy, if left to his own devices, would begin his career by murdering his father and raping his mother. Rousseau, who never knew his mother, apparently had no inkling of the Oedipus complex, though he was plentifully endowed with almost every other variety.

The practical application of Rousseau's theoretically unsound principles of pedagogy has been evident in all modern or "pro-gressive" education since his days, with more or less fortunate results. Rousseau himself applied his ideas in a rather original manner. He asserted that he had five children from his common-law wife, the terrible Thérèse Levasseur, and that he sent all five to the French state institution for foundlings. In his words, "in letting them become working people and peasants rather than adventurers and fortune seekers, I believed that I was acting as a good citizen and father, and regarded myself as a member of Plato's republic." His subsequent contrition and his repudiation of such rationalizations never sounded quite sincere. His estimate, moreover, of the beneficent qualities of the foundling homes and orphanages of his time was strangely optimistic. And yet, if they improved in later ages, this was due largely to Rousseau's con-tribution—not the contribution of his five children, but the con-tribution of his thought, which was to bear fruit in the work of his fellowcountryman Johann Heinrich Pestalozzi.

V

In character, Rousseau and Pestalozzi were as day and night. Rousseau was suspicious, petty, and ungrateful. Pestalozzi, from his earliest childhood, was trusting to the point of foolishness; though he clearly saw through people, he knew no resentments. His indestructible gentleness could be read in his face. It is strange to see that even in their upbringing the two underwent exactly opposite experiences. While Rousseau was motherless, Pestalozzi, who was born in Zurich in 1746, lost his father, a surgeon, at the age of five and was brought up in very straitened circumstances by his mother. Pestalozzi was one of seven children, of whom only three had survived early childhood. Rousseau's father, who kept his little son awake till the early morning hours by reading romances to him, was hardly fit to instill domestic discipline into his progeny. Pestalozzi's mother, who hardly allowed her children to budge from their livingroom for fear that they might tear their clothes or run holes in their shoes, was of a different caliber. Pestalozzi, in his later years, deplored his lack of male company during his childhood. "I regarded the world as a mere extension of my mother's livingroom."

The mother somehow managed to scrape enough money together to give Johann Heinrich a liberal education—again in contrast to Rousseau, who never received any formal education at all. Though a fairly good student, Pestalozzi was considered by his schoolmates something of a half-wit. He was what would now be called a "one hundred percent sucker," ready to take the rap for anything.

At the *Collegium Carolinum* in Zurich, Pestalozzi came under the influence of the champions of liberal patriotism—men like Bodmer, who was professor of history, young Fuseli, the painter, and Lavater—he who was to become famous as a writer on physiognomy. Rousseau and the Elder Mirabeau—the high priest of physiocracy and self-styled Friend of Mankind—were the patron saints of this group, and the corruption of the age was the dragon they were fighting.

Already Pestalozzi was dreaming of vast reforms to be operated in the field of morals and education by means of distributing, "gratis, or for not more than one shilling," simple printed directions on how to bring up one's children. It did not take long for the group to get itself into trouble with the government by inopportunely pressing lawsuits against corrupt officials, printing propaganda against the military intervention of Zurich in the civil troubles of Geneva, and other such radical activities. Pestalozzi escaped the attention of the authorities, but Fuseli and Lavater were obliged to flee their country.

It was around that time—1767—that Pestalozzi fell in love and became engaged to a rich pastry manufacturer's daughter, Anna Schultess. Though Anna was more than seven years his elder, her parents tried (not very successfully) to keep her as secluded as though she were still in her early teens and opposed her marriage to Pestalozzi with all their might. Pestalozzi, in the meantime, fired by love and by Dr. Quesnay's *Economic Chart*, had decided to seek his fortune in agriculture.

For this purpose he left Zurich in the fall of 1767 and spent what he considered an apprenticeship on the farm of a Bernese friend named Johann Rudolf Tschiffeli. Tschiffeli's economic principles were bold. With a little cleverness and speculation, Pestalozzi gathered from him, nothing was easier than to gain vast fortunes from farming. Three years later, Tschiffeli was saved from bankruptcy by winning the first prize in a lottery—a new but hazardous device of husbandry. But Pestalozzi was all optimism. Borrowing the necessary capital from a banker and from relatives, he leased some farmland near Zurich in 1769, ordered the construction of some ambitious buildings, and married Fräulein Schultess, whose parents let her take with her no more than her clothes and her piano.

Perhaps Dr. Quesnay's celebrated Table was not entirely right. Perhaps Pestalozzi had underestimated the amount of capital necessary to make the doctor's zigzags come out properly. Or perhaps he just was not a good farmer. At any rate it did not take him long to sink shoulder deep into debt. Mrs. Pestalozzi seemed to think that her husband's interests were perhaps too catholic, in fact she confided to her diary that her dear beloved lacked religion and was a little bit peculiar. Pestalozzi, for his part, was struggling with his conscience. "When will my evil heart let itself be guided by God and cease to be tossed on the wild waves of base vice?" Just what the base vices of the good man were, nobody knows.

In 1770, a year before the couple moved to their new house, the Neuhof, a son was born to them. Now was the time to test *Emile* in practice. Had Rousseau tried to educate his children instead of sending them to state institutions, it is doubtful that he would have insisted for long on the maxim that a child should never be made to obey. Pestalozzi, at any rate, threw that part of Rousseau's theory overboard at an early stage. For the rest, however, he stuck by his principles with an earnestness worthy of Mr. Shandy, Sr.

Rousseau had said that children should never be taught any more than they can fully comprehend. Perhaps, Pestalozzi thought, he was driving his three-year old son too fast. "How much in accordance with nature it would have been not to let him say 3 before he had apprehended 2 in all its applications. How naturally he would thus have learned to count, and how much my haste has made me deviate from the path of Nature!"

Materially, things were going from bad to worse with the Neuhof. But Pestalozzi seems to have shared a curious trait with almost all those Swiss who were to become benefactors of mankind: he thought that he was a good businessman, he combined his humanitarian impulses with his material interests, he went bankrupt as far as his material interests were concerned, and he emerged as an idealist champion of humanitarianism. More specifically, Pestalozzi hit upon the idea that by transforming his farm into an institute for poor children he would attain the double advantage of getting his accounts out of the red and of being a benefactor to mankind.

It is curious, and perhaps a little dismaying, to see how neatly Pestalozzi's humanitarian theories dovetailed with his material interests, how promptly he dismissed whatever did not fit them in the Rousseauan and physiocratic schemes as unpractical dreams. The main object in the education of the poor, he proclaimed, was to educate them to be poor. Why bring up an institutionalized child in idleness, why teach him unnecessary knowledge, if he is going to spend his life as a farmhand or as an industrial worker? "The poor should not shy from the dampness of the weaver's basement . . . they should be used to the cotton dust . . . the disgusting grease of sheeps' wool should not seem repellent to them."

Talk about factory work disquieted his physiocratic friends, through whose generosity he was able to keep up his institution. He reassured them. It is said, he wrote, that factories, with their unhealthy air, would transform children into machines and bring them up in an irresponsible and immoral atmosphere. This was not so. "Spinning or grazing, weaving or plowing—there is nothing in these things that makes one either moral or immoral." It all depends on the efforts of the employer. Very true—factories need not be dens of sin—but what about their tendency to transform children into machines? Pestalozzi was so much concerned with moral virtue that he forgot to answer that.

The sad fact is that Pestalozzi had the thirty or so children on his farm work most of the day, either in the fields or on cotton looms. Instruction—the three R's—was kept at a minimum, while moral lectures were frequent. That the children were not particularly happy (they often complained to their mothers and occasionally ran away), Pestalozzi ascribed to the corrupt training they had undergone before they came to him. The economic advantages he had hoped for failed to materialize. In 1780 he was obliged to close his institution and to sell most of his land, and even his best friends began to doubt his sanity when they saw him roaming distractedly over the fields which had once been his.

During the following few years Pestalozzi, unabashed by failure, produced a vast literary output. In *Lienhard und Gertrud*, a novel which appeared between 1781 and 1787 in four installments, he painted a picture of village life which was to pillory the abuses of his time and point out the remedies. The villain was the local magistrate, who combined his office with the profession of innkeeper, a rascal whom nothing could daunt in his fight against virtue, as represented by the honest working couple Lienhard and Gertrud, the parish priest, and a humanitarian landowner. Salvation is shown in moral upbringing, symbolized by the living room in which the mother rules like a pious and industrious divinity.

In the same period Pestalozzi turned to a more specific question. A German society had proposed a prize for the best essay on the question, What are the best practical means to prevent child murder? Pestalozzi's answer, which was not completed in time for the competition, was first printed in book form in 1783. Leaning heavily on Beccaria's pioneering work *On Crime and Punishment*, but adding his own original thought, Pestalozzi pointed out that legal measures could not possibly affect the deeper motivations for child murder. Immorality and criminality were the results of insufficient ethical education; the home, not the courthouse, was the place where reform should begin. The State should see to it that young people could marry at an early age, but it should not absolve the father of an illegitimate child from the obligation to provide for it, nor should it take away from the mother the task of bringing it up. It is the law that breeds lawlessness. For the conventional symbol of justice, the blind, deaf, and immovable statue, he had no use. A new justice, with the primary needs of mankind as its mean objective, was necessary.

The same plea was made in a periodical which Pestalozzi published for a few ephemeral months, the *Schweizer Blätter*. The highest purpose of all legislation and policing, he declared, was to ensure domestic well-being for every working and virtuous citizen. Poverty had remained his ideal, but at the same time he realized ever more clearly that not only wealth but misery as well endangered morality.

Poverty was to be respectable. The rich should honor the poor, but they should also be taught not to despise money, for how could they realize the needs of the poor if they were ignorant of the value of money? A return to nature and to agriculture was all well and good, but a state could not be economically sound without a certain amount of bourgeois prosperity. Rousseau and the physiocrats he now rejected as theoretical dreamers who inspired intellectual chimeras rather than the direct action which was necessary.

Two years after Pestalozzi had published the last volume of *Lienhard und Gertrud*, the Rousseau-inspired theoretical dreamers in France had come pretty much to the same conclusion. By August 26, 1792, they had suspended their king, declared war on Austria, and, incidentally, conferred the honorary citizenship of France on Pestalozzi, along with Friedrich Schiller, George Washington, and some other distinguished foreigners.

Pestalozzi hailed the Revolution, and upon hearing the news of his honorary citizenship he offered his services to the French government. Their appreciation, however, was more symbolic than anything else, for his offer went unheeded. Pestalozzi, whose career as a writer was due only to the fact that he had found no opportunity as yet to teach by deeds rather than words, had ample time to write more books.

A visit by Fichte, the German philosopher, in 1793, encouraged him to embark on an ambitious project, a philosophy of politics. In this book, tersely entitled *My Researches on the Course of Nature in the Development of the Human Race*, Pestalozzi sought to order and clarify the conflicting thoughts and emotions which the French Revolution had inspired in him. Though based on Rousseau's premise that Man, in his natural state, was innocent and unspoiled, Pestalozzi's development of the theme represented a radical and original departure from Rousseau.

According to Pestalozzi, natural and unspoiled Man turned into natural but corrupt Man as soon as his instincts no longer enabled him to satisfy his sensual needs. From an unspoiled animal, he turned into a violent barbarian. In this new state he soon felt threatened in his instinct of self-preservation. The violence done to other men might one day be done to him. Thus, he invented law and social order for the simple purpose of being able to satisfy his animal instincts peacefully and securely. Corrupt natural Man had become corrupt social Man, yet basically he still was an animal.

Society, by assigning different functions to different classes, stunted Man. "The smith's right arm alone is stronger than both his feet; the tailor bobs as he walks; the plowman has the same gait as the ox with which he plows." In fact, "social existence is but the continuation of a war of all against all—a war which takes its origin in the corruption of the natural state and which merely has changed forms in the social state." It is a jungle in which "everywhere the powerful deploy all possible means to be the masters of a social community without really respecting social law."

How can Man extricate himself from the jungle? Not by renouncing social order or by reforming the social order but by reforming himself. The animal instincts, cause of all the struggle for power, oppression, and injustice, must be overcome in the soul of Man. Having passed from the natural to the social state, he now must pass from the social to the ethical state. Man must make himself.

As for revolutions, they can never be lawful. However, they occur only where law has been usurped and has become meaningless. The guilt does not lie with the rebels; it lies with those against whom they have revolted. As Franz Werfel was to put it a considerable time later, "Not the murderer, but the murdered is guilty."

Early in 1798 French troops entered Switzerland. The Helvetic Republic was set up and Pestalozzi, who immediately offered his services to the new government, was appointed editor of a periodical intended for the enlightenment of the rural population. In the very first issue he declared that the events of the Revolution had sufficiently proved the weakness of all property based on power. Only one hope remained; "ethical enlightenment."

At long last, in 1799, Pestalozzi found the opportunity of acting out what he preached. In the village of Stans the French invaders had massacred some three hundred men, women, and children, and an orphanage was to be founded for the surviving children. Pestalozzi was appointed its director.

VI

With the orphanage of Stans begins the Pestalozzi legend. The image of a benign and disheveled father, surrounded by a happy flock of grateful children, has ever since been conjured up by the simple mention of his name. Actually, Pestalozzi had barely begun to gain the confidence of his new wards and of the distrustful Catholic countryfolk when the orphanage was closed down to be transformed into a French military hospital. Pestalozzi transferred his activities to Burgdorf, in the canton of Berne, where he began to work out the principles of his instruction technique by teaching the three R's to the youngest classes of a school for well-to-do children.

The aim was to simplify all instruction by reducing it to its basic elements, which he conceived to be "number, shape, and name." Some men, like Goethe, felt that Pestalozzi's super-rational approach threatened to mechanize education. No, Pestalozzi replied, he was "psychologizing education." Utmost simplification was indispensable, for ideally education should not be given in schools at all, but at home, by the mother. To show how this could be done he published books such as *How Gertrude Taught Her Children* and *Instructions to Mothers on how to Make Their Children Observe and Speak*, and several abstract textbooks.

The concept of the living room as the fountainhead of all ethical values and of the mother as their chief dispenser, now became almost an obsession. In 1802 Pestalozzi had visited Paris as a member of the Swiss delegation convoked by Bonaparte to help him settle the internal quarrels of Switzerland. (Pestalozzi's party, favoring centralization, lost out; the Act of Mediuation of 1804 was a blow to him.) While in France, he observed that Frenchmen had become mere wheels. The "cursed Revolution," as he now called it, had destroyed their individualism. Terms such as "collective society" and "propertyless masses" were to become more and more frequent in his writings, and he dreaded what they stood for.

Yet he saw no real way out of the dilemma between a collective social existence and individual self-development. Both had to exist side by side, he recognized, and unending conflict was inevitable. However, he did not develop this idea through Hegelian dialectics: instead, he merely specified that collective requirements never should be allowed to take the upper hand. To prevent this, nation-wide education of all as ethical individuals was more pressing than ever, and nothing apparently was more likely to produce ethical and selfless individuals than his own basic principles of education.

When, in 1805, the town of Yverdon in Vaud put its castle at Pestalozzi's disposal, his fame had spread throughout Europe, and foreign visitors, come to learn how to educate their respective nations, marveled at the miracles he worked by such newfangled methods as making children repeat phrases in a chorus. His new school at Yverdon was planned primarily as a practical seminar for future teachers—in an optimistic moment Pestalozzi thought that with two hundred disciples he could change the world—and the victims of the experiment included French, English, German, and Russian children.

Nowhere were Pestalozzi's ideas welcomed more enthusiastically than in Prussia. Fichte, in his *Addresses to the German Nation*, developed the plan for national education as a remedy to Prussia's moral and political prostration. He had friends in the Prussian government, and in 1808 it began to send young teachers to Yverdon to learn Pestalozzi's method. In his own country, however, Pestalozzi was no prophet. Reaction had set in, and to the

Swiss Diet any plan aimed at raising the educational level of the common people seemed dangerous. An investigating commission was sent to Yverdon in 1809 and reported unfavorably on Pestalozzi's effort "to raise . . . men arbitrarily from the natural station to which Providence has assigned them." The report did the school great financial harm. The number of pupils fell, intrigues and quarrels among the teachers were chronic, and in 1810 a visiting Prussian official was so appalled by the level of the instruction and the chaotic financial situation of the school that he did not give it more than a year to continue in existence.

It would be interesting to know how much ethical values the pupils absorbed under such conditions—unfortunately, most studies and dissertations on Pestalozzi, for some reason known only to students of education, seem to be far more concerned with the thoughts of the teachers of the institution than with the fate of the pupils. Surely, the pupils must, at times, have wondered at their odd and unkempt apostle.

Indeed, Pestalozzi was, as his wife had early noted, peculiar. In 1814, when the invading allied armies planned to use his school for a hospital, Pestalozzi, without being asked to do so, forced his company on two deputies sent by Yverdon to the allied headquarters in Basel to protest against the plan, which endangered public health. The two deputies were rebuffed, but Pestalozzi, breaking out into dithyrambic pleas, literally cornered Tsar Alexander I, inviting him to cancel the hospital order, to establish national education in Russia, and to free all serfs. With his back against the wall, the tsar found no other way to extricate himself than to embrace Pestalozzi and to promise him everything.

Still stranger must have been the scene at the funeral of Pestalozzi's wife, in 1815. Feeling that he had not made her quite as happy as he might have done, Pestalozzi, standing over her open grave, held a funeral oration in the form of a dialogue, in which he supplied his wife's answers himself. The audience, it is said, was deeply moved.

The worst was yet to come. In 1815 the evil spirit of efficiency arrived at Yverdon in the form of Joseph Schmid, a former pupil, who immediately took not only the school but Pestalozzi himself in his own hands. The practical results were excellent, and

Yverdon began to flourish once more. However, the nickname given to Schmid by the pupils was not, perhaps, entirely in conformity with Pestalozzian ideals: they called him the police chief.

Before long, uncontrolled enmity began to divide the teachers into two parties. The anti-Schmidians were led by Pastor Johannes Niederer, who had been associated with Pestalozzi since 1803 and somehow regarded himself as his warden. Niederer brutally accused Pestalozzi of having betrayed his ideals. Pestalozzi, in one scene among many, declared that Schmid was his guardian angel, sent by God to rescue his work, and with tears streaming over his face went from teacher to teacher, imploring, pressing hands, and embracing.

Niederer finally left in 1817. For the next ten years he poisoned the life of Pestalozzi with the most heartless attacks, insinuations, and even lawsuits involving contested sums of money. His frantic crusade to rescue the idea of Pestalozzi from the man Pestalozzi forced the old man to close down his school in 1825 and to spend his last two years in defending his conduct through his memoirs.

It is, perhaps, irrelevant whether in such a poisoned atmosphere Pestalozzi's methods actually benefited his pupils or not. As he himself wrote in his memoirs, the only important and lasting effect of his work was the stimulus which he had given, throughout the world, to the idea of popular education. Even in the last troubled years Pestalozzi added to his pioneer work by combining his regular school at Yverdon with a school for the poor of which he had also assumed the leadership. Rich and poor, boys and girls, all lived and learned together, to the great scandal of Yverdon society.

Pestalozzi's achievements were of such deep and lasting value throughout the world that it cannot be said that Switzerland, which had treated him quite ungratefully, was more deeply affected by them than any other country. It was rather in Germany that his ideas were most fully developed, thanks to his pupils Herbart and Froebel, and the present system of public education in Switzerland is modeled more closely on that of Germany than on a direct tradition derived from Pestalozzi.

However, the Pestalozzian spirit was a typical product of his country. Experimental and progressive schools—devised for the very rich foreigners rather than for the Swiss poor—have mush-roomed in Switzerland ever since his days. Pedagogues with un-conventional methods and theories—and usually equipped with considerable financial acumen, a virtue Pestalozzi lacked—were never found wanting. Switzerland became the country of *pensionnats* and preparatory schools. In this respect it was favored by the fact that three languages could be learned there. In their enthusiastic efforts to attract students, cities such as Neuchâtel began to make the extraordinary claim that their inhabitants spoke purer French than was spoken anywhere in France—a claim which, by sheer force of repetition the Neuchâtelois now have come to believe themselves. What generally characterizes those private schools is a phenomenon which could already be dis-cerned at Yverdon: everybody seems enthusiastic about their ethi-cal and high-minded aims and methods, with the possible excep-tion of the pupils.

In some instances the truly creative mind of Pestalozzi has found worthy successors. The reform in the teaching of music propagated by the Genevese Emile Jaques-Dalcroze was an original extension of Rousseau's and Pestalozzi's principles of natural self-development. For better or for worse, it has revolu-tionized music teaching the world over. A more recent tribute to Pestalozzi's spirit is the children's village founded at Trogen, near Appenzell, for orphans of the recent war, in which some four hundred children of formerly enemy nations are being trans-formed from hopeless wrecks into human beings. Fittingly enough, the village is named after Pestalozzi.

It may be doubtful if the world can be saved through education. It is improbable at any rate, that Pestalozzi's principles can ac-complish that task. But the very core of Pestalozzi's thinking—that Man must make himself, that only unselfish love can produce unselfish beings—this, it would seem, is a fairly reasonable prop-osition. It is a pity that the Swiss, who for so long have displayed a definite talent for pedagogy, were obliged by the nature of things to exploit their reputation as a source of income, much as they have exploited their landscape. It is not always easy to combine unselfish love with the task of earning a living.

IX: Humanitarians, Humanists, and Mediators

WITHOUT FANFARE the Swiss government, and, especially, Swiss individuals have given aid to millions of victims of the recent war—above all to children. They have distributed food, sent medical missions, and taken into their homes thousands of starving or maimed children for their rehabilitation.

A traditional refuge for the persecuted since Reformation days, Switzerland could not absorb or admit the sudden tremendous influx that swamped the rest of Europe since Hitler seized the power in Germany in 1933. Yet, relatively speaking, it proved more hospitable than other countries that could more easily have absorbed great numbers of refugees; even so, a large proportion of the Swiss population felt that they were not liberal enough. What the Swiss could—and did—do, at any rate, was to send as much relief abroad as they could manage.

Strangely enough, their medical and humanitarian missions rarely ran into iron curtains or hostile and suspicious officials—nor did their members return with their pockets stuffed with manuscripts of books exposing the countries they had visited. Funds were raised, aid was organized, as if by miracle, without the assistance of a single movie star. Simple appeals sufficed. Incredible though it may seem, it was not found expedient to coat the bitter pill of humanitarianism with a sweet, crunchy crust of promised economic returns, or to wrap it in the cellophane of an anti-Communist crusade. Somehow, the Swiss did not even seem to believe that they had come to rescue the world. They simply felt that the sight of hunger edema and of children whose limbs had been torn off was painful. In their impulsive susceptibility they decided that they could contribute their little drop in the bucket, completely forgetting to inquire if their beneficiaries approved of the capitalist system in Switzerland or were willing to thank them nicely in their newspapers. Yet, for sentimental dreamers they worked rather efficiently.

It is true that Switzerland has suffered little during the war years. It lost no lives and no property except through some inadvertencies like the bombing of Schaffhausen by United States aircraft in 1944. Its sufferings were confined to such minor annoyances as rationing, lack of heating fuel, and the hardships wrought by the general mobilization. Swiss humanitarianism is perhaps motivated, to some extent, by the bad conscience that often goes with wealth, especially if the wealth has been preserved through being neutral while others bled.

It must also be said that the Swiss as a nation never actually went so far as to deprive themselves of anything essential in order to assist others. Even their hospitality for refugees is qualified: they may stay in Switzerland only if they do not work. This qualification is necessary in a country which has only a limited employment capacity, but at the same time it tends to restrict the right of asylum to refugees who own some money.

Switzerland is not the only country with a record of humanitarian work without political strings attached. Norway, after the First World War, certainly did more than its share to relieve famine-stricken Europe. Sweden, another neutral, has done work much along the same lines as that of the Swiss. Switzerland is, moreover, very limited in the kind of aid it can extend. Aside from dairy products, it can spare no food. If it wishes to keep a favorable balance of payments, it cannot spend money or credits on the purchase of food abroad for the purpose of redistributing it gratis. Medical and pharmaceutic supplies, technical skill, and experience in social work are the only articles the Swiss can offer —aside from unselfish and devoted men and women.

Thus the Swiss approach to humanitarianism has developed differently than elsewhere. Human sympathy, selfless work, and the qualities of the heart in general have been placed above the material wherewithal of charity. There is a considerable margin between Pestalozzi and Herbert Hoover. Between Andrew Carnegie and Henri Dunant (the founder of the Red Cross) few parallels are possible.

In some countries a humanitarian is a person who sacrifices large sums for noble purposes—the larger the sum, the greater his humanitarianism. Unfortunately, this definition makes it as difficult for ninety-nine percent of the population to be humanitarians as it is for a camel to smoke a doctor. In Switzerland the rich and the poor have divided their labor in these matters: the banker who gives money is a philanthropist; the poor man who gives his life is a humanitarian.

Usually Switzerland's humanitarians started out as would-be philanthropists. Only after adverse experiences did they reluctantly accept the fact that business and Christian charity do not mix. What made them great is that, once arrived at this point, they opted for Christian charity, no matter what its consequences. This was, by and large, the story of young Pestalozzi; it was also that of Henri Dunant.

II

There were all kinds of reasons why the Red Cross should have been founded in Switzerland and why its international headquarters should be located there. Switzerland's neutrality was guaranteed by the major European Powers; the Swiss government, as a disinterested party, was ideally suited to promote an idea like the Red Cross; the central location of Switzerland made it a natural headquarters. None of these, however, were immediate reasons. The immediate reason was the obsession of one man.

Henri Dunant was born in Geneva, in 1828, of a solid family of businessmen. He spent a sheltered youth, and as a young man he sowed his first humanitarian oats by completely abandoning himself to the favorite pastime of his native city. He visited the poor, joined young Christian men's associations, and fought vice with immense earnestness. His family, disquieted at seeing him make a primary activity out of what should merely have been a hygienic exercise for his soul, encouraged him to serve God in more positive ways by increasing the family fortune.

Henri went to Algeria, only recently conquered by the French. Temporarily dismissing theological speculation, he enthusiastically threw himself into grain speculation. He bought some land, on which he built several gigantic mills, only to discover that he needed more land to give work to the mills. To buy more land, he thought, would be easy. Back in Geneva, he painted the potentialities of Algeria in the most glowing colors and brought glitter into the eyes of the Genevese. A share-holding society— *Société anonyme des moulins de Mons-Djémila*—was founded, and not a small part of his family's fortune was sunk into it. This eventually proved to be Dunant's undoing, as well as a great boon to humanity.

The lands which he wanted to acquire, it turned out, were not to be acquired easily. The French authorities stalled, raised objections, and ended by selling land to other concessionaires, who apparently were abler wire-pullers than Dunant. His mills were slowly going to pieces, his capital began to crumble, and the shareholders began to ask questions. Dunant, who had petitioned about everybody in the French government except Napoleon III himself, decided to try his last chance.

His approach to the emperor was thoughtful and indirect. To obtain land for his mills, Dunant sat down to write a book entitled, *The Empire of Charlemagne Reestablished; or, The Holy Roman Empire Reconstituted by His Majesty the Emperor Napoleon III, by J. -Henry Dunant, director and president of the Financial and Industrial Society of Mons-Djémila (Algeria), member of the Asiatic Society of Paris, of the Oriental Society of France, of the Geographic Societies of Paris and Geneva, of the Historical Society of Algiers, etc.* The book, which conclusively proved that Napoleon was heir to Augustus and of which one magnificent sample copy was printed, was intended to help Dunant gain the emperor's ear. To approach Napoleon, Dunant chose a most opportune moment: the eve of the battle of Solferino (June 24, 1859), which was to decide the issue of the Italian *Risorgimento.*

Somehow Dunant did not seem to have given much thought, before that day, to the fact that wars were made of battles and that his Algerian mills or Charlemagne's succession were of no particular concern to anybody at that particular moment. To his great surprise, he found himself caught in one of the bloodiest engagements in the history of warfare, an engagement which cost some thirty-three thousand casualties within ten hours. The tidy and well-mannered Dunant, in impeccable white clothes, with the re-established empire of Charlemagne in his pocket and the mills of Mons-Djémila in his mind, suddenly forgot why he had come.

Before his eyes an unceasing stream of wounded and dying were dumped and left to their own devices. The military surgeons had not expected fifty-five casualties per minute, and there was nothing, it seemed to them, that they could do. Dunant, however, did not reason. As in a trance, he began to wash their wounds, to call the townspeople to his aid, to give orders, to distribute tasks, to round up surgeons, to procure bandages, water, and food. In the nearby town of Castiglione he continued his work, two days after the battle, without having slept and hardly having eaten.

The unknown civilian, in his crumpled white suit, was now a legendary figure. It was not till June 28 that he remembered Charlemagne. Napoleon could not receive him, but he glanced at the book which Dunant finally managed to have transmitted to him. To his regret, His Majesty could not accept the dedication in view of political circumstances.

After busying himself in several military hospitals in northern Italy, Dunant returned to Geneva via Paris. It was not easy to shake himself from the nightmare he had witnessed. Mons-Djémila was still pending, but there was nothing to do but wait. In the meantime he wrote a book and relived his nightmare.

Un Souvenir de Solférino was an impressive account of what he had seen and a powerful plea for the establishment of a neutral organization for the care of the wounded in war. Published in 1862, it immediately made a profound impression. The queen of Prussia recommended it to her husband, and Monsieur Gustave Moynier, president of the Society for Public Usefulness of Geneva and member of at least half a dozen international charitable societies, felt that Dunant had a good idea. Gustave Moynier was a philanthropist rather than a humanitarian; efficient rather than warmhearted. Under his auspices a committee was founded and an international conference was planned for the end of 1863. Dunant set out on a tour to conquer the courts of Europe for his project. His frantic pleas, his relentlessness were irresistible. One is reminded of old Pestalozzi driving Alexander I against a wall. By the end of the year an unofficial conference took place in Geneva, with delegates from sixteen countries attending, and in the following year the Swiss government arranged for an official conference.*

Dunant's fundamental and only original idea—the neutral status of the projected organization—was opposed from the start by Moynier. That it was, nevertheless, adopted by the preparatory conference was Dunant's last triumph.

In 1864, when the first Geneva Convention was signed, General Henri Dufour was president of the conference, Gustave Moynier was vice president, and Dunant was a spectator. The philanthropists had fully succeeded in crowding out the humanitarian. This, however, was merely the beginning of a long series of disappointments which ultimately transformed the humanitarian into a misanthropic paranoiac.

The catastrophe of Dunant's life came three years after he had founded the Red Cross. In 1867 Napoleon III, who had received Dunant very politely on a previous occasion, cut short his Algerian hopes. He had no control over the sale of lands, he claimed. Dunant already had lost a small fortune in stock exchange speculations through which he had hoped to save the mills. Bankruptcy was inevitable now. It was all very well for Dunant to have been the savior of hundreds of thousands of future lives—but this weighed as nothing against the gravest sin that his century, and particularly his city, could conceive of: he had squandered capital. To his dying day neither his creditors nor the Society for Public Usefulness were to forget or forgive his crime. Dunant left Geneva, a black sheep, a wastrel, a frivolous dreamer who had spent thousands of his creditors' francs for the promotion of irresponsible humanitarianism.

Dunant almost vanished from the scene. He had other projects in the meantime—a Universal International Society for the Reno-

---

* It was in deference to the Swiss government that the Geneva Convention adopted as its symbol the Swiss flag with inverted colors: a red cross.

vation of the Orient, among others, through which he planned to place the Levant under Napoleon's protection and to create a Jewish state in Palestine—but they understandably came to nothing. He still frequented the powerful and the titled, but as soon as he left their doorsteps he was a tramp, homeless and often without food. Undermined by illness and still pursued by his indefatigable Genevese creditors, he drifted between Paris, London, and Germany. His family, ashamed of his vagrant existence, finally sent him a small pension.

In 1887 Dunant gave up his wanderings. In the small village of Heiden, in the canton of Appenzell, he entrusted his breaking health to a doctor and began to live a hermit's life. He was practically forgotten and was but slowly emerging from the darkness of his persecution mania when a Swiss-German newspaperman made the discovery that the founder of the Red Cross was living in destitution in a small village. Other newspapers immediately took up the story, and the hermit of Heiden, with his patriarchal white beard, suddenly re-emerged into publicity. Pilgrims began to arrive to see the great man, collections were taken, and pensions were showered on him. In 1901 he was awarded the first Nobel Peace Prize, along with Frédéric Passy, the founder of the Interparliamentary Union for Arbitration and Peace.

One would be mistaken, however, in assuming that his creditors had forgotten or forgiven. When Dunant was awarded the Nobel prize, they even attempted to have it seized in settlement for his debt. Nor was his position as founder of the Red Cross universally recognized—at least not in Geneva. Dunant, who was not exempt from vanity, spent a large part of his time establishing his historical share in the adoption of the Geneva Convention by re-editing his *Souvenir de Solférino*, by newspaper articles, and by writing a work on *The Origins of the Red Cross*. It was the one achievement of his life to which he constantly returned, for all else was failure.

It was in a querulous mood that the misanthropist of Heiden spent his last ten years. His humanitarianism became entirely restricted to humanity in the abstract; his passion became a passion for public recognition. His hatred of Geneva, which had denied him recognition, now extended to all organized states, to all organized religion—but it subsided as soon as a grand duchess or an ambassador flattered him with their friendship. Indeed, the true Henri Dunant, the active humanitarian had died long ago; when the rest of him died, in 1910, it was a frustrated philanthropist, who found great satisfaction in leaving his Nobel prize money to the charitable institutions of Norway and Switzerland rather than to his creditors, whose claims had lapsed.

III

Don Quixote in Switzerland is a dreamer, a preacher, or a teacher. Like Rousseau, Pestalozzi, and Henri Dunant, he is more likely to write books than to read them. Where Don Quixote tried to save humanity with his lance, they hoped to achieve the same end by persuasion and education. In fact, they were prisoners who had broken loose from their ivory towers. Life had somehow forced them into action, and they usually were lost and bewildered in their unexpected freedom.

They were typical of their nation only in so far as every nation has its own typical exceptions. The rule for the Swiss thinkers was the ivory tower rather than the wide world; humanism rather than humanitarianism. Yet, if the typical Swiss humanitarian was actually a humanist who had broken loose, the typical Swiss humanist was a humanitarian who did not quite dare to break loose. He stayed in his ivory tower, but from there, unlike other humanists, he sought to reach and influence the multitude outside.

Switzerland was a center of the humanities even before there was a Switzerland and before there was such a thing as humanism. The abbey and school of Saint Gall began to flourish at the time of Charlemagne and became one of the very few beacons of learning of the early Middle Ages. By the time the first Swiss league came into existence, however, the abbey and the school had already greatly declined. When Switzerland reached the height of its political power, at the close of the fifteenth century, Swiss cultural life had sunk to its lowest.

At the same time, the growing prosperity and the central location of the Swiss cities began to attract some of the foremost men of their age. Foremost among these cities was Basel, where Eras-

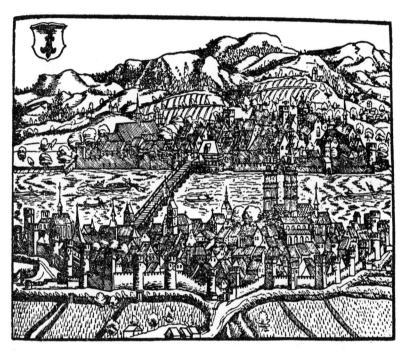

BASEL IN 1548

Woodcut in a sixteenth-century chronicle

mus of Rotterdam fixed himself in 1521. With the printer Fro-
ben, Erasmus published the first printed editions of the religious
and classical Greek and Roman texts. His contemporaries in Basel
included Hans Holbein, and that most inspired of all quacks,
Theophrastus Bombastus von Hohenheim, better known as
Paracelsus. Though Erasmus left Basel after the introduction of
the Reformation, the city has remained a center of humanism to
this very day. With its venerable university and through its location at the intersection of the Swiss, French, and German frontiers, it certainly was ideally suited for its role. Its aristocratic
government, moreover, and the narrowness of its territorial resources, lent it a character very similar to that of Geneva.

It is true that at times the intellectual atmosphere of Basel became so rarified—particularly in the seventeenth and eighteenth
centuries—that there seemed to be little left except the university.
For one thing, the city suffered from a concentration of mathe-
matical geniuses. The Bernoulli family, Leonard Euler, and lesser
lights contributed more to the progress of mathematics in barely
a century than whole nations during their entire existence. Isak
Iselin, the humanitarian friend of Pestalozzi and physiocracy's
ambassador to Switzerland, though he thought of himself as a
humanist, left nothing of permanent value. It was only in the
nineteenth century that Basel came into its own again, thanks
mainly to the presence of Jakob Burckhardt.

Jakob Burckhardt is chiefly known as the author of *The Culture of the Renaissance in Italy*. Ever since Professor Lynn Thorn-
dike, of Columbia University, has proven that the Renaissance
never existed, Burckhardt has fallen into discredit. However, the
existence or non-existence of the Renaissance was entirely irrelevant in the case of Burckhardt. If it did not exist, it had to be
invented, for to the man Burckhardt it was absolutely essential
that it should have existed. Born in 1818, the son of a clergyman
and the scion of an old patrician family, Burckhardt studied for
the ministry to please his father, but his interests, from the very beginning, lay elsewhere. He had planned and built his ivory tower
to his own specifications while still a young man, and by 1839 it
was ready for occupancy. In that year, with the consent of his
father, he switched from theology to the study of history.

Possibly the image of an ivory tower is out of place in Burck-hardt's case—at least it would seem so in the light of a poem which he wrote during his youth, containing the following lines:

> Let me sink deep in the Tyrrhenian sea!
> It is the stillest of all graves!
> There lie, since times of old, the naves
> Of Carthaginian silver ships. Let me
> Of such antiquities be curator,
> And let devour each other the rabble of knaves,
> That silence may return as once before.

Burckhardt believed with all his soul—and every one of his writings expressed that belief—that the highest achievement of man lies in art, that everything else is merely instrumental. For him there was no progress in history; there were no nations, only cultural units. The fountain of all culture was in Italy, a country which in itself had become a work of art.

For politics he had no interest whatever. One day he entered his lecture room in the university of Basel, where he had taught since 1858, and pulled a newspaper out of his pocket. A minor riot had taken place in London because of increased bread prices. The trouble occurred in Pall Mall. Now Pall Mall was not far from the Royal Academy, and in the Royal Academy there hung a cartoon by Leonardo da Vinci which had never been copied. What if it had been destroyed? The lesson of the bread riot, Burckhardt concluded, was that as many works of art as possible should be photographed.

This was a most un-Rousseauan attitude, a most un-Pestalozzian way of viewing things, but it was not far from Henri Dunant's, except that Burckhardt was too contemplative to consider the foundation of a neutral international organization for the pre-vention of damage to works of art in wartime and revolutions. Nor was his attitude typically un-Swiss. As neutrals during all the recent conflicts, the intellectuals of Switzerland by and large felt called upon to deplore the destruction of cultural values with far greater intensity than the destruction of humans, and at the same time were contemplating the general carnage with a philo-sophical detachment which would have done honor to Burck-hardt.

If Burckhardt had merely written books, he would have been —despite Professor Thorndyke and others—one of the finest historians in the tradition of Voltaire and one of the very few great humanists of modern times. Yet he also had another side: he was a great and inspiring teacher. He was not writing for a small, scholarly coterie, but for the educated public at large, and he was not contented with imparting the dry results of his investigations to his students, but made them live in the world of beauty in which he lived. His ivory tower was large enough for all humanity, if they but cared to come in. He cared nothing for the large and ugly world in which he lived—and at the same time he was an intense local patriot who cultivated even the dialect of his native city, refused all offers to teach at the great universities of Europe, and took part with utmost conviviality in the local social life. In fact, with his belief in the existence of the Renaissance and the supremacy of beauty, he was a very enviable man. Without realizing it, he—who lived but in the fifteenth and sixteenth centuries—was to remain one of the most attractive monuments of the Victorian age.

Among Burckhardt's friends was his fellow professor at the university of Basel, Friedrich Nietzsche. Nietzsche was German, not Swiss, but his long sojourn in Basel (from 1869 to 1879) certainly was the most important formative period of his life. It was Burckhardt who was Nietzsche's guide through the Renaissance; it was Burckhardt who, by raising the state to an esthetic ideal, prepared—unwittingly, perhaps, the ground for Nietzsche's identification of beauty with power. In this respect, it is true, both were equally endebted to a Frenchman, Stendhal, who was the first to glorify unscrupulous Renaissance villains as heroic embodiments of vital force.

Burckhardt, Nietzsche, and Wagner, this outwardly disparate trinity of the nineteenth century, cannot be thought of independently of each other. Was it pure accident that all three spent the most important years of their lives in the same country, and in intimate contact with each other? Wagner's synthesis was, it may well be argued, an attempt at the same esthetic culmination that Burckhardt saw in the Renaissance; and Nietzsche's break with Wagner occurred only when Wagner began to backtrack into Christian renunciation, while Nietzsche more and more positively affirmed every manifestation of the vital force. Among the three, only Burckhardt kept his head.

I V

It has been said that Burckhardt was the historian of the Renaissance, Nietzsche its prophet, and Conrad Ferdinand Meyer its poet. Such preoccupation in the most inhibited of all centuries with the least inhibited era of Christian civilization may seem puzzling. A clue to the puzzle, if needed, may be found in the approach of these three men to their favorite subject. Nietzsche proclaimed what he lacked most to be the principle of life: power. Burckhardt escaped from action into contemplation of action. Meyer fled from life, which he was constitutionally unable to live fully, into a dream world of historical fiction.

In Zurich, where Conrad Ferdinand Meyer was born in 1825, the literary life was not overshadowed, as it was in Basel, by the university. From 1336 to 1798 the town had been ruled as a corporative state by its aristocracy and its prosperous artisan and merchant guilds. As a silk and textile center it began to rival Lyons by the seventeenth century. With industrial expansion came intellectual activity—an activity which in the late eighteenth century made Zurich the capital of Swiss nationalist and liberal aspirations. The nationalists and liberals, it is true, clashed with the ruling oligarchy, but shortly after Meyer's birth the inevitable happened: Zurich adopted a liberal constitution and from that time on grew by leaps and bounds into a small-scale metropolis. The arts and the intellect found in Zurich a market place where they could profitably sell their finished products; but their raw materials, their inspiration, was largely imported from elsewhere.

Conrad Ferdinand Meyer was closer in spirit to Basel's humanism than to Zurich's preoccupation with material values. His spiritual home was in Italy, which he knew as intimately as Burckhardt knew it. From what he had seen and learned there he constituted for himself an ideal of esthetic classicism which gave his novels, short stories, and poems finish and perfection, but only at the expense of spontaneity. Few writers have been more admired and less read, despite the intriguing titles of some of his books: *The Shot from the Pulpit; Plautus in the Nunnery; The Monk's Wedding; Pescara's Temptation;* and *Angela Borgia.*

Except the great novel *George Jenatsch* and the briefer *Gustav Adolf's Page,* which take place in the Thirty Years War, Meyer's novels were all laid in a Renaissance setting. Their refined elegance, their perfection of style, their delicate irony, their cameo-like quality call for a comparison with Anatole France. It is an unfortunate comparison, for it reveals only too plainly how far Meyer was removed from the Latinity for which he strove and in which he had chosen to build his dream world. Meyer's Italy, like the Italy of a Burckhardt or a Nietzsche or even a Goethe, was always an Italy seen by a German temperament, a longed-for and nostalgic refuge—how different from the Italy of a Fabrizio del Dongo, the concrete, unmetaphysical Italy!

It was, moreover, an Italy seen by a Swiss, for Meyer could never quite forget that he was a son of Zwingli's Zurich. To him, esthetic values never could transcend ethical values. When he died, in 1895, he had begun to write a work dealing with the Reformation in Zurich, a work in which he intended to praise Zwingli, but Zwingli, though certainly representative of the Renaissance, did little to further its esthetic ideals. Burckhardt, who in one of his works spoke of a "special dispensation from moral law" as applying to extraordinary individuals, almost kept spiritual company with Stendhal's Julien Sorel and Dostoevski's Raskolnikov. Meyer never really strayed so far from his native ground. Toward the end of his life he was right back where he had begun, at one in mind with his solid countrymen Johannes von Müller and Sismondi.

Gottfried Keller, Meyer's contemporary on Zurich's literary stage, was in some respects his antithesis. Whereas Meyer, like Amiel, had escaped from the life of action into humanism and esthetics, Keller escaped from the world of esthetics into the world of action. Having lamentably failed as an art student in Munich, he vigorously embraced the Liberal cause, taking part in the armed partisans' raids on the reactionary cantons which preceded the Sonderbund War. Finally, after several years of hardship in Berlin, he returned to Zurich, with the realization that his mission was to be a writer. Yet in his writings he did not flee into the past. His chief works, the novels *Der Grüne Heinrich* and *Martin Salander*, were concerned with the vital problems of his time. They were *Bildungsromane*—development of character novels—somewhat in the tradition of Jeremias Gotthelf's *Uli*, though they shunned Gotthelf's realism and were, from the artistic point of view, closer to Goethe's *Wilhelm Meister*.

The bourgeois, Carlylian, goggle-eyed admiration for the unscrupulous hero, the irresponsible artist, which flourished in the nineteenth century until Tolstoy deflated it with mighty jabs—held no attraction for Keller, who in Munich had had first-hand experience with the shoddier side of artistic irresponsibility. However, unlike Tolstoy, who went all the way back to Rousseau, and past Rousseau to primitive Christianity, Keller was a nineteenth-century bourgeois himself, and a Swiss one at that. His *Der Grüne Heinrich*, largely autobiographical, approvingly described the transformation of an irresponsible bohemian into a responsible citizen. Keller himself, in 1861, combined his literary activities with the office of First Secretary of the Canton of Zurich.

Even his political opinions slowly underwent a metamorphosis. The radical of 1848, the sharp critic of Gotthelf's complacent conservatism, turned into a conservative himself. Like Burckhardt or Nietzsche, he had little use for the industrial revolution and for the petty materialism, the cheap get-rich-quick philosophy, that seemed to have taken hold of his countrymen. But where the humanists had taken refuge in their ivory towers of estheticism, Gottfried Keller remained deeply rooted in his country: the spirits of Haller and Gotthelf descended upon him, the ideal of the rough and rustic simplicity of the old Swiss became the text of his sermons. The *People of Seldwyla*, a sharp criticism of his countrymen's new way of life, was written in the form of delightful short stories. It was followed by the more ponderous *Martin Salander*, the long-winded Swiss equivalent of Turgeniev's brief and elegant *Fathers and Sons*. Keller was not artistically detached, as Turgeniev was. He roundly condemned his own generation, the materialist ex-revolutionaries, and hopefully represented the younger generation as harking back to older and

simpler times. With all his outward appearance of a nineteenth-
century writer, Keller, the most representative of all Swiss
authors, should be named in a breath with Haller rather than
with Meyer.

v

An entirely different kettle of fish was Carl Spitteler, perhaps
the most baffling figure on the modern literary scene. Almost unknown on this continent, Spitteler is usually classified as an
anachronism, and thus disposed of. Yet there is nothing anachronistic about him except the fact that he chose to express himself
through epic poems. In all other respects he was the perfect
product of the late nineteenth century and, particularly, of Burckhardt's and Nietzsche's Basel. It was a disquieting product.

Though born in Liestal, the chief town of Basel-Land, where
rancor against Basel-City was still rife, Spitteler studied at the
university of Basel. There the tutelary deity was Schopenhauer,
from whose founts Burckhardt, Nietzsche, and Wagner were already drinking in deep draughts. Whereas these three were only
taking from Schopenhauer what they needed, Spitteler took
everything. His mind became filled with Hindu philosophy,
pantheism, Oriental, Christian, and Greek myths, Nietzschean
supermen, Wagnerian world cataclysms, and Dostoevskian symbols. In due time, by the turn of the century, Dr. Freud added his
bit, and the progress of the machine age added Wellsian visions to
an already generous imagination.

With all this, Spitteler had a leaning toward Swiss monu-
mentalism: the epic poem was his dish. Taking the figures of
Greek mythology, he changed gods into supermen and Olympus
into a superworld. Of the myths, he kept only what suited him
and invented the rest, associating Behemoth with Prometheus,
Zeus with Christ, metampsychosis with messianism. The gods
mingle with robots, elevators transport passengers through the
celestial spheres, and majestic speeches and images alternate with
burlesque modernisms. This is true of his first epic, *Prometheus
and Epimetheus,* which he later recast into *Prometheus the Suf-
ferer,* and of *The Olympic Spring,* for which he invented his own
metric system. Most of his other works, except the autobio-

graphical prose novel, *Imago,* he regarded as mere preparatory exercises.

The Olympic Spring undoubtedly was Spitteler's greatest and most disquieting parable—disquieting not because of what Spitteler meant, but because of what might be made of it. In the first part the "chosen manhood of a coming generation," issuing from the womb of night, is led by a "Führer" to the brink of day and, via the Christian Paradise, ascends to its ultimate destination, Olympus. The next part describes the struggle for the possession of the "bride," Hera—the symbol of power. The artist and the strong one—who already were the antithetical pair in Prometheus and Epimetheus—are the contestants. The artist wins, but the strong one seizes the power by ruse; at last the two make peace, and the community of supermen can now develop in full freedom. This development fills the third part of the epic; the fourth and last part deals with the salvation of the base generations of non-Olympian manhood, effected through Messiah, the son of the strong one. By suffering the fate of mankind without succumbing to its weight he shows humanity the way to salvation, which is found in Olympus, "the workshop where a better life is made."

The extraordinary poetic power of Spitteler's epics has never been questioned. Their philosophical content is something else again. Offhand, it would seem like a blending of all great myths, a reconciliation between Nietzsche and Christ. On second thought, it may just as well be so much confused and pseudo-mystical hogwash, which found its culmination in the writings of Messrs. Alfred Rosenberg and Adolf Hitler. What seems certain is that Spitteler achieved neither a synthesis nor a transvaluation of all values, but succeeded admirably in expressing the confusion that besets the poetic mind in a world divorced from any unified spiritual tradition. Spitteler was not anachronistic. His timeliness was merely hidden by his poetic genius, but in truth it may be said that with him the reign of the swami in the world of Western letters had begun. There is, as yet, no end in sight.

Spitteler * died at the end of 1924, an Olympian himself both

* Official confirmation of his genius was made in 1919, when he received the Nobel Prize in literature.

in his outward aspect and in his detachment from the events of the baser world. A few months later died Dr. Rudolf Steiner, founder of the anthroposophic movement, a doctrine which is as difficult to define as to pronounce. A native of Austria-Hungary, Rudolf Steiner found his haven, fittingly enough, at Dornach near Basel. He had dabbled in theosophy before he decided that the universe had to be explained in the terms of Man, whatever that means. To this effect he wrote spiritualist and occult guides and constructed the Goetheanum at Dornach, the anthroposophist high temple which somehow was supposed to represent the fundamental proportions of Man. The Goetheanum, which burned down completely, but has been reconstructed, is now flourishing under Steiner's widow. The leadership of the anthroposophists passed to Steiner's Swiss disciple, Albert Steffen, the most important of contemporary Swiss writers.

As a writer rather than a high priest, Steffen, who was born in Berne in 1884, makes an almost normal impression. The reason for this is that he is firmly rooted in the Swiss tradition. His mysticism is not extravagant, as Spitteler's was, and his practical approach to life is essentially in agreement with Haller's and Jeremias Gotthelf's; his hatred of big cities and his longing for the simplicity of nature are the same.

His metaphysics is something else again. Here oriental and occidental mysticism are fused, but with a strong admixture of Pestalozzian pedagogy. The chief enemy of man is the animal in him; love is the only means by which man can save himself; religion is mutual social responsibility. Innocence, in his scheme, is not personified by the animal, but by the plant, and the plant in turn is a symbol of childhood, and so forth. Steffen tried to improve mankind through his parables. His philosophy of sweetness, love, and light, not very unlike that of Maeterlinck, was extremely popular in Germany around 1933. Anthroposophy, it would seem, has not succeeded any better than simple Christianity. It is still going strong, though, and like the Burckhardtian humanists, like the Spittelerian Olympians, the Steinerian anthroposophists continue to look upon the world with considerable contemplative wisdom from their comfortable little corner in Switzerland.

VI

In 1916, in a Zurich cabaret named Voltaire, an earnest youth, aged twenty, who cultivated an impassive eye under a beribboned monocle, could be heard holding forth in French. "Put all words into a hat," he said, "and draw them by lot." The object of the procedure was the writing of poetry. The name of the now forgotten young man was Tristan Tzara. The school of poets he fathered became known, for several depressing years, as Dadaists. It was not the first time that Switzerland had functioned as a literary maternity hospital, nor was the occasion, spectacular though it may seem, of enduring consequence.

Swiss literature, in a sense, is a contradiction in terms. There is a German-Swiss literature, a French-Swiss literature, and—though only just beginning—an Italian-Swiss literature. A certain spiritual affinity exists in all three, but there has been very little direct mutual influence. The French-Swiss have rarely condescended to read the products of their Alemannic cousins. The German-Swiss were less impervious, but they, in their turn, usually looked upon French-Swiss literature as on something foreign. On the other hand, Swiss literature as a whole, be it written in French or in German, has greatly influenced the writers of Switzerland's neighbors. The most important function of Swiss writers has always been one of mediation. This function became clearly defined by the middle of the eighteenth century, when the high priests of Swiss letters began to spread the gospel of Milton and Shakespeare on the Continent.

Muralt, with his *Lettres sur les Anglais et les Français*, had made a beginning. But Muralt was a gentleman, not a prophet. The prophets, the destroyers of the French idols of classicism, were two young citizens of Zurich: Johann Jakob Bodmer (1689–1783) and Johann Jakob Breitinger (1701–1776). The first of the two Johann Jakobs was an ex-student of theology who had turned into a bookseller and a professor of Swiss history; the second was a professor of Hebrew. Both were immensely learned and immensely earnest. They began, modestly enough, by founding a magazine called *Discourse der Mahlern* (*The Painters' Discourses*), inspired as they were by Steele's *Spectator*. In it they crusaded against the Baroque excesses of German poetry, against the "unnatural" stiffness of the French, and proclaimed the virtues of the English, who were to serve as models for a true German literature.

In their war they found inspiration in two rather disparate sources: Milton and Rousseau. Milton suited their Puritanism; Rousseau suited their longing for what they considered natural simplicity and freedom of emotions. *Paradise Lost*, in their eyes, was the meeting ground of both Milton and Rousseau. Here Man was painted in his natural goodness, and the devils, with all their artillery, which struck Voltaire as ludicrous, struck Bodmer and Breitinger as the protagonists of destructive civilization. No wonder, then, that Bodmer, though not overfamiliar with the English language, translated Milton's epic. He also translated Butler's *Hudibras* and Thomas Percy's ballads. At the same time he and Breitinger poured forth numerous critical and esthetic writings, which soon were to clash with a belated champion of French classicism, the stiff and ponderous Saxon, Johann Christoph Gottsched. It was a battle of giants, where each of the contestant parties tried to crush the foe under ever heavier loads of pedantry and ever deadlier shafts of academic scorn.

When all was over, the two Swiss emerged as the victors. Their triumph was aided by the fact that actually they had been beating dead dogs, but perhaps it would have been delayed a little longer but for the intervention of a talented young German writer. Gotthold Ephraim Lessing enthusiastically embraced the cause of the young Zurich rebels, adding his own polemic artillery to theirs till poor Gottsched lay gasping in the dust and expired while his persecutors were still mercilessly hacking away at him. However, while the two Johann Jakobs were arid pedants, Lessing was able to create living works.

It was at about that time that Shakespeare began to become a German author. Even before Lessing, in his *Hamburgische Dramaturgie*, blew mighty fanfares to welcome the newly naturalized citizen, the Swiss had been doing some spadework for the Bard. The first German translation of twenty-two of Shakespeare's dramas was the work of Christoph Martin Wieland. The most celebrated German poet of his time, Wieland had spent many years in Zurich, where the translation was published and splendidly illustrated by Solomon Gessner.

Another German friend and disciple of Bodmer and Breitinger was Klopstock, the author of the tedious epic poem *The Messiah* and of a number of inflated odes, but nonetheless an influential figure, for he completed Lessing's work of putting German literature on its own feet. The scene was set for *Sturm und Drang* and for romanticism. Racine had been slain, Rousseau's *Nouvelle Héloïse* had filled rivers of tears since 1761, *Ossian* had been wailing and plucking his harp since 1765, and in 1774 *Werther* appeared and caused an epidemic of suicides. With *Werther*, Goethe turned the tables on European literature. For the first time Frenchmen were reading a German author and actually imitating him.

VII

Not only Lessing, Wieland, Goethe, and Herder stood in debt to Switzerland. Kant digested and incorporated into his system a large port of Rousseau. Fichte was inspired by Pestalozzi. Schiller was planning to write a William Tell. By the year 1800 these men were only vaguely known outside their country. It took another Swiss mediator to introduce them to the rest of Europe. This time it was a woman.

Germaine Necker was born in the Paris in 1766. Her father was Jacques Necker, the Genevese banker and, it was hoped, financial wizard, who was entrusted with the impossible task of saving France from bankruptcy in 1776 and again in 1789. Her mother was Suzanne Curchod, who in her brilliant salon in Paris never regretted for a moment that she had not married her erstwhile suitor Edward Gibbon. Brought up in Paris, Germaine knew little of Geneva except that Rousseau came from there. By 1786 she had grown up to be a not very attractive, but intellectually formidable, young lady and was married off to a Swedish diplomat, Baron Staël-Holstein, who later became ambassador to the French Republic. Four years later her father left France, accompanied by the jeers of the court as well as the rabble, and fixed himself on his estate at Coppet, on the Lake of Geneva. While he busied himself writing on the financial causes of the

French Revolution, Germaine, who mildly welcomed the fall of the *ancien régime*, stayed on in Paris.

Shortly after the September massacres of 1792, Madame de Staël decided that things were becoming too hot and left France. After a stay at Coppet, she proceeded to England, where she graced the circle of liberal emigrés headed by Talleyrand, and after Robespierre's fall, in 1794, she returned to her old hunting ground in Paris. Her husband, who had granted her an amicable separation in 1797, had the good grace to die not long afterward.

During the happy years of the Directory, Madame de Staël lorded it over all that was fashionable, important, and artistic. Her salon, though perhaps less polished, was no less brilliant than her mother's had been. She made politics, she made reputations, and she wrote books. *Delphine*, published in 1802, though some readers thought that its style sounded like a translation from the German and that it was written in "Swiss," was an immediate success. Nevertheless, had it not been for Madame de Staël's personal quarrel with Napoleon, she probably would be all but forgotten.

The reason for her quarrel, according to Madame de Staël, was her disapproval of Napoleon's dictatorial ambitions. According to others, her anger dated from the day when the First Consul refused to admit her, on the pretext that he was in his bath and in no state to receive a lady. "But a genius has no sex!" Germaine is said to have exclaimed. It is not clear whom she meant—herself or Napoleon.

Whatever the reasons for the quarrel, it became plain that one of the two had to leave Paris. Since Bonaparte was even more firmly entrenched than Germaine, it was she who was ordered to leave and forbidden to set foot within a radius of forty leagues. Her exile was in many ways providential. By sharpening her conflict with Napoleon, it forced her into an increasingly outspoken opposition, which she had not at first intended, until in her great posthumous work, her *Considerations on the Principal Events of the French Revolution*, she formulated the guiding doctrines of French liberalism under the Bourbon Restoration. A more immediate consequence of her exile was her reluctant decision to undertake a journey to Germany, where, she hoped, her triumphal reception would wipe out the injury done her by Napoleon. She had not been in Germany long when she discovered a whole new world of revolutionary ideas; she made it her mission to communicate them to France.

During her long exile at Coppet and Geneva, which was interrupted by trips to Italy, Austria, and France, Madame de Staël worked on the book of her life, *De l'Allemagne*. The occasion for this work was a whirlwind visit through Germany in 1803, during which she managed to assimilate everything there was to be known about Germany, the Germans, German philosophy, and German literature, and all this despite the fact that she never ceased talking to the men whom she had come to interview. Goethe, on the news of her approach, took to flight, but was finally cornered. She found him stiff and pedantic. Goethe found her intrusive.

Having talked philosophy with the philosophers, politics with the statesmen, literature with the poets, religion with the pastors, and love with all, the impetuous lady steamrollered back home, and with the assiduity of an American newspaperman just back from Russia, wrote her book. She had loved everything in Germany. France—particularly Napoleon's France—had everything to learn. The Germans were peace loving. They had no national prejudices. They were honest and always kept their word. The daughters of German pastors were blonde and virtuous. German philosophy was sublime. German poetry was the poetry of the future.

Napoleon had the complete edition of her book impounded and stamped into pulp. The work, he declared, was "un-French."

When Napoleon fell, Madame de Staël's book triumphed in France. It was the clarion call for romanticism. Its very shortcomings suited it better for the role. She understood neither Goethe nor Kant, but she knew how to make both Goethe and Kant palatable to the average educated Frenchman. Nearest to her heart was not the awe-inspiring Olympus of Weimar, but the Gothic medievalism of the brothers Schlegel, whose opinions break forth from almost every one of her pages. Her Germany was the fairytale world of Tieck and Delamotte-Fouqué. Her success was remarkable. It was so complete that even to the present day little is known outside Germany of German literature other than Hoffmann's Gothic tales, Grimm's fairy stories, and other assorted collections of spooks, elves, monsters, and shining knights. Goethe largely remained a mere name; Madame de Staël's Germany became an association of ideas.

On Switzerland, Madame de Staël had little influence. Her mansion in Coppet, where she spent her years of exile, became a sort of latter-day Ferney, where Constant, Sismondi, Châteaubriand, Mme Récamier, August Wilhelm Schlegel, and an unceasing stream of visitors rubbed elbows with each other and paid homage to their hostess. But one would not have suspected that Coppet was laid in the landscape of Julie and Emile; it was rather a Parisian salon in exile. Admirer though she was of the simple and virtuous ways of German pastors' daughters, Madame de Staël failed to appreciate these qualities in her own Switzerland. Indeed, she had the misfortune of not merely having the opportunity to admire the innocent rustic scene, but of also having to live in it. This was asking too much from a woman who had been brought up in the drawing room of Suzanne Necker. "Here I am," she wrote from Geneva to Madame Récamier in 1811, "here I am in this town where I have been bored for the past ten years."

To give appropriate expression to her tedium, she married, in the same year, a consumptive Swiss officer twenty-three years younger than she. It must be added that she must have possessed a prodigious capacity for boredom; lesser mortals would not have complained. Stendhal called the intellectual reunions of Coppet the "States-General of European public opinion." Even Suzanne Necker, who counted Diderot, d'Alembert, and Hume among her domestic animals, never was paid such a compliment.

Half a century after Madame de Staël's death Amiel called Geneva the city of ethnographic neutralizations. The phrase might be applied to nineteenth-century Switzerland as a whole. Formerly the Swiss had gone abroad; now the foreigners came to Switzerland. The whole country became a drawing room, with Alpine scenery instead of tapestries. Pulmonary romantics, syphilitic philosophers, and slightly unbalanced revolutionists arrived from all points of Europe to improve their health. It was all very stimulating, but Switzerland, by dint of acting as mediator, was in danger of losing its personality. It was in the process of becoming a Magic Mountain. Reaction was bound to set in.

VIII

Switzerland was ailing from overintellectualization. A young Swiss writer from Cully, in the canton of Vaud, who in 1902 had uprooted himself and settled in Paris, had fully awakened to that realization by the time the First World War broke out. His name was Charles Ferdinand Ramuz. He went back to Cully in 1914; he stayed in Cully till his death, in 1945. When he died, the Swiss government proclaimed a national day of mourning. This was unprecedented.

Ramuz was a peasant. He was rooted in his native Vaud more firmly than a tree. His mountains were no magic mountains; his countryside was no drawing room. He, too, was a mediator, but he did not feel called upon to mediate between national literatures or civilizations. In fact, his great merit consisted of his realization that the one thing with which creative writing is definitely not concerned is literature. In his native Vaud, he knew what he was writing about. It was nature. Not Rousseau's Nature, just plain nature: people, mountains, cows, grass, marriage, death, fear, anything. He felt called upon to mediate—but what is there that a poet should mediate between if not inarticulateness and articulateness? His nature was, naturally, inarticulate; but he possessed the magic gift to communicate it.

Like Spitteler's temperament, Ramuz's was essentially epical, but his world was not peopled with supermen. In Ramuz's world, which is everybody's world, all beings and all objects are symbols of themselves. They are *symbols* as well as *things*, because they are inarticulate. They require no supersymbols to represent them, for only articulate beings have lost the second, the symbolic half of their entity, and consequently stand in need of projecting themselves onto supersymbols.

In Ramuz's epics of men's—not Man's—struggle with nature, there is a complete return to primitive relationships. Even his language, contemptuous of grammar, ponderously deliberate, clumsily circumlocutionary, especially in dialogued passages, conveys the brute rather than the man. It is a constant grappling of the primitive mind with phenomena beyond its comprehension. There are no glib mythologies *à la* Spitteler. Ramuz's complete identification of himself, his style, and his people with his native land makes it, of course, almost impossible to translate him. One cannot uproot a passage like the following: "Les montagnes, c'est beau, mais ça n'entend pas . . . ça fait clair devant vous dans l'air et blanc, mais ça ni ne vous voit ni ne vous écoute. Ça ne s'occupe pas de vous. Elles sont mille, mille, et mille—et vous, vous êtes tout seul."

There is no cheap attempt at the use of dialect. Ramuz goes to the very roots of language—the order of words, the sequence of ideas, the struggle for articulation. In one of his novels, *La Séparation des races*, the importance of language to the primitive mind is fully implied. The northern crest of the Valaisan Alps is a sharp linguistic divide between Romanic and Alemannic dialects. To the north, as one of the characters in the novel puts it, "they speak another tongue, they believe in another God." One of the Valaisan villagers commits the crime of crossing the line of separation. He falls in love with a blonde Bernese girl. He ravishes her and brings her back into his own village, where she contrasts strangely with the small, dark, Valaisan girls, a foreigner in a land but a few miles distant from her own. She refuses to become his, but in the following spring, when the others drive their cattle up to the alps, she persuades him to stay in the village. There he is over-powered by a band of Bernese peasants, who have crossed the divide to avenge the girl. They burn down his village and hang him on the gable of his own house. The taboo of language is safe again.

There are other taboos. In *La Grande peur dans la montagne* it was a certain grazing alp, where in old times a disaster had taken place and which had been avoided ever since by the Valaisan herdsmen in the nearby valley. One summer, despite the warnings of the older men, the villagers decided to drive their cattle to that alp. From that moment inexplicable events begin to happen. The cattle die, driven to insane self-destruction by strange noises; a sense of impending catastrophe takes hold of the villagers' minds, growing to ever more terrifying proportions, till at last the mountain avenges itself and obliterates the village by drowning it in the suddenly released water of a glacier.

Again, in *Le Règne de l'Esprit Malin*, the Devil gains power over a whole mountain community—but the Devil is not the Christian Devil, he is a pagan evil spirit, born out of the mountain. Pious Catholics though they may be, the Valaisan peasants somehow seem to possess no control over the natural forces amid which they live. Their strength is in their instinctive acceptance of their littleness and of the infinite greatness of the mountain. This also is essentially the theme of *Derborence*, the only one of Ramuz's novels that is reasonably well known in the United States, under the title *When the Mountain Fell*.

To say that Ramuz was the personification of his native Vaud is not entirely true. Most of his greatest novels are laid in the Valais, which has an entirely different landscape, and where the population is Catholic, while Vaud is Protestant. It is true, however, that once Ramuz had completely understood his own native land and identified himself with it, once he had learned the secret language of the inarticulate, he was able to understand other regions with equal penetration. His writings are by no means regional literature. They are concrete poetry, poetry with a definite root in a definite spot—and by that very fact their scope is universal.

Swiss nature worshipers such as Rousseau and Pestalozzi—and a goodly number of lesser ones—were in a sense neurotic peasants. They were uprooted, divorced from nature, and their very obsession with the idea of nature was an index of their distance from it. The phenomenon was not limited to the Swiss. Even a writer like Knut Hamsun, in many ways kindred in spirit to Ramuz, never could shake from himself the neurotic bitterness that city life had given him. Ramuz was not warped. His happy collaboration with Stravinsky (to which *L'Histoire du soldat* is owed) shows that Ramuz could express himself through the medium of urban sophistication whenever it suited him. In Paris he did not feel that he was among enemies; he merely felt that he was among strangers and that he was not happy. Quietly he went home and found himself. Yet localism and nationalism were alien to him, for he was above all a European, a moralist, and an artist.

By giving articulate expression—just barely articulate enough—
to the innermost nature of his country he enriched the literature
of Europe and, incidentally, helped to restore their identity to his
countrymen. Strangely enough, they were grateful to him. In
France, Ramuz is among the most highly esteemed writers in the
French language. In Switzerland, he is a national symbol.

X: The Philosopher's Stone

THE PRECEDING chapters might easily create the impression that the Swiss are a nation of dreamers. This impression would be very wrong. They are essentially sober realists. Their great number of dreamers is only the result of the inevitable reaction of exceptionally sensitive minds to their environment. The English, for instance, one of the most level-headed nations, have produced more cranks and eccentrics than any other; in Italy, a country inhabited by people who tend toward dreaming and relish emotions, these cranks and eccentrics, instead of being members of the House of Lords, would be closely guarded by brawny men in white.

It may be further noted that as a rule the dreamers of Switzerland were rarely very successful in their country. No man is a prophet in his home—this is true everywhere—but a Swiss prophet is hardly even a man in his home. This really is as it should be, for the Swiss cannot afford many prophets. Switzerland is in itself a poor country and needs sober realists above all. It also needs adventurers, for it is too small for its population. The world is full of Swiss adventurers and their descendants.

The statement that the Swiss had little use for dreamers must be qualified. They had little use for dreamers such as Rousseau, Pestalozzi, or Amiel, but they had considerable use for dreamers such as Sutter, Lefort, or Necker—for fortune hunters and imaginative bankers. When it came to dreaming up new ways of transforming ideas into cash, the Swiss displayed such a wealth of genius and imagination, such a degree of audacity and perseverance, as can be found only with difficulty in other small nations. Even in the ideas of Rousseau and Pestalozzi, after a first spell of blindness, they soon discerned practical potentialities of financial exploitation which such professional dreamers as Rousseau and Pestalozzi would never have dreamed of. The Swiss did not discover the philosopher's stone, but they came pretty close to it.

At present, Switzerland is one of the richest nations in the world. It has more gold than it needs to cover every penny of its currency. It can buy abroad anything it needs, and the Swiss franc is in even greater demand than the American dollar. The Swiss standard of living, by and large, is at least as high, if not higher, than that of the United States. And yet Switzerland's only natural resources consist of some Alpine grazing land, forests, and some very insufficient agricultural acreage—nothing more. It has not even an outlet to the sea, like the similarly barren Norway or Scotland. How did it get where it is?

The answer is simple: the very limitations under which the Swiss have been laboring for hundreds of years have developed in them several qualities which have become their second nature. For one thing, they are hard working and tenacious; for another, they are frugal and thrifty. These qualities would not have been enough, however, if they had not also acquired an uncanny flair for seeing potential gains where unimaginative human eyes could detect nothing.

It has been shown in previous chapters how the early Swiss in the pastoral regions solved their problems of overpopulation and insufficient agricultural production by transforming military service into an export article and by abandoning agriculture altogether in favor of a pastoral economy. Organized on a thoroughly businesslike basis, the idea was entirely new. By lending out its manpower instead of allowing it to emigrate and colonize foreign lands or to hire itself out at its own terms, the state kept its capital intact, created employment, collected fees for its human loans, and even had the advantage of seeing its capital increase by the painless process of sexual reproduction. The bill, moreover, was footed entirely by foreigners.

It will be said that here necessity was the mother of invention. But why, if this is so, did the Scots or the Norse allow their human resources to go to waste, spending their strength and enter-

prise in faraway lands with no appreciable benefit to the home
countries? Emigration, conquests, raids—surely these were solutions to overpopulation, but they were crude solutions. Possibly
the Swiss, not being a seafaring nation, were less indifferent to
leaving their homes permanently than were the Normans or the
Vikings. At any rate, the necessity which was the mother of Swiss
intervention was psychological as much as economic.

The Norwegians and the Scots are centrifugal peoples; the
Swiss are centripetal. Five to ten percent of the population is
obliged to live abroad at all times. But the majority are not emigrants. They are businessmen, business apprentices, technicians,
teachers, mostly young people, and they ultimately return to
Switzerland. It is usual for the upper middle classes to send their
sons to foreign lands, a practice which is facilitated by the numerous affiliations of Swiss firms throughout the world. Wherever
there is money to be made, be it in London or Rio de Janeiro, in
Shanghai or in the Belgian Congo, one will always meet a Swiss.
Some remain abroad, yet even in their third or fourth generation
the Swiss in foreign lands often continue to look upon Switzerland
as their homeland, and Swiss citizenship laws allow them to retain
their nationality as long as they wish.

With the advent of the Reformation, the larger part of the
Swiss became so pronouncedly centripetal that even foreign
service appeared to them a drain on the nation. Well it might, for
wars had become dangerous and bloody business. The Protestant
cantons greatly restricted the trade, which remained profitable
only for the members of the aristocracy—officers and generals
who gained wealth and fame in Europe's armies. Agriculture, in
these cantons, was not the unprofitable business it was in the
Catholic regions; their peasants, moreover, were overwhelmingly
members of the subject class, and thus more tractable than those
of the Catholic cantons, where a large part of them constituted the
sovereign body of the people.

The Reformation also seems to have developed, wherever it
took root, certain characteristic virtues and abilities. Among the
upper classes, banking and finance, next to theology, became a
form of toil which Providence blessed with bountiful rewards.
Among the lower classes, cotton spinning and weaving became

epidemic. In France the Huguenots mightily took to watch-making—possibly because a watch, with its intricate mechanism in which the slightest vice leads to catastrophe, somehow repre-sented the perfection of their virtue. By the seventeenth and eighteenth centuries, cotton, wool, and silk textile industries and embroidery manufactures were firmly establised in Zurich and in eastern Switzerland, notably St. Gall and Appenzell; banking flourished in Geneva, Basel, and Zurich, not to mention hun-dreds of Swiss banking establishments abroad, ranging from Rus-sia to North America; and the Huguenot refugees had made Geneva and the Jura the world center for the manufacture of watches, clocks, and music boxes. Swiss investments abroad were considerable in the eighteenth century, and Swiss financiers were creditors to all Europe. The world acknowledged Swiss efficiency and financial genius. François Lefort, a Genevese, created the modern Russian army and navy under Peter the Great; Jacques Necker, a Genevese, became minister of finance under Louis XVI; Albert Gallatin, a Genevese, was made secretary of the United States treasury under Jefferson.

Swiss prosperity was, of course, helped by Swiss neutrality, but not to the extent one might believe. In the first place, neu-trality did not prevent internal wars or, between 1798 and 1815, foreign invasions, which proved costly. Second, prosperity during war years, as during the Thirty Years War, was regularly fol-lowed by depression due to economic overexpansion. Only in the last two wars can Switzerland's neutrality be said to have aided its prosperity—and then only in the sense that it enabled Switzer-land to exist at all, for in all other respects the last war and its sequels shook Swiss economic stability more seriously than is realized.

By 1815, at any rate, Switzerland was economically in a pre-carious position. Napoleon's Continental System had, on the one hand, forced an industrial expansion which suddenly met the challenge of British competition, especially in the manufacture of textile goods. On the other hand, it had retarded technological progress, in which England was far ahead. Export industries no longer sufficed to balance the import of food and raw materials. Unemployment, and even famine, resulted and caused a major wave of emigration. It was a serious sign, for ordinarily the Swiss went into the world as individual fortune seekers rather than as anonymous emigrants. Swiss ingenuity was now needed more than ever if prosperity were not to become merely a fond memory. Unless new natural resources were discovered, Switzerland was bound to sink to the economic level of, for instance, Scotland. The Swiss discovered new natural resources.

They were no longer able, as they had been in the fifteenth century, to transform their problematic excess population into export capital; but they were able to import a new raw material which paid for itself—tourists. Now, an imported raw material which pays for itself is a fair equivalent of a natural resource. The Swiss were able to import large quantities of tourists because they were quick to realize that, while no one wanted to spend money to purchase worthless rocks or icefields, everybody was glad to pay a price for the privilege of gaping at them. By the time the imported raw material crossed the Swiss border on the way home, he had spent enough money to help feed a few more Swiss.

In short, the tourist industry might be defined as a chemical process in which one unproductive raw material (the tourist), if put into contact with another unproductive raw material (rocks), produces gold. The gold the tourist leaves behind is as good as the profit obtained through the export of a finished product. Thus, the tourist trade has come to be regarded as a sort of "hidden export." The simplicity of the trick does not detract from its cleverness. Indeed, many another country has tried to do likewise, but none ever succeeded to the same degree.

The secret of Swiss success in this particular field was that, as in the case of the mercenary trade, they put the tourist trade on a rational and thoroughly unsentimental business basis from the very beginning. The Swiss were, beyond any doubt, the founders of the science of hotel management and all allied arts; generations of managers all over the world were trained in Switzerland or by Swiss hoteliers who had established themselves abroad, with César Ritz as their patron saint. Their fertile imagination has not yet stopped inventing new schemes and devices for the rational exploitation of human *Wanderlust*.

Of course, the tourist trade of Switzerland is by no means the most important national industry. In fact, it employs but 3.5 percent of the working population and provides but a minor fraction of the national income; just how much it is impossible to calculate, for obvious reasons. However, in normal times such small fractions are vital to Switzerland, for they signify the difference between increase or decrease of the nation's total wealth.

How providential the poetic flights of a Rousseau or a Lord Byron proved in that particular respect has already been amply hinted. Similar benefits were reaped from the exploitation of Switzerland's pedagogical reputation. But it was for the realization of the economic potentialities of pulmonary tuberculosis and other diseases that the Swiss genius deserves its fullest praise. Swiss watering places have been exploited since antiquity, but it was the discovery of the virtues of thin air that made Switzerland the international health resort it is. Mountain air is, admittedly, beneficial—yet it is no more beneficial in Switzerland than in many other countries. Swiss climate is, in fact, rather rougher than in many another place. It was by combining all their "know-how" in the allied fields of medicine and hotel management with their gist for persuasive salesmanship that the Swiss succeeded in transforming their most barren canton, the Grisons, into an inexhaustible gold mine.

In due time—that is, after the Swiss unification in 1848—the industrial lag was made good. Internal trade restrictions were removed. The right to free settlement of citizens of any canton anywhere within the Confederation was guaranteed by the new constitution and put an end to a situation in which idle manpower was accumulated in one canton and labor shortage prevailed in another. Engineering and technological skill, for which the nation displayed great aptitude, were immensely stimulated by the foundation of the Federal Polytechnical School at Zurich, which was to turn out some of the world's greatest engineers and a few capable physicists like Albert Einstein.

New industries were created: solid chocolate, canned foods, and pharmaceutic articles began to boost Swiss exports to a considerable degree. Old industries were diversified. Watchmaking, for instance, came to include the manufacture of precision instruments, with the result that the industry no longer depended entirely on the fluctuating demand for just one article. Technical skill in watchmaking also came to find its uses in the manufacture of armaments: the Oerlikon works soon were to supply, with the most admirable impartiality, guns to the entire world.*

II

In one respect the Swiss were singularly tardy in exploiting their potentialities: transportation and transit trade. In the early nineteenth century it was cheaper for Switzerland's neighbors to transport the goods they exchanged over long detours rather than directly across Switzerland. This situation was unnatural, for the Swiss, despite their landlocked position, were in a way more favorably situated than the English. England, with all her Navigation Acts, never could entirely force international trade to recognize her as its middleman. In Switzerland, a few good roads and reasonably low tariffs would have been sufficient to channel a large part of European traffic through its passes.

If the Swiss were late in realizing this potentiality, the reason lay chiefly in their political disunity. Nevertheless, they anticipated England by several years in making free trade their avowed economic policy, and the Swiss example served as a frequent subject of debate in the House of Commons when England was about to follow a similar course. That Switzerland resumed protectionism late in the century was not the fault of the Swiss. The policy was imposed on them by the practices of the large nations.

Swiss engineering accomplished its supreme achievements in the building of roads, railroads, and bridges. Within the four decades between 1870 and 1910 Switzerland became one of the hubs of the European transportation network. The development of the railroads came relatively late, but when it came it surpassed in technical daring everything that had been done before.

The expansion of the Swiss road and rail nets was the direct result of political centralization. In 1872 the constitution was amended so as to place all major communications directly under federal control. However, the cost of the projected constructions

---

* For figures on Swiss industrial production and exports, see Appendix II.

was as formidable as were the technical obstacles to be overcome, and it was necessary to mobilize all available capital. One of the first questions to come up was, of course, whether railroads should be publicly or privately owned. As early as 1852 Robert Stephenson, the son of the inventor of the locomotive, was called by the federal government as an advisor and expressed his preference for government ownership—an attitude which may appear positively treasonable to the more outspoken advocates of private enterprise. The solution, however, was adopted only after considerable floundering, in 1897, when it was also resolved to electrify the entire Swiss railroad system. No private corporations could possibly have shouldered the cost. Indeed, for every mile of Swiss railroad track there was a corresponding debt of more than $70 as late as 1945.*

The electrification of the Swiss railroads grew out of necessity. Switzerland is obliged to import practically every lump of coal it uses. On the other hand, it possesses unlimited resources of hydroelectric power. Just as they had transformed rocks into bread, the Swiss were to change water into coal. But it was a profitable change in the very long run only so far as railroads were concerned. Its immediate advantages were limited to an increased economic independence and to increased comfort for passengers. The latter advantage was offset by the invention of the automobile. As for independence from coal imports, it was only partially achieved by 1939. Immense concessions had to be made by the Swiss government to Germany during the last two world wars in order to make sure of an adequate coal supply.

If the invention of the automobile did great damage to the Swiss Federal Railroads, it greatly benefited the Swiss federal postal service, which operates all major bus lines. According to the official statistics of 1943, it is true, a few horsedrawn coaches are still in operation on about 130 miles of roads which are too difficult to manage by bus. This fact, however, should be mentioned merely as a curiosity. On the major routes buses are in operation which surpass in magnificence anything a greyhound ever dreamed of and are driven at fearful speed, with a few inches

---

* The debt, however, is being rapidly absorbed and will be paid within a few years. Electrification is practically completed.

to spare between walls of rock and abysmal precipices, by a race of men whose nerves are surgically removed from their bodies a few hours after birth.

III

The story of the construction of the major Swiss roads and of such railroad lines as the St. Gotthard, the Lötschberg, and the Simplon contains enough material for several epics, beginning with the times of Caesar's legions, or possibly Hannibal's elephants, and continuing to the present day. As samples, a few highlights will have to do here.

The first of the great Swiss trans-Alpine rail lines was the St. Gotthard, which runs, roughly speaking, along the St. Gotthard road from Lake Lucerne to Bellinzona. This passage, which rises up to nearly 7,000 feet, came into use relatively late (about 1237), but was, from the very beginning, an extremely important highway. Since it was passable only by mules, Napoleon Bonaparte, in 1800, ordered the building of a regular military road, a task which was accomplished within six years by an army of 30,000 workingmen, headed by one Italian and one French engineer. Between 1817 and 1859 the road was rebuilt to suit carriage traffic, and subsequent improvements have kept it up to date.

For the railroad construction there was no real precedent inside or outside Switzerland, except the Mont Cenis line, a direct link between France and Italy, which was built between 1859 and 1871. But the technical problems of the Gotthard line were of a quite different order.

The actual work, undertaken by the firm of L. Favre of Geneva, was begun in 1873. Previously, agreements had been reached by the Italian, Swiss, and German governments, all of which were vitally interested in the construction. Italy was to contribute 45 million gold francs, Switzerland and Germany 20 million each. These figures were later revised upward.

The line as a whole, which links the valley of the Reuss with that of the Ticino, comprises no less than fifty-three tunnels, totaling 25.5 miles in length; seven galleries, to protect the tracks from avalanches; five viaducts; and forty-two bridges. Seven of its tunnels are spirals within the mountain, and at several points

SWISS WARRIORS SURPRISED BY AN AVALANCHE AT THE
ST. GOTTHARD PASS

Pen drawing from a chronicle, c. 1500

they pass under themselves. As for the principal tunnel section, the St. Gotthard proper, it runs for 9⅓ miles in a straight line due south from Göschenen in Uri to Airolo in Ticino. Its grade on the northern slope is 5.82 percent, on the southern slope, 2 percent; it is about 20 feet high, and is doubled-tracked. The drilling proceeded from both ends, and necessitated thirteen turbines, 21 compressors working at the pressure of 14 atmospheres, 236 drills, and 3,874 workers, of whom 601 were maimed and 246 killed in accidents.

Work was carried on in a temperature of more than 90° F, with water often reaching up to the knees, and in a humidity beyond the saturation point. Among other discomforts were cave-ins, sudden jets of hot water which, with a pressure of several atmospheres, burst out of the rocks, and a general feeling that the mountain might slide any time. Indeed, it was found that contrary to expectations the mountain was not all hard rock and that any injudicious shift of pressure might cause several thousand feet of mountain to move elsewhere. Another difficulty was that all calculations had to be obtained through indirect triangulation. It was, therefore, with considerable excitement that the engineers, on February 29, 1880, witnessed the final junction of the two drilling parties which had been working from opposite ends. They were fourteen inches off laterally and two inches vertically.

The St. Gotthard line was officially opened on January 1, 1882. In 1897 a ventilating system was installed, and between 1920 and 1924 electrification was completed. The Simplon tunnel, which was begun in 1898 and inaugurated in 1906, was planned from the beginning for an electric railroad. Its problems were, if possible, even more challenging.

The longest railroad tunnel in the world (12¼ miles), and also the lowest of the great mountain tunnels (its average altitude is 2,313 feet, while the Monte Leone, towering above it, reaches 11,684 feet), the Simplon was built in several stages. A first tunnel, accommodating one track, was completed in 1905; a second, narrower tunnel, constructed at the same time, was to be used at first as a service tunnel to facilitate work on the larger one. It subsequently was widened, and the sixty foot wall separating

the two tunnels was broken through at regular intervals. Aside
from a cave-in which occurred on November 19, 1901, the
builders encountered the already familiar troubles caused by unexpected jets of hot and cold water and a temperature up to

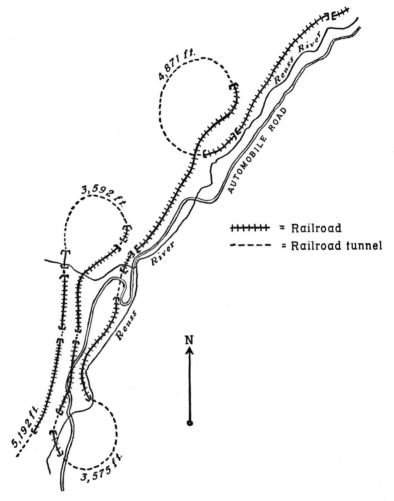

NORTHERN APPROACH TO THE ST. GOTTHARD TUNNEL

132° F. One of the chief engineers, Alfred Brandt, died of in-
juries received from falling rock. Unlike the St. Gotthard, which
is entirely situated in Swiss territory, more than half the Simplon

tunnel runs in—or rather under—Italian soil. It was undertaken by
a Swiss firm, Brandt, Brandau and Co., of Winterthur, but it was
built largely by Italian labor. The war of 1914–18 delayed the
widening of the second tunnel, which was not completed until
1921.

The examples of the St. Gotthard and the Simplon tunnels
may give an idea of the titanic labor which placed Switzerland
third among the world's nations (next to England and Belgium) in
miles of railroad track per square mile of territory. From the technological point of view, the record is not less impressive than
that of the United States, all proportions duly considered. From
the point of view of national usefulness, it was a great achievement. From the financial point of view, it was almost a fiasco.

The reason for this failure was the overambitious scope of the
project. Nineteenth-century Switzerland was, like the rest of the
world, brimming over with optimistic speculators of the Lesseps
type. In their enthusiasm for progress and their visions of gain,
they enormously overestimated the actual need for the railroads
they planned. Usually sober and realistic, the Swiss were in the
clutches of megalomania when it came to railtracks. Incorrigible
enthusiastics are still talking of a tunnel through Mont Blanc, to
link Geneva and Turin, but on the whole their imagination has
fortunately turned to more promising plans, especially the dam-
ming up of artificial lakes and the building of power stations.
Swiss accomplishments in this field are no less grandiose than in
the matter of railroads. The artificial lake atop the Grimsel Pass
and the power station near Sion in the Valais, which are among
the dozens of projects completed between the two world wars,
are merely preludes to an all-out electrification of Swiss industry.
The French Rhone project, near Bellegarde on the Swiss border,
will ultimately make the Rhone navigable from the Lake of
Geneva to its mouth on the Mediterranean and furnish enough
power to change the economic structure of the Geneva area.

IV

Few of these projects could have been carried out by private
enterprise alone, without any kind of government supervision or
co-ordination. This was demonstrated by the history of Swiss

railroads. It was, fittingly enough, the question of the railroads which brought the problem of private enterprise versus state ownership before the Swiss people. On February 20, 1898, the Swiss electorate endorsed the federal law which transferred the railroads from private to public ownership.

There was little question of state socialism at that time, and and there was little discussion of the abstract principles underlying the change. The only question was: did the community derive greater benefit from a private or from a public ownership of a rail system? It was, perhaps, an intelligent idea to weigh such matters according to their individual merits and to submit the problem to the most interested party, the people. In the case of hydraulic power, which also began to assume national importance at the beginning of the century, the Swiss people decided, by a referendum in 1908, to place its exploitation under federal control; it is the government that grants concessions to private corporations. The government, moreover, has monopolies or semi-monopolies such as the operation of bus lines by the postal service. Salt mines, the only important mining industry of Switzerland, are also monopolies exploited by cantonal governments, and there is a federal alcohol monopoly.

There are other restrictions of private enterprise. By a constitutional clause, the manufacture of arms and explosives was placed under the exclusive control (but not ownership) of the federal government. All forests are—also by a constitutional provision—under the direct protection of the state. However, all these restrictions, are primarily fiscal, policing, and conservation measures, and are not aimed at weakening the position of private capital.

Switzerland is as capitalistic a country as one could wish. With the exceptions mentioned above, all industrial enterprise is in private hands. The whole political and economic outlook of the majority of the Swiss is based on the sanctity of private property. In fact, Switzerland is so imbued with the spirit of capitalism that it not only refused to recognize Soviet Russia until 1945 but also refused to lose money by not carrying on trade with the same Soviet Russia.

More serious than governmental restrictive measures, as a challenge to capitalism, is the tremendous development of consumers' and producers' co-operatives, which in 1937 had 443,000 members in Switzerland, or more than 10 percent of the population. Almost all farmers and dairy producers operate through these associations. But the challenge is more apparent than real. The smallness of Switzerland has made it necessary to abandon certain competitive practices on which American business is said to be based. Competition takes place less on the Swiss domestic market than on the world market, so that even if all Swiss production were put under a single monopoly that monopoly would still be barely powerful enough to compete with the gigantic "nonmonopolistic" enterprises of countries like the United States.

Assuming the fantastic hypothesis that the Swiss, without external pressure, should nationalize all their industries and banks, one would still have to concede that Swiss prosperity would hinge on the maintenance of the capitalist system in other countries.

Switzerland is—and has been for more than two hundred years —primarily an industrial and commercial nation. Forty-five percent of its population depend on industry, and almost 10 percent on commerce, banking, and insurance; the balance between industry and agriculture—on which only 25 percent are dependent —inclines definitely to industry. But the preponderance of industry and commerce appears ever more striking when one considers that Swiss agricultural production covers only three fifths of the nation's total need and that a large percentage of it serves to produce raw material for the Swiss food industry. Despite the efforts of the Swiss government to increase the area of productive land—the program was initiated in the late thirties in anticipation of the impending war—Switzerland is only slightly less dependent on food imports than is Great Britain.

Of the industries, the larger part are necessarily designed to produce export goods—not only to balance the food imports but also for the simple reason that there is almost no domestic market. In other words, the situation is exactly the reverse of that in the United States, where in normal times the domestic market is all-important. Some of the principal industries, watchmaking for instance, export 90 to 95 percent of their total production. In

1923, Switzerland manufactured 14,368,000 watches and watch movements, or nearly four watches for every Swiss man, woman, and child.

Most Swiss exports consist of consumer goods, much of which might be qualified as luxury or semi-luxury articles. The reasons for this specialization are both historical and economic. Historically, the early development of highly skilled craftsmanship gave Switzerland the lead in certain industrial fields which it would have been folly to abandon. The economic reasons are obvious: since most raw materials must be imported, it is essential that their volume be kept at a minmum and that they be transformed into finished articles in which labor and skill represent almost the entire value. Watches, jewelry, precision instruments, chemicals, silk, and fine fabrics are such finished articles. Heavy industry, which is centered chiefly around Winterthur, in the canton of Zurich, is largely confined to the manufacture of machinery, locomotives, and trucks, mostly for home use.

Any fluctuation in foreign markets is consequently bound to affect Swiss economy. Switzerland is all the more sensitive to such fluctuations because consumer and luxury goods are the first to feel the effects of diminishing purchasing power. While in wartime there always exists a great demand for Swiss precision instruments, chemicals, and machinery, this demand falls off abruptly when war ceases and is replaced by demand for precisely those products that Switzerland cannot furnish: capital goods, basic food staples, and essential raw materials.*

A similar effect would be produced if any of the countries that import heavily from Switzerland were to undergo an abrupt change from capitalism to socialism, unless its industry were already so highly developed that no change in its basic economic structure need accompany the change.

In normal years Swiss exports alone would not suffice to balance imports, not even, in all likelihood, if "hidden exports" were included in the balance. The gap is filled by services—transit

---

* This falling off usually occurs only a few years after the cessation of hostilities, for at first there is increased demand for consumer goods—especially in countries which, like the United States, have come through the war relatively unscathed. But as soon as these countries reach their normal production level, their imports from Switzerland fall off.

and insurance rates—and by investments abroad. To give a meaningful figure for Swiss investments in foreign countries is difficult, for it has long been a practice for non-Swiss to cloak their investments under the mantle of Swiss names. What seems certain, at any rate, is that the normal interest of Swiss investment abroad considerably exceeds in total value the interest produced by foreign investments in Switzerland.

Swiss investments are placed not only in foreign shares or obligations but also in Swiss enterprises abroad. Swiss firms such as Nestlé, Omega, Universal Genève, Longine have branches in many countries and are relatively independent of their home establishments. It can be imagined how here, again, any major economic changes abroad would affect the whole structure of Swiss economy.

There remains the matter of banking. If it is difficult to tell just how large a part of the Swiss investments abroad is really Swiss, it is an insuperable problem to figure out how much of the assets and the deposits in Swiss banks is actually owned by Swiss nationals. The question has been the subject of slightly acid conversations between the American and the Swiss governments ever since the armistice of 1945. At that time the United States government began to claim on behalf of the Allied Control Council the German assets in Switzerland, which, it said, amounted to $750,000,000. The Swiss maintained that the figure did not exceed $250,000,000, a sum far less than the debt owed them by Germany, and that they would yield to no pressure.

Whatever the correct figures, they are impressive only on account of the smallness of the country. They are a symptom rather than a cause of Swiss prosperity. Capital is abundant in Switzerland, interest rates are low, and service fees charged to gold depositors are high. Yet these healthy signs would quickly disappear if Swiss exports and the yield of Swiss investments were to sink below their normal level. As a result, the Swiss government and Swiss private banks are more than willing to extend loans and credits to foreign countries. Political considerations hardly enter into these agreements, which are essential to the maintenance of Swiss production.

V

How delicate an organism the apparently solid Swiss economy is can be seen by the effects it suffered during the crises that followed the end of the First World War. The watch industry, for instance, was set back so sharply in the early nineteen twenties that it never fully recovered. Within three years the value of watch exports fell from 215 million francs to 169 million. Thousands of the most highly skilled workers suddenly became unemployed and were obliged to take up coarse work, which spoiled their hands and blunted their skill. From artisans they became proletarians.

The watch industry itself became somewhat proletarianized. In 1918 more than four million gold watch cases were produced; in 1939 the number had sunk to about 365,000. Prices had to be reduced to compete with the American and Japanese industries. By and large, Swiss watches still lead the world market by combining workmanship, accuracy, and low cost, but old watchmakers tend to shake their heads sadly at the difference between old and new production methods.

Watchmaking is one of the most specialized of industries as far as division of labor is concerned, and the necessary adjustments undergone by the industry in recent years have caused the virtual disappearance of one of the oldest specialties of the trade: the manufacture of watch cases. Importing countries such as the United States adopted protectionist measures and began to manufacture watch cases themselves, importing only the movements from Switzerland. It was largely for this reason that Swiss firms began to open affiliated branches in the United States. This move may have been profitable to the manufacturers, but it certainly did not help the Swiss makers of watch cases who had been thrown out of work.

In recent years the fluctuations of the export markets for watches had thrown the industry into such chaos that it became necessary to organize the various firms into a cartel for export purposes. The benefits of the cartel to the industry made themselves quickly felt, and a certain stability was achieved. At present, with the German market virtually closed, the United States has become the principal customer for Swiss watches; however, though it imports about seven million Swiss watches or movements annually, the figure is still too low for Switzerland.

Another sensitive spot is the tourist industry, one of the most reliable barometers of international economic conditions. Once hotels were geared to luxury travelers who stayed for extended periods. Since the great depression they have had to accommodate chattering busloads of lower middle-class tourists, traveling under the auspices of travel agencies, at fixed prices, spending little, damaging much, and leaving after one night in a whirl of dirty sheets and towels. Though hotel keepers have succeeded in adjusting their budgets to the new democratic trend, it had nonetheless aggravated them somewhat.

During the great depression, when the number of foreign tourists fell to an unprecedented low, considerable ingenuity was displayed in increasing the volume of domestic tourism and thus making the hotel industry less dependent on the ups and downs of foreign economies. This shift of emphasis, though it did nothing to redress an unfavorable balance of trade, stimulated the circulation of currency, checked unemployment and was, moreover, planned in such a manner that it gave families with a low income the opportunity to see their country and to strengthen their health.

At present, Switzerland has a pronouncedly favorable balance of trade, and foreign tourists are not particularly needed. In fact, the excellent shape of Swiss economy has brought about the paradoxical situation in which the Swiss government limits the amount of money foreigners may spend. The cause of this apparently perverse attitude is that Switzerland has no need for foreign currencies, which it would accumulate if tourists bought up large quantities of Swiss francs. While the English and the French voluntarily undergo privations in order to accommodate American tourists and thus to accumulate dollar credits, the Swiss sit back comfortably. They largely confine their tourist propaganda to publicity for the Swiss airlines. How long they will remain able to indulge in such superior indifference it is difficult to say.

That the Swiss have until now succeeded in maintaining their prosperity must be credited very largely to their resourceful approach to economic problems. As businessmen, the Swiss are famous for their toughness and stubbornness. At the same time they are always quick to adjust themselves to changing circumstances. Yet every economic crisis, every sign of ill health in world capitalism tends to tax their resourcefulness anew—and, after all, it cannot be inexhaustible.

As other nations increase and perfect their industries, there will be less and less need for Swiss products. In other words, Swiss economy is threatened not only by international economic crises but also by the prospect of international economic prosperity. There is little that non-Swiss nations import from Switzerland that they could not produce themselves, a fact which puts Switzerland into much the same boat as England. Even where the Swiss still possess a monopoly in technical skill and know-how they will not be able to perpetuate the monopoly and they will, furthermore, be obliged to neglect their standards of workmanship in favor of low-cost mass production. Switzerland is, consequently, obliged to secure markets in countries which will be likely to depend on imports from Switzerland for a considerable time.

At present, the United States is Switzerland's most important single customer, but without a market in Eastern Europe the United States will not suffice. Dependent though it is on capitalism, Switzerland cannot afford to take anything but a neutral position between the two opposing systems of free enterprise and collectivism. When Swiss economic neutrality can be no longer maintained, it will be almost as bad for Switzerland as if political neutrality had broken down. The result, in all likelihood, would be the slow disintegration of Switzerland, for as soon as the Swiss can no longer supply their neighbors, their neighbors will have to supply them—and they will not do so without a price.

XI: Animal Oeconomicum

I⊤ WOULD NOT be an exaggeration to consider the whole of Switzerland as just one big business concern. Actually, of course, this should be true of any country, for the existence of every nation rests on its economy. But few nations have apprehended their economic needs and limitations as fully as have the Swiss. The problems and intricacies with which every Swiss, particularly every Swiss businessman, must be familiar are not commensurate with the size of the country.

In the United States even a large manufacturer or retailer can do business successfully, though he may have only faint notions about international finance, foreign trade and markets, cartelization, and such matters—let alone foreign languages. This is not so in Switzerland, where not only manufacturers and businessmen, but everybody else must be familiar with these matters if he wishes to reach an intelligent decision affecting his business or his country. There are more financial experts per capita in Switzerland than anywhere else. If Switzerland is to exist at all, its policy, internal and external, can have but one object: to do business.

Voltaire once said that the Japanese admitted no Christians into their country except the Dutch, because they considered the Dutch as merchants, not as Christians. Like the Dutch, the Swiss have managed to subordinate their convictions to their interest. They cannot be particularly blamed. In a world in which it is the duty of every government to attend to the welfare of its own people only, they have done very well. This is proved by the fact that the vast majority of the Swiss nation are very well satisfied with their past and present policy. They are the stockholders of the vast business concern, and they hold stockholders' votes.

At the top of the Swiss holding company is a board of directors, seven in number, which is known to the public as the Federal Council. Each Federal Councillor heads one department, and their chairman is known as the president of the Swiss Confederation. The board is elected every four years by the assembled deputies of the shareholders, popularly known as the Federal Assembly—or rather, they are *re*-elected every four years, for membership in the Federal Council is almost tantamount to life tenure. The chairmanship and vice-chairmanship of the Council rotate among the members. Every year the Federal Assembly elects two of them as president and vice-president, respectively, so that a Federal Councillor can become president over and over again, at regular intervals, provided he lives long enough. The late Giuseppe Motta was president on and off so often that his name became almost familiar to attentive newspaper readers, who may have drawn the mistaken inference that such repetitiveness was a sign of popularity. It was not. It was merely a sign of longevity.

As in most corporations, the board of directors is not particularly representative of the vast mass of small stockholders. In the National Council, elected by proportional representation, the Social-Democrats now hold approximately 27 percent of the seats; in the Federal Council, they are represented by only one member, or roughly 14 percent. The Catholic Conservatives, on the other hand, who represent but 22 percent of the electorate, furnish two members to the Federal Council, or twice as many as the Social-Democrats. The reason for this peculiar phenomenon is that the Federal Councillors are elected jointly by both chambers of the Federal Assembly. Now, the Council of Estates is not elected by proportional representation, and moreover a small canton like Uri has as many representatives in it as a large one like Zurich—two for each, following the American model.

There are three interesting points in the Swiss constitutional setup. They apply to the federal, as well as to the cantonal, governments. In the first place, there is no single man at the head of any of the executive branches. The title "president" merely designates a chairman. In the second place, the executives—the federal and cantonal cabinets—are all elected, either directly or indirectly. They are not, as in most other democratic governments, appointed by the chief of state. Lastly, all cabinets are, and of necessity must be, coalition cabinets, in which the principal parties are represented. Consequently, Swiss politics are unlikely to be swayed overmuch in one direction or the other, as they are in countries where either the Greens or the Blues, the Big-Endians or the Little-Endians, the Democrats or the Republicans take over the entire administration after each election or *coup d'état.**

The two legislative chambers which constitute the Federal Assembly are, in fact, consultative rather than legislative. They almost always agree with the Federal Council; with the people they occasionally disagree. In these instances the people have the final word through the practice of the popular initiative and referendum.

Any Swiss who can gather 30,000 signatures can subject a Federal legislative act to the referendum, except where legislation is involved which necessitates the utmost expedition. Even those legislative acts or decrees which are not subject to the referendum can be made subject to it since the introduction of the popular initiative in 1891. Through the right of initiative, every Swiss who can collect 50,000 signatures can propose to the electorate the partial or total revision of the constitution. By introducing legislation in the form of a constitutional amendment, the practice of the initiative has virtually obliterated the distinction between a legislative act and a constitutional provision.

That there has been substantial agreement between the government and the electorate can be seen by the record of constitu-

---

* The following table shows the distribution of seats among the four principal parties in the National Council, the Council of Estates, and the Federal Council.

		1938	1940	1947
Social-Democrats	National Council	50	49	54
	Council of Estates	3	3	6
	Federal Council	0	0	1
Radical-Democrats	National Council	48	50	47
	Council of Estates	15	14	11
	Federal Council	4	4	3
Catholic Conservatives	National Council	42	44	43
	Council of Estates	18	18	19
	Federal Council	2	2	2
Farmers, Workers, & Middle Class Party	National Council	21	21	22
	Council of Estates	3	4	4
	Federal Council	1	1	1

tional amendments accepted or rejected. Between 1874 and 1938 thirty-eight amendments were accepted; of these, only six were due to popular initiative. During the same period, twenty-nine projected amendments were rejected; of these, only eight emanated from the Federal Assembly, and twenty-one were due to popular initiative. Of the six initiatives accepted, only two were of fundamental importance. The first, adopted in 1918, made proportional representation the method of electing the lower house; the second, adopted in 1921, made international treaties which were binding for more than fifteen years subject to the referendum. As a result, a vote had to be taken before Switzerland entered the League of Nations.

To visualize the Swiss method of government one would have to imagine that nearly every act of the United States Congress might, upon the request of about ten million voters, be subject to popular revision or that any American citizen, if he could gather about sixteen million signatures, could propose legislation of his own. In as large a nation as the United States, it would be a rather cumbersome procedure. In Switzerland, the system works very smoothly.

The larger part of federal legislation falls into the category of police measures, economic measures, and social measures. Thus, as early as in 1890 an amendment was put into the constitution which made accident and sickness insurance compulsory for certain categories of citizens. Free and compulsory primary education is guaranteed, and in 1902 the electorate endorsed the grant of federal subsidies to the cantons for this purpose. Through another referendum the manufacture and sale of absinthe has been forbidden since 1908. The right of the Confederation to set up public grain reserves and to compel millers to store up grain was adopted by the electorate in 1929. The establishment of a federal income tax was promulgated by the Federal Assembly in 1933 as an emergency measure. The emergency has lasted ever since. Regulations regarding labor, tariffs, subsidies, and similar problems form the usual topics under discussion of the Federal Assembly.

In the matter of foreign policy, the Swiss attitude is so clearly

and permanently defined that it required little debate in the
legislative halls. There were, however, a few notable exceptions.
One was the problem of Switzerland's entry into the League of
Nations, which was accepted by a narrow margin of the electorate
and only after Switzerland had been exempted from participation in military sanctions as a League member. In 1936, on the
occasion of the economic sanctions voted against Italy after her
aggression on Ethiopia, the subject of Swiss neutrality was under
debate once more. The one-hundred percenters won out, and
Switzerland freed itself from even the obligation of observing
economic sanctions. The last major debate on foreign policy
occurred in 1945, when Russia began to accuse the Swiss of having
favored the Axis. This particular debate had a spectacular end,
for the Federal Councillor in charge of foreign affairs, Marcel
Pilet-Golaz, was forced to resign before diplomatic relations
with Russia, interrupted after the October Revolution, could be
resumed.

The Russian accusation was not entirely unfounded. If only
because of economic necessity, the Swiss had been obliged to
co-operate with the German war machine in order to obtain food
and coal. The few chartered ships which sailed under the Swiss
flag from Genoa would not have sufficed to supply Switzerland,
and, besides, the shipments could easily have been stopped between Genoa and Switzerland. The danger of a German invasion,
moreover, existed until 1944. However, even with these mitigating
circumstances, there is no denying that the Swiss government
complied, perhaps, a little easily. The Swiss press was curbed to
avoid giving offense to the Germans, and more business deals
were concluded than were strictly necessary. Rumors that high
Swiss officials were secretly favoring National Socialism had circulated in Switzerland even before the war, and there is little
doubt that many important figures in Swiss banking and industry
did not look unfavorably upon Fascism.

By and large, however, even those Swiss who thought that
Hitler and Mussolini had accomplished splendid things in their
respective countries felt little inclined to imitate them in Switzerland. As for the Swiss who favored the democratic nations, few

among them would have gone so far as to compromise Switzerland's security by advocating a positive stand against the Axis Powers. Almost all realized that it was Switzerland's business to produce, to sell, and to buy and that there was little point in asking prospective buyers and sellers any questions that did not strictly relate to buying and selling.

This attitude is not likely to change. Far from it; the Swiss are at present less committed in international politics than they were after the First World War, since they have decided to maintain neutrality in its most literal sense rather than to join the United Nations as a full member.* The dominating organs of public opinion in Switzerland yield nothing to their American counterparts when it comes to denouncing Communism, which most Swiss ardently wish to see crushed. Yet, in the event of a conflict, it is unlikely that the Swiss would take a position. They know that they could not contribute anything that would turn the course of events, and it would be very much against sound business principles to make a sacrifice with no possible gain in sight.

The literal interpretation of neutrality which the Swiss government has adopted has led it to great extremes of caution. Taking a long range view of the German future, it avoided as much as was possible, even after the German surrender, committing any act that might later be held against it by a revived Germany. The Swiss position with regard to German assets in Switzerland brought them into conflict with the nation whose economic and political outlook is closest to their own—the United States. But they did not allow ideological sympathies to interfere with their position. It is likely that the American Department of State has met in the Swiss the most determinedly stubborn negotiators next to the Russians. In the end, an agreement was reached which was far closer to the Swiss stand than to that of the Americans. On the other hand, Swiss relations with the Communist-dominated world have become quite cordial. The Russians regard the Swiss much as Voltaire's Japanese regarded the Dutch.

---

* As of July 1, 1947, Switzerland was a member of the following subsidiary bodies of the United Nations: International Labor Organization; Food and Agriculture Organization; International Civil Aviation Organization; and World Health Organization.

II

Even the soberest businessmen must let off steam if they are not to perish in frustration. Since foreign policy offers the Swiss little opportunity for serious political debate, and since federal politics are so excruciatingly stable, political passion takes refuge in local politics.

There are, strictly speaking, no national parties in Switzerland. Each canton has its own party system, and it is only by approximation that the parties represented in the Federal Assembly can be grouped as Radicals, Conservatives, Catholics, and Social Democrats. The Social Democrats are at present the strongest single party, but since they are the only large party left of center, it is the conservative element that prevails. This has been the case ever since the Radicals, in the last century, settled down and became conservative. It has not been the case in the individual cantons.

The passion and hate expended by the Swiss in cantonal politics would not be misplaced in vaster theaters. It is particularly bitter in those cantons where a proletariat has developed and where socialism has gained a foothold. In some cantons, as in Berne and Zurich, the Social Democrats have, by dint of co-operation with the other parties, gained a certain respectability. In others, as in Geneva, to call oneself a Socialist has become the equivalent of a self-imposed social ostracism. It is in those cantons that a body of citizens has developed who do not consider themselves shareholders in the Swiss business concern, for the simple reason that they receive no dividends—or at least they think that they receive none. But the members of this body can vote just as the shareholders do, and at times they have been in the majority. Now, to have your business run by people who hold no shares in it is an unpleasant experience. It is this unpleasantness rather than mere prejudice which accounts for the violent opinions entertained by the middle and upper classes on the subject of Socialists.

The only time when socialism really represented a threat to the political stability of Switzerland was in the nineteen thirties, when the depression added a large number of middle-class votes to those of the Socialist proletariat. In Geneva, where Socialist leadership was most aggressive, a Socialist majority was in power for one term. After that, the depression was largely overcome, and the middle classes returned to the respectable fold.

On November 27, 1940, the Communist party was outlawed throughout Switzerland, and the Social Democrats adopted a general trend to the right. This was only normal, since the major part of the Swiss population, including the great number of highly skilled and well-paid workers, have a middle-class mentality and see little to be gained by socialization. As in most of Western Europe, the Social Democrats were actually nothing but trade unionists. In certain regions, however, a proletariat had undeniably developed. Shortly after the outbreak of the war, the left minority wing of the Swiss Socialists combined with the former members of the outlawed Communist party. These dissident Socialists recently formed a new party under the leadership of the former Socialist president of the canton of Geneva, Léon Nicole. The importance of this party depends largely on the fate of Swiss economy. There can be no doubt that in the case of a depression it would gather considerable strength.

Aside from Nicole, there is only one colorful political leader in Switzerland. Gottlieb Duttweiler, the head of the Independent party, had the original idea of frankly reducing all political problems to problems of business management. Early in his youth he went to Brazil, where he was a coffee grower. Returning to Switzerland in 1924, he decided to put into practice his theory that goods could be sold much cheaper and yet bring in profit. For the purpose, he acquired several trucks, which he fitted out as ambulant grocery stores; these delivered his goods to certain points in the suburbs and the country where housewives would congregate, make their purchases, and save themselves much trouble. The housewives also saved money, for Duttweiler's *Migros,* as his enterprise was called, undercut everybody else. His prediction that the system would prove profitable came true. He soon owned a whole fleet of trucks all over Switzerland, with chain stores, and warehouses. In 1935 Duttweiler decided to go into politics. He was elected on an independent ticket. In the same year he proposed a highly original hotel plan in a book called *The Hotel Plan—Sportsmanship in Economics,* and also published another opus entitled *Back to Cheese!* The *Migros* he ultimately transformed into a consumers' co-operative.

Though Duttweiler's party is small, it is highly articulate, and his reputation among his followers might be compared favorably with Joan of Arc's. His efforts to give the domestic market a more important place than it has hitherto held in the Swiss economy and his proposals for reducing the cost of living are, no doubt, to be taken seriously. But as a political party his group has hardly a chance to compete with the others.

What characterizes the Swiss political scene as a whole is the almost entire absence of graft and of machine politics, which seem so indispensable to the democratic process among other nations. Political offices are no sinecures in Switzerland; if a Swiss wants to make money he goes into business. As for political machines, they cannot very well exist in a country where proportional representation is the usual method of electing candidates. The electorate is educated and familiar with the problems on which it has to give its vote. The general political atmosphere is little conducive to wardheeling.

To the Swiss, politics is not the game which it still is to many Americans, for they cannot afford waste of any kind. Passions and animosities are not whipped up for the occasion of elections and then buried as if the whole contest had been a mere sportive bout. They are deep, permanent, and fundamental, and for this very reason seldom assume undignified expression. Combining the obstinacy of a theological dispute with the earnestness of a parish meeting and the solemnity of a stockholders' assembly, the Swiss are not likely to let themselves be swayed into participating in the unrealistic debate which divides the rest of the world into two camps. So long as the majority remain stockholders in the common concern, they will continue to reach their decisions unsentimentally, on the basis of francs and centimes, leaving to their writers and thinkers the task of taking position in the larger issues of the day.

III

Switzerland has weathered many a storm in the six and a half centuries of its existence. Such hardiness was only partially due to the realism of its citizens, who knew when to sacrifice ideological convictions to concrete interests. Indeed, Switzerland would, in all likelihood, have disappeared from the map long ago had it not been for the balance of power of the European states. When this balance was endangered, as in the time of Louis XIV, Switzerland was little more than a French protectorate; when the balance was destroyed, as in the Napoleonic era, Switzerland ceased to exist altogether. It was at the Congress of Vienna, when the principle of the European balance reached its most complete expression, that the Great Powers agreed to make Switzerland a No Man's Land.

At the time, the Great Powers considered neutral Switzerland their ward. In 1847, after European intervention in the Sonderbund War had proved abortive, the wardenship of Swiss neutrality passed from the hands of the Great Powers into the hands of the Swiss themselves. So it did, at least, from the point of view of the Swiss, but it would be difficult for them to maintain the principle for long if the Great Powers did not consent. Their consent was expressed in the Treaty of Versailles, in their willingness to grant Switzerland special dispensations as a member of the League of Nations, and in the general practice of using the good offices of the Swiss diplomatic representatives in countries with which they have ceased to maintain diplomatic relations.

With the outcome of the Second World War, the European balance was destroyed. It is doubtful whether or not the remaining two Great Powers, neither of which borders on Switzerland, will continue to respect Swiss neutrality. At any rate, it is questionable if they will be willing to accept Swiss neutrality at the terms of the Swiss. So long as there is peace, or a reasonable equivalent thereof, the Swiss themselves will probably succeed in clinging to their present status, even if it means a thorough readjustment of their economy, but in the event of war, they can no longer even dream of defending it.

There is one hope for the Swiss. Just as in the past Swiss neutrality was respected because of Switzerland's crucial strategic situation, so in the future is it likely to be respected because new methods of warfare have made Switzerland strategically unimportant. It is a feeble hope, for a cataclysm such as another war is bound to be will make the very concept of neutrality meaningless.

Neutrality presupposes the existence of a free interplay of competing powers and ideologies. There will be nothing left for the Swiss to be neutral between.

The disintegration of Switzerland without a war is inconceivable unless a complete collapse of the Swiss economic structure should occur. That such a collapse is possible cannot be doubted, since the Swiss economic structure is an even more artificial edifice than that of England. To the Swiss, disintegration would mean partition among Germany, Italy, and France. In none of these countries could they ever hope to recover their high standard of living. From the political and cultural points of view, partition would mean the complete disruption of centuries of tradition. Everything is possible in this world, but imagination has to be stretched to the breaking point to visualize the Swiss as living under German, French, or Italian rule.

To the rest of the world, the disappearance of Switzerland would not mean very much. Economic effects would be felt for some time, but they would be relatively minor. Switzerland's role with regard to the outside world has been primarily moral and intellectual; even if it is still fulfilling its mission in these fields, the outside world no longer seems to display much interest.

The disproportionately important part which the Swiss have played in Western intellectual life was due to the special condition of their country—its focal situation, its attraction to many independent minds in other nations, and, paradoxically, its smallness, which forced many of its own most ambitious citizens to find a field of action abroad and thus to spread the traditions of Swiss thought among other nations. It will also be observed that an overwhelming majority of those Swiss who contributed most in the fields of art, letters, philosophy, ethics, or religion were Protestant. This is true now as much as ever: the architect Le Corbusier, the writers Ramuz and Denis de Rougemont, the composers Honegger and Jaques-Dalcroze, the psychoanalyst Jung, the theologian Karl Barth, all are, or were, Protestants. The single exception among internationally known contemporaries of Swiss origin seems to be Ernest Bloch, who is a Jew. Such preponderance of the Protestant element, which represents only little more than half the Swiss population, is no mere accident.

CONTEMPORARY DISASTER OR TOTAL FREEDOM
OF SPACE

Drawing by Le Corbusier, from his *Œuvre complète*,
1938–46, Vol. IV; by permission of the Verlag für Ar-
chitektur A. G., Erlenbach-Zurich

With the only possible exception of New England, Switzerland was the only country in the world where Calvinism became a national way of life in all its manifestations. The great historical function of Switzerland was the Reformation. The constant self-probing, the inescapable spiritual isolation of the Calvinist, his almost unlimited capacity for re-examining all problems, his never-ending thirst for certainty—these are qualities which cannot fail to produce original and revolutionary thought. Le Corbusier's cities of glass on pillars are the product of an uncompromising Calvinist conscience. It does not matter that Calvinism itself has been discarded on the way.

The example of Le Corbusier, the prophet of modern architecture, is illustration enough in itself that the historical role of Switzerland is not finished. Jung's departure from orthodox Freudianism may also, in part, be explained by his Puritan background, which never could reconcile itself with the supremacy of the flesh. Karl Barth's attempt to formulate a dialectical Christian doctrine on the basis of dogmatic Calvinism is probably the most revolutionary contribution to modern theology. To the average human, these names mean little; yet if human civilization were permitted to pursue its normal progress, their contributions would be lasting. It might be argued that such contributions, revolutionary as they are, are being made in a vacuum. For one who does not possess the gift of prophecy, it is difficult to argue the point.

Whether or not Swiss thinkers will be able for long to continue their contributions to human civilization depends very largely on whether human civilization will be allowed to exist for long. Barring its total extinction, however, the Swiss have a better chance than most others.

Supposing that a future war does not obliterate the globe altogether—for in that case speculations would be misplaced—one may venture that countries like Switzerland would escape total ruin more easily than others. Even if all the rest of Europe were reduced to a shambles, the Swiss would be able to avoid annihilation for a long time. Blast damage in mountainous terrain is very limited, as was proved by the preservation of large sections of Nagasaki after the atomic bomb was dropped. The Alps would constitute excellent shelter. There would be little deliberate bombing, for the belligerents would hardly find it worth while to waste their precious explosives on the Swiss. Even gas and bacteriological warfare would be less effective in Switzerland than in flat terrain, since it would affect only the valleys, which could be evacuated. If the war were extended, the Swiss would die of starvation, but it is unlikely that such fury as an atomic war could continue for long.

Once the Swiss can emerge from their natural shelters, they might easily find that they are the only Europeans left who have preserved the technical know-how of prewar years. They would be in great demand wherever they went. Hunger would force them to help other nations reorganize their resources. About that task they would go with an efficiency and a determination of which other peoples would no longer be capable. Swiss engineers, Swiss physicians, Swiss agricultural and financial experts, and Swiss Red Cross workers would roam through the devastated lands like a race of supermen. Sensibly and rationally they would survey the potentialities of the ruins, make reports, and draft plans for the reorganization of Europe on a solid business basis, with no political nonsense allowed to interfere. They probably would do an excellent job.

The speculation is fantastic and improbable—but the point is that it is not impossible. No nation has less desire to expand than the Swiss. They had a chance to acquire Upper Savoy in 1866, and they missed it; they might have claimed Mulhouse in 1870, but they refrained; in 1919 the Austrian province of Vorarlberg voted in favor of joining Switzerland as a canton, and the Swiss did not even take cognizance of the offer. There is danger in expansion. Yet if they had to expand, they probably could do so more efficiently than many a nation that feels itself invested with a historical mission. The Swiss business concern is a highly concentrated organization. It has enough experts in every field to suffice unto a whole continent.

Appendix A

EXTRACTS FROM THE FEDERAL CONSTITUTION OF SWITZERLAND

"In the name of the Almighty God! The Swiss Confederation, desiring to strengthen the alliance of the confederates, to maintain and increase the unity, power, and honor of the Swiss nation, has adopted the following federal constitution.

CHAPTER I. GENERAL PROVISIONS

1. The peoples of the sovereign twenty-two cantons of Switzerland . . . together form the Swiss Confederation.

3. The cantons are sovereign inasmuch as their sovereignty is not limited by the federal constitution; as such, they exercise all the rights not delegated to the federal authority.

4. All Swiss are equal before the law. There are in Switzerland neither subjects nor privileges. . . .

6. The cantons must request from the Confederation the guarantee of their constitutions. This guarantee will be given, provided that (a) these constitutions contain nothing contrary to the provisions of the federal constitution; (b) they ensure the exercise of political rights in accordance with republican procedures—either by representation or through [direct] democracy; (c) the constitutions must have been accepted by the people and they must be open to revision whenever the absolute majority of the people shall so demand.

8. The Confederation has the exclusive right to declare war and to make peace, as well as to make alliances with foreign States. . . .

9. In exceptional cases, the cantons reserve the right to conclude treaties with foreign States affecting their economies, their regional relations, and policing. . . .

10. Official relations between the cantons and foreign governments . . . take place through the mediation of the Federal Council. However, the cantons may correspond directly with the subaltern authorities and the employees of a foreign State whenever the matters mentioned in the preceding article are involved.

13. The Confederation does not possess the right to maintain permanent troops. No canton or half-canton can maintain more than 300 men as permanent troops without the authorization of the federal authority. . . .

18. Every [male] Swiss is bound to military service. . . . Every soldier receives, free, his original issue of weapons, equipment, and clothing. The weapon remains in the hands of the soldier. . . .

19. The federal army consists of (a) the corps of cantonal troops; (b) of all those Swiss who, not belonging to those corps, are nonetheless obliged to do military service. The right to govern the army . . . is vested in the Confederation. . . . The cantons govern the military forces [originating in] their territories. . . .

24. The Confederation has the right of supervision over the policing of dikes and forests. . . .

24*bis*. The exploitation of hydraulic power is placed under the supervision of the Confederation. . . .

24*ter*. The power to legislate concerning navigation is vested in the Confederation.

26. The power to legislate concerning the construction and exploitation of railroads is vested in the Confederation.

27. The Confederation has the right to create, besides the existing Federal Polytechnical School, a federal university and other establishments of higher education, or to subsidize establishments of this kind. The cantons shall provide for elementary education, which must be adequate and placed under exclusive direction of the civil authority. [Primary education] shall be compulsory and, in public schools, free. Public schools shall be open to adherents of all religious denominations, who shall not be obliged to suffer in any manner whatsoever regarding their freedom of conscience and their beliefs. The Confederation shall take appropriate measures against cantons which fail to fulfill these obligations.

27*bis*. Subsidies shall be allocated to the cantons in order to help them to fulfill their obligations in the field of primary education. . . .

28. All matters concerning tolls are within the power of the Confederation. . . .

30. The revenue from tolls belongs to the Confederation. . . .

The cantons of Uri, Grisons, Ticino, and Valais shall receive, beginning on January 1, 1925, yearly indemnities . . . in view of their international alpine roads. . . .

32*bis*. The Confederation has the right to legislate concerning the manufacture, importation . . . and sale of distilled liquors. . . . Half of the net receipts derived by the Confederation from the tax on distilled liquors will be distributed among the cantons in proportion to their . . . population; every canton shall use at least ten percent of its share [in order] to combat alcoholism, its causes and effects. The other half of the receipts remains in the possession of the Confederation; it will be allocated for old-age insurance. . . .

34. The Confederation has the right to prescribe uniform rules concerning child labor in factories, concerning the length of working hours that may be imposed on adults, and concerning the protection to be accorded to workers against employment in unhealthful and dangerous industries. . . .

34*bis*. The Confederation shall introduce legislation to provide for accident and sicknes insurance, taking into account the already existing insurance agencies. The Confederation may declare participation in such insurance to be compulsory for certain designated categories of citizens.

34*quater*. The Confederation shall introduce legislation to provide for old age insurance and benefits. . . .

37. The Confederation exercises supervision over roads and bridges the maintenance of which is in its interests. . . .

37*ter*. The right to legislate concerning aviation is vested in the Confederation. . . .

38. The Confederation exercises all the rights connected with the mint. . . .

39. The right to issue bank notes . . . is exclusively vested in the Confederation. . . .

41. The manufacture, acquisition, trade, and distribution of gunpowder . . . arms, munitions, and other war matériel is reserved to the Confederation. . . .

43. Every citizen of a canton is a Swiss citizen. . . .

44. No Swiss national can be expelled from the territory of the Confederation or of his original canton.

49. Freedom of conscience and of belief is inviolable. No one can be constrained to become a member of a religious association, to take religious instruction, to fulfill a religious act, or to incur penalties of any kind because of a religious opinion. . . . No one may for re-

ligious reasons free himself from any civic duty. No one shall be obliged to pay taxes the produce of which is specifically allocated to cover the specific expenses of a religious cult to which he does not belong. . . .

50. Freedom of worship is guaranteed within the limits compatible with public order and morality. . . . No episcopal dioceses may be created on Swiss territory without the approval of the Confederation.

51. The order of Jesuits [*sic*] and the societies affiliated with it cannot be admitted into any part of Switzerland, and all activity in the church and in schools is forbidden to its members. This interdiction may be extended . . . . to other religious orders whose actions endanger the State or trouble the relations between the denominations.

52. It is forbidden to found new convents or religious orders or to re-establish those that have been suppressed.

55. The freedom of the press is guaranteed. However, cantonal laws shall lay down the necessary measures to prevent abuse; these laws must be submitted to the Federal Council for approval. The Confederation may also establish penalties to repress abuses directed against itself or its authorities.

56. Citizens have the right to form associations, provided there be nothing in the aim of these associations or in the means they use that is illegal or dangerous to the State. Cantonal laws shall be promulgated in order to insure appropriate measures to prevent abuses.

58. No one may be estranged from the jurisdiction of his natural judge. Consequently, no extraordinary tribunals may be set up. Ecclesiastical jurisdiction is abolished.

61. Decisions in civil cases made in one of the cantons are binding throughout Switzerland.

64. The Confederation has the right to legislate on criminal law. . . .

65. No death sentence may be imposed for political crimes. Corporal punishment is forbidden.

CHAPTER II. FEDERAL AUTHORITIES

71. Reservation being made for the rights of the people and of the cantons . . . the supreme authority of the Confederation is vested in the Federal Assembly, which is composed of two sections or councils, namely, (*A*) the National Council; (*B*) the Council of Estates.

72. The National Council consists of the deputies of the Swiss people, elected in the proportion of one member for 22,000 souls of

the total population. Fractions larger than 11,000 souls are accounted as 22,000. Each canton and, in the divided cantons, each half-canton, shall elect at least one deputy.

73. Elections to the National Council are direct. They shall take place on the principle of proportional representation, with every canton or half-canton forming an electoral college. . . .

74. The right to participate in elections and to vote is accorded to every [male] Swiss having completed his twentieth year who is not otherwise disqualified as an active citizen by the legislation of the canton in which he resides. . . .

75. Every [male] Swiss citizen who is not of the clergy and who has the right to vote is eligible to the National Council.

76. The National Council is elected every four years and is wholly renewed at each election.

79. The members of the National Council are remunerated by the federal treasury.

80. The Council of Estates consists of forty-four deputies of the cantons. Each canton nominates two deputies; in the divided cantons, each half-canton elects one deputy.

83. The deputies to the Council of Estates are remunerated by the cantons.

84. The National Council and the Council of Estates deliberate on all matters which the present constitution reserves for the Confederation and which are not [specifically] placed under another federal authority.

86. The two councils shall meet once a year, in ordinary session, at a date fixed by regulation. They may be called in extraordinary session by the Federal Council, or upon the demand of one fourth of the National Council, or by request of five cantons.

88. In the National Council and in the Council of Estates decisions are reached by the absolute majority of votes.

89. No federal law, federal decree, or federal order can be issued without the consent of the two councils. Federal laws shall be submitted to the people for adoption or rejection if a demand for such action is made by 30,000 active citizens or by eight cantons. The same applies to federal orders of a general scope which are not of an urgent nature. International treaties concluded for an indeterminate period of time or for longer than fifteen years shall also be submitted to popular adoption or rejection if a demand is made by 30,000 active citizens or eight cantons.

92. Each [of the two] councils deliberates separately. However,

the two councils shall assemble together . . . for the purpose of electing [the Federal Council, the Federal Tribunal, the federal chancellor, and the commanding general of the federal army]. . . .

93. [Parliamentary] initiative is the privilege of each of the two councils and each of their members. The cantons may exercise the same right by writing.

94. As a rule, the sessions of the councils are public.

95. The highest executive and directing authority of the Confederation is vested in a Federal Council composed of seven members.

96. The members of the Federal Council shall be appointed for four years, by the united councils, and chosen from among all Swiss citizens eligible to the National Council. However, not more than one member of the Federal Council may be chosen from any one canton. The Federal Council shall be wholly renewed after each renewal of the National Council. . . .

98. The Federal Council is presided over by the president of the Confederation. It shall have a vice-president. The president of the Confederation and the vice-president of the Federal Council shall be nominated for one year, by the Federal Assembly, from among the members of the [Federal] Council. . . .

101. The members of the Federal Council shall possess an advisory voice in the two sections of the Federal Assembly, as well as the right to initiate proposals concerning the matters under discussion.

103. The business of the Federal Council shall be distributed among its members, [each of whom heads one or more] departments. All decisions are made on the authority of the Federal Council [as a whole]. . . .

105. A federal chancellery, headed by the chancellor of the Confederation, shall act as secretariat of the Federal Assembly and of the Federal Council. . . .

106. There is a Federal Tribunal to administer justice in all federal matters. There is, moreover, a jury for criminal cases.

107. The members . . . of the Federal Tribunal shall be named by the Federal Assembly, which shall take into account the equitable representation of the three official languages. . . .

110. The Federal Tribunal shall take cognizance of disputes in civil law (1) between the Confederation and the cantons; (2) between, on the one hand, the Confederation, and, on the other, corporations or private individuals if the said corporations or private individuals are the plaintiffs and whenever the dispute reaches a degree of importance to be determined by federal legislation; (3) between cantons; (4) be-

tween, on the one hand, the cantons, and, on the other, corporations or private individuals, whenever one of the parties requests it and whenever the dispute reaches a degree of importance to be determined by federal legislation. It [the Federal Tribunal] shall take cognizance, moreover, of all disputes involving loss of nationality as well as all disputes that may arise among the communes of different cantons regarding birth right.

112. The Federal Tribunal, assisted by the jury, which shall pass on the facts, shall take cognizance in matters of penal law (1) of cases of high treason against the Confederation, and of revolt or violence against the federal authorities; (2) of crimes and offenses against international law; (3) of political crimes and offenses which are the cause or the consequence of disturbances entailing the intervention of the federal army; (4) of charges made against officials nominated by a federal authority, if the said authority lays the charges before the Federal Tribunal.

113. The Federal Tribunal takes cognizance, moreover: (1) of conflicts of competence between the federal authorities on the one hand and cantonal authorities on the other; (2) of disputes among cantons, whenever these disputes involve public law; (3) of complaints involving the violation of constitutional civic rights, as well as of claims made by private individuals involving the violation of concordats or treaties. . . .

116. The German, French, Italian, and Romansh languages are the national languages of Switzerland. German, French, and Italian are hereby declared the official languages of Switzerland.

118. The federal constitution may be revised at any time, in its entirety or partially.

120. If one of the two sections of the Federal Assembly decrees the total revision of the federal constitution, and if the other section refuses consent, or if 50,000 Swiss citizens entitled to vote request a total revision, the question whether or not the federal constitution should be revised is, in both these cases, submitted to the vote of the Swiss people, by "Yes" or "No" [ballot]. If in either case the majority of the Swiss citizens taking part in the vote declare in favor of revision, the two councils shall be newly elected for the purpose of working on the revision.

121. Partial revision may take place either by means of popular initiative or through the procedure provided by federal legislation. Popular initiative consists of a request, presented by 50,000 Swiss citizens entitled to vote, proposing the adoption of a new constitu-

tional article or the repeal of an old constitutional article or the modification of certain articles of the constitution in force. If, by means of popular initiative, several different proposals are presented . . . each one of them must form the object of a separate initiative. The request offered by the initiative may be presented either as a proposal couched in general terms or as a specifically stated bill. If the request . . . is couched in general terms, the Federal Chambers, if they approve it, shall proceed to draft the partial revision in the desired meaning and shall submit the project to the people and the cantons for acceptance or rejection. If, on the contrary, they disapprove, the question of partial revision shall be submitted to the vote of the people; if the majority of Swiss citizens participating in the vote declare themselves in the affirmative, the Federal Assembly, conforming to the popular decision, shall proceed to draft the revision. If the request is in the form of a specifically stated bill, and if the Federal Assembly approves it, the bill shall be submitted to the people and the cantons for adoption or rejection. If the Federal Assembly disagrees, it may elaborate a separate bill or it may recommend to the people the rejection of the bill and submit to the vote its counterproposal or its proposal for rejection at the same time that it submits the bill which originates in the popular initiative.

123. The revised federal constitution or the revised part of the federal constitution becomes law if it has been accepted by the majority of the Swiss citizens participating in the vote and by the majority of the cantons. To establish the majority of the cantons, the vote of a half-canton is counted as half a vote. The result of the popular vote in each canton is considered the vote of the canton.

Appendix B

ECONOMIC TABLES

TABLE 1. THE PRINCIPAL SWISS INDUSTRIES

INDUSTRY	WORKERS EMPLOYED		EXPORTS (In 1,000,000 Swiss francs)		
	1920	1939	1920	1939	1945
Machines	80,854	83,810	302.3	226.2	233.4
Watches	62,833	41,443	325.8	195.7	492.6
Other metal products	80,547	101,622	214.8	228.2	427.7
Construction	161,141	112,633	...	...	...
Clothing	148,905	81,637	...	...	...
Textiles	142,640	81,477	1,569.2	230.4	240.4
Foodstuffs & tobacco	73,418	91,785	217.6 [a]	73.8 [a]	8.9
Graphic arts	19,043	32,048	...	...	...
Chemicals	18,861	22,428	309.0	255.9	210.2
Public utilities	12,557	11,654	...	...	...

[a] The breakdown of food exports in 1920 was as follows: chocolate, 43 percent; condensed milk, 22 percent; cheese, 4 percent; other foods, 31 percent. In 1939 a complete reversal had taken place: chocolate, 2 percent; condensed milk, 7 percent; cheese, 67 percent; other foods, 24 percent.

TABLE 2. EXCESS OF IMPORTS

YEAR	MONEY VALUE (In Swiss francs)	PERCENTAGE OF EXCESS
1888	154,018,000	18.6
1914	291,521,000	19.7
1920	965,716,000	22.8
1939	591,782,000	31.3
1945	−248,330,000	−20.3

TABLE 3. POPULATION BY OCCUPATIONS

OCCUPATION	PERCENTAGE OF POPULATION DEPENDING ON OCCUPATION	
	1888	*1930*
Agriculture	41.2	25.1
Industries & crafts	39.9	44.9
Commerce, banking, insurance	4.9	9.5
Hotel industry	2.3	3.5
Communications & transportation	3.6	6.0
Administration & professions	4.2	5.7
Domestic service, etc.	3.9	5.3

Selected Bibliography

Akeret, Erwin. Regierung und Regierungsformen der schweizerischen Eidgenossenschaft. Andelfingen, 1941.

Baud-Bovy, Daniel, and others. La Vie romantique au pays romand. Geneva, 1930.

Berlepsch, H. A. Die Gotthardt-Bahn, in *Dr. Petermanns Mittheilungen aus Justus Perthes' Geographischer Anstalt* (Gotha, 1881), Vol. XIV.

Birchner, Ralph. Wirtschaft und Lebenshaltung im schweizerischen "Hirtenland" am Ende des 18. Jahrhunderts. Lachen, 1938.

Blavignac, J. D. Etudes sur Genève. 2 vols. Geneva, 1872–74.

Bonjour, Edgar. Swiss Neutrality. Geneva, 1944. Eng. tr., London, 1946.

Brandner, Gertrud. C. F. Ramuz, der Dichter des Waadtlandes. Würzburg, 1938.

Brockmann-Jerosch, Heinrich. Schweizer Volksleben, Sitten, Bräuche, Wohnstätten. 2 vols. Erlenbach-Zurich, 1929–31.

Brooks, Robert Clarkson. Civic Training in Switzerland. Chicago, 1930.

Burckhardt, Walther. Kommentar der schweizerischen Bundesverfassung. Berne, 1931.

Chaponnière, Paul. Voltaire chez les Calvinistes. Paris, 1936.

Cherbulliez, A. E. De la démocratie en Suisse. 2 vols. Paris, 1843.

Dändliker, Karl. Geschichte der Schweiz. 3 vols. Zurich, 1893–95.

Dierauer, Johannes. Geschichte der schweizerischen Eidgenossenschaft. 6 vols. Gotha, 1887–1931.

Diethelm, Ernst. Der Einfluss der Theorie der Volkssouveränität auf die eidgenössischen und kantonalen Verfassungen nach 1798. Pfäffikon-Zurich, 1939.

Dubi, Heinrich. Der Alpensinn in der Litteratur und Kunst der Berner von 1537–1839. Berne, 1901.

Dubler, Hans. Der Kampf um den Solddienst der Schweizer im 18. Jahrhundert. Frauenfeld, 1939.

Egli, Karl. Schweizer Heereskunde. Zurich, 1916.

Ernst, Fritz. Die Schweiz als geistige Mittlerin von Muralt bis Jacob Burckhardt. Zurich, 1932.

Faesch, Remy. The Swiss Army System. New York, 1916.

Frauchiger, Friedrich. Der schweizerische Bundesstaat. Zurich, 1922.

Fueter, Eduard (1876–1928). Die Schweiz seit 1848. Leipzig, 1928.

Fueter, Eduard (1908–   ). Grosse schweizer Forscher. Zurich, 1939.

Gagliardi, Ernst. Der Anteil der Schweizer an den Italienischen Kriegen, 1496–1516. Zurich, 1919.

—— Geschichte der Schweiz. Rev. ed. 2 vols. Zurich, 1934–37.

Gessler, E. A. Die schweizer Bilderchroniken. Zurich, 1941.

Gigon, Fernand. L'Épopée de la Croix-Rouge. Paris, 1943.

Godet, Philippe. Histoire littéraire de la Suisse française. 2d ed. Paris, 1895.

Greyerz, Hans von. Studien zur Kulturgeschichte der Stadt Bern am Ende des Mittelalters. Berne, 1940.

Gruner, Erich. Das bernische Patriziat und die Regeneration. Berne, 1943.

Heusler, Andreas. Schweizerische Verfassungsgeschichte. Basel, 1920.

Hoffmann-Krayer, Eduard. Feste und Bräuche des Schweizervolkes. Zurich, 1913.

Jenny, Ernst. Die Alpendichtung der Deutschen Schweiz. Berne, 1905.

Jenny, Ernst, and Virgile Rossel. Geschichte der schweizerischen Literatur. 2 vols. Berne, 1910.

Korrodi, Eduard. Geisteserbe der Schweiz. Erlenbach-Zurich, 1943.

Kuhl, Erich. Die Natur des Menschen und die Struktur der Erziehung bei Rousseau und Pestalozzi. Stettin, 1926.

Le Corbusier (*pseud.* of Jeanneret-Gris, Charles Edouard). Œuvre complète, Vol. IV. Erlenbach-Zurich, 1946.

Loosli, C. A. Ferdinand Hodler. 4 vols. Berne, 1921–24.

Major, Emil, and Erwin Gradmann. Urs Graf. Basel, 1941.

Medicus, Fritz. Pestalozzis Leben. Leipzig, 1927.

Monnier, Marc. Genève et ses poètes du XVIe siècle à nos jours. Paris, 1874.

Mühlestein, Hans. Ferdinand Hodler. 2 vols. Leipzig, 1914.

Nadler, Josef. Der Geistige Aufbau der Deutschen Schweiz (1789–1848). Leipzig, 1924.

—— Literaturgeschichte der Deutschen Schweiz. Zurich, 1932.

Oechsli, Wilhelm. History of Switzerland. Cambridge, 1922.

Pestalozzi, Johann Heinrich. Sämtliche Werke. 18 vols. Berlin, 1927–43.

Rambert, Eugène. Ecrivains de la Suisse Romande. Lausanne, 1889.

Rappard, W. E. Le Facteur économique dans l'avènement de la démocratie moderne en Suisse. Geneva, 1912.

—— Les Fondements constitutionnels de la politique économique suisse. Zurich, 1942.

—— The Government of Switzerland. New York, 1936.

Raymond-Duchosal, Claire. Les Etrangers en Suisse. Paris, 1929.

Reynold, Gonzague de. Bodmer et l'école suisse. Lausanne, 1912.

Rosli, Joseph. Die Bestrafung der aufständigen Berner im Bauernkrieg von 1653. Berne, 1931.

Rossel, Virgile. Histoire littéraire de la Suisse romande. 2 vols. Paris, 1889–91.

Rougemont, Denis de, and Charlotte Muret. The Heart of Europe. New York, 1941.

Rousseau, Jean-Jacques. Œuvres complètes. 13 vols. in 7. Paris, 1885–1907.

Schmidt, Peter Heinrich. Die schweizer Industrien im internationalen Konkurrenzkampfe. Zurich, 1912.

Schweizer, Paul. Geschichte der schweizer Neutralität. Frauenfeld, 1895.

Sévery, William de. La Vie de société dans le Pays de Vaud à la fin du dix-huitième siècle. 2 vols. Lausanne, 1911–12.

Singer, Samuel. Literaturgeschichte der Deutschen Schweiz im Mittelalter. Berne, 1916.

Spink, J. S. Jean-Jacques Rousseau et Genève. Paris, 1934.

Swiss-American Historical Society. The Swiss in the United States. Madison, Wis., 1940.

Swiss Federal Government. Die eidgenössischen Abschiede aus dem Zeitraume von 1245 bis 1798. 8 vols. Published in various places, 1856–86.

—— La Suisse Economique et sociale. 2 vols. Einsiedeln, 1927.

Tarabori, A. U. Pannochie al sole; note di letteratura, d'arte e d'ambiente Ticinese. Bellinzona, 1930.

Ticino, Dipartimento della Pubblica Educazione. Scrittori della Svizzera Italiana. 2 vols. Bellinzona, 1936.

Tobler, J. L. Schweizerische Volkslieder, in *Bibliothek älterer Schrift-*

werke der Deutschen Schweiz und ihres Grenzgebietes (Frauenfeld, 1882–84), Ser. 1, Vols. IV–V.

Vinet, Alexandre (1797–1847). Littérature et histoire suisses. Lausanne, 1932.

Voltaire. Œuvres complètes. 52 vols. Paris, 1877–85. Also Kehl edition (1785–89), especially Vol. XII.

Weck, René de. Opinions sur Ramuz, in *Les Cahiers Romands*, No. 6. Lausanne, 1929.

Weber, Ella. Pestalozzis Stellung zum Problem der Nationalerziehung. Menziken, 1944.

Wehrli, Max. Das geistige Zürich im 18. Jahrhundert. Zurich, 1943.

Weiss, Richard. Volkskunde der Schweiz. Erlenbach-Zurich, 1946.

DICTIONARIES

Dictionnaire biographique des Genevois et des Vaudois. 2 vols. Lausanne, 1877.

Dictionnaire géographique de la Suisse. 6 vols. Neuchâtel, 1902–10.

Dictionnaire historique et biographique de la Suisse. 7 vols. Neuchâtel, 1921–33.

Neue schweizer Biographie. Basel, 1938.

Sammlung bernischer Biographie. 5 vols. Berne, 1884–1906.

Schweizer Gesellschaft für Statistik und Volkswirtschaft. Handbuch der schweizerischen Volkswirtschaft. 2 vols. Berne, 1939.

Schweizer Lexikon. 7 vols. Zurich, 1945–48.

Schweizerisches Zeitgenossenlexikon. Berne and Leipzig, 1932.

Swiss Federal Government. Statistisches Jahrbuch der Schweiz. Berne, 1891– .

Index